INTRODUCTION: STOPPING TO BUY SPARKNOTES ON A SNOWY EVENING

Whose words these are you *think* you know.
Your paper's due tomorrow, though;
We're glad to see you stopping here
To get some help before you go.

Lost your course? You'll find it here.
Face tests and essays without fear.
Between the words, good grades at stake:
Get great results throughout the year.

Once school bells caused your heart to quake
As teachers circled each mistake.
Use SparkNotes and no longer weep,
Ace every single test you take.

Yes, books are lovely, dark, and deep,
But only what you grasp you keep,
With hours to go before you sleep,
With hours to go before you sleep.

CONTENTS

CONTEXT

T HE BELL JAR is an autobiographical novel that conforms closely to the events of the author's life. Sylvia Plath was born to Otto and Aurelia Plath in 1932 and spent her early childhood in the seaport town of Winthrop, Massachusetts. Otto Plath died when Plath was eight years old, and she moved with her mother, younger brother, and maternal grandparents to Wellesley, an inland suburb of Boston. Plath excelled in school and developed a strong interest in writing and drawing. In 1950, she won a scholarship to attend Smith College, where she majored in English. *The Bell Jar* recounts, in slightly fictionalized form, the events of the summer and autumn after Plath's junior year. Like Esther, the protagonist of *The Bell Jar,* Plath was invited to serve as guest editor for a woman's magazine in New York. After returning to Wellesley for the remainder of the summer, she had a nervous breakdown and attempted suicide.

Plath went on to complete a highly successful college career. She won the prestigious Fulbright scholarship to study at Cambridge University in England, where she met the English poet Ted Hughes. They married in 1956, and after a brief stint in the United States, where Plath taught at Smith, they moved back to England in 1959. Plath gave birth to her first child, Freda, the following year. The same year, she published *The Colossus,* her first volume of poetry. Her second child, Nicholas, was born in 1962. Hughes and Plath separated shortly afterward; her instability and his affair with another woman had placed great strain on their marriage. Plath and her children moved to a flat in London, where she continued to write poetry. The poems she wrote at this time were later published in a collection titled *Ariel* (1965). In February 1963, she gassed herself in her kitchen, ending her life at the age of thirty-one.

Plath most likely wrote a first draft of *The Bell Jar* in the late 1950s. In 1961 she received a fellowship that allowed her to complete the novel. *The Bell Jar* was published in London in January 1963 under the pseudonym Victoria Lucas. Plath chose to publish the work under a pseudonym in order to protect the people she portrayed in the novel, and because she was uncertain of the novel's literary merit. The novel appeared posthumously in England under her own name in 1966, and in America, over the objections of her mother, in 1971. *The Bell Jar* has received moderate critical acclaim, and has long been valued not only as a glimpse into the psyche of a major poet, but as a witty and harrowing American coming-of-age story. Plath is primarily known not as a novelist, but as an outstanding poet. *Ariel* cemented her reputation as a great artist. Her other volumes of poetry, published posthumously, include *Crossing the Water* (1971), *Winter Trees* (1971), and *The Collected Poems* (1981), which won the Pulitzer Prize.

Sylvia Plath's literary persona has always provoked extreme reactions. Onlookers tend to mythologize Plath either as a feminist martyr or a tragic heroine. The feminist martyr version of her life holds that Plath was driven over the edge by her misogynist husband, and sacrificed on the altar of pre-feminist, repressive 1950s America. The tragic heroine version of her life casts Plath as a talented but doomed young woman, unable to deal with the pressures of society because of her debilitating mental illness. Although neither myth presents a wholly accurate picture, truth exists in both. *The Bell Jar* does not label its protagonist's life as either martyred or heroic. Plath does not attribute Esther's instability to men, society, or Esther herself, although she does criticize all three. Rather, she blames mental illness, which she characterizes as a mysterious and horrific disease.

Plot Overview

ESTHER GREENWOOD, A COLLEGE STUDENT from Massachusetts, travels to New York to work on a magazine for a month as a guest editor. She works for Jay Cee, a sympathetic but demanding woman. Esther and eleven other college girls live in a women's hotel. The sponsors of their trip wine and dine them and shower them with presents. Esther knows she should be having the time of her life, but she feels deadened. The execution of the Rosenbergs worries her, and she can embrace neither the rebellious attitude of her friend Doreen nor the perky conformism of her friend Betsy. Esther and the other girls suffer food poisoning after a fancy banquet. Esther attempts to lose her virginity with a UN interpreter, but he seems uninterested. She questions her abilities and worries about what she will do after college. On her last night in the city, she goes on a disastrous blind date with a man named Marco, who tries to rape her.

Esther wonders if she should marry and live a conventional domestic life, or attempt to satisfy her ambition. Buddy Willard, her college boyfriend, is recovering from tuberculosis in a sanitarium, and wants to marry Esther when he regains his health. To an outside observer, Buddy appears to be the ideal mate: he is handsome, gentle, intelligent, and ambitious. But he does not understand Esther's desire to write poetry, and when he confesses that he slept with a waitress while dating Esther, Esther thinks him a hypocrite and decides she cannot marry him. She sets out to lose her virginity as though in pursuit of the answer to an important mystery.

Esther returns to the Boston suburbs and discovers that she has not been accepted to a writing class she had planned to take. She will spend the summer with her mother instead. She makes vague plans to write a novel, learn shorthand, and start her senior thesis. Soon she finds the feelings of unreality she experienced in New York taking over her life. She is unable to read, write, or sleep, and she stops bathing. Her mother takes her to Dr. Gordon, a psychiatrist who prescribes electric shock therapy for Esther. Esther becomes more unstable than ever after this terrifying treatment, and decides to kill herself. She tries to slit her wrists, but can only bring herself to slash her calf. She tries to hang herself, but cannot find a place to tie the rope in her low-ceilinged house. At the beach with friends, she

3

attempts to drown herself, but she keeps floating to the surface of the water. Finally, she hides in a basement crawl space and takes a large quantity of sleeping pills.

Esther awakens to find herself in the hospital. She has survived her suicide attempt with no permanent physical injuries. Once her body heals, she is sent to the psychological ward in the city hospital, where she is uncooperative, paranoid, and determined to end her life. Eventually, Philomena Guinea, a famous novelist who sponsors Esther's college scholarship, pays to move her to a private hospital. In this more enlightened environment, Esther comes to trust her new psychiatrist, a woman named Dr. Nolan. She slowly begins to improve with a combination of talk therapy, insulin injections, and properly administered electric shock therapy. She becomes friends with Joan, a woman from her hometown and college who has had experiences similar to Esther's. She is repulsed, however, when Joan makes a sexual advance toward her.

As Esther improves, the hospital officials grant her permission to leave the hospital from time to time. During one of these excursions, she finally loses her virginity with a math professor named Irwin. She begins bleeding profusely and has to go to the emergency room. One morning, Joan, who seemed to be improving, hangs herself. Buddy comes to visit Esther, and both understand that their relationship is over. Esther will leave the mental hospital in time to start winter semester at college. She believes that she has regained a tenuous grasp on sanity, but knows that the bell jar of her madness could descend again at any time.

CHARACTER LIST

Esther Greenwood The protagonist and narrator of the novel, she has just finished her junior year of college. Esther grew up in the Boston suburbs with her mother and brother. Her father died when she was nine years old. Esther is attractive, talented, and lucky, but uncertainty plagues her, and she feels a disturbing sense of unreality.

Mrs. Greenwood Esther's mother, she has had a difficult life. Mrs. Greenwood lost her husband when her children were still young. Because her husband had inadequate life insurance, she struggles to make a living by teaching typing and shorthand. Practical and traditional, she loves Esther and worries about her future, but cannot understand her.

Buddy Willard Esther's college boyfriend, he is an athletic, intelligent, good-looking man who graduated from Yale and went to medical school. Buddy cares for Esther but has conventional ideas about women's roles and fails to understand Esther's interest in poetry. He represents everything that, according to society, Esther should want but does not.

Doctor Nolan Esther's psychiatrist at the private mental hospital. Esther comes to trust and love Dr. Nolan, who acts as a kind and understanding surrogate mother. Progressive and unconventional, Dr. Nolan encourages Esther's unusual thinking.

Doreen Esther's companion in New York, a blond, beautiful southern girl with a sharp tongue. Esther envies Doreen's nonchalance in social situations, and the two share a witty, cynical perspective on their position as guest editors for a fashion magazine. Doreen represents a rebellion against societal convention that Esther admires but cannot entirely embrace.

Joan Gilling Esther's companion in the mental hospital. A large, horsy woman, Joan was a year ahead of Esther in college, and Esther envied her social and athletic success. Joan once dated Buddy, Esther's boyfriend. In the mental ward, Esther comes to think of Joan as her double, someone with similar experiences to Esther's whom Esther does not particularly like, but with whom she feels an affinity.

Jay Cee Esther's boss at the magazine, an ambitious career woman who encourages Esther to be ambitious. She is physically unattractive, but moves self-confidently in her world. She treats Esther brusquely but kindly.

Betsy A pretty, wholesome girl from Kansas who becomes Esther's friend when they both work at the magazine. Esther feels she is more like Betsy than she is like Doreen, but she cannot relate to Betsy's cheerfulness and optimism.

Constantin A UN simultaneous interpreter who takes Esther on a date. Handsome, thoughtful, and accomplished, he seems sexually uninterested in Esther, who is willing to let him seduce her.

Marco A tall, dark, well-dressed Peruvian who takes Esther on a date to a country club. Marco expresses dashing self-confidence, but also a hatred of women. Violent and sadistic, he believes that all women are sluts.

Irwin Esther's first lover, he is a tall, intelligent, homely math professor at Harvard. Irwin is charming and seductive but not particularly responsible or caring.

Doctor Gordon Esther's first psychiatrist, whom she distrusts. He is good-looking and has an attractive family, and Esther thinks him conceited. He does not know how to help Esther, and ends up doing her more harm than good.

Philomena Guinea A famous, wealthy novelist who gives Esther a scholarship to attend college and pays for Esther's stay in the private mental hospital. She is elderly, generous, and successful.

Mrs. Willard A friend of Esther's mother and the mother of Esther's sometime-boyfriend, Buddy Willard. Mrs. Willard, who feels protective of her son, has traditional ideas about the roles men and women should play.

Lenny Shepherd Doreen's love interest, Lenny is a New York DJ and smooth older man. He wears cowboy-style clothes and has a cowboy-style home.

Eric A past acquaintance of Esther's with whom she had her most open conversation about sex. He is a southern prep school boy who lost his virginity with a prostitute and now associates love with chastity and sex with behaving like an animal.

Dodo Conway The Greenwoods' neighbor, Dodo is a Catholic woman with six children and a seventh on the way. She lives unconventionally, but everyone likes her.

Jody A friend of Esther's, with whom she is supposed to live while she takes a summer writing course. Jody is friendly and tries to be helpful, but cannot reach Esther.

Valerie A friend of Esther's in the private mental hospital. Valerie has had a lobotomy, and is friendly and relaxed.

ANALYSIS OF MAJOR CHARACTERS

ESTHER GREENWOOD

Esther Greenwood is the protagonist and narrator of *The Bell Jar*. The plot of the novel follows her descent into and return from madness. *The Bell Jar* tells an atypical coming-of-age story: instead of undergoing a positive, progressive education in the ways of the world, culminating in a graduation into adulthood, Esther learns from madness, and graduates not from school but from a mental institution.

Esther behaves unconventionally in reaction to the society in which she lives. Society expects Esther to be constantly cheerful and peppy, but her dark, melancholy nature resists perkiness. She becomes preoccupied with the execution of the Rosenbergs and the cadavers and pickled fetuses she sees at Buddy's medical school, because her brooding nature can find no acceptable means of expression. Society expects Esther to remain a virgin until her marriage to a nice boy, but Esther sees the hypocrisy of this rule and decides that like Buddy, she wants to lose her virginity before marriage. She embarks on a loveless sexual encounter because society does not provide her with an outlet for healthy sexual experimentation. Plath distinguishes Esther's understandably unconventional behavior from her madness. Even though society's ills disturb Esther, they do not make her mad. Rather, madness descends on her, an illness as unpreventable and destructive as cancer.

Largely because of her mental illness, Esther behaves selfishly. She does not consider the effect her suicide attempts have on her mother, or on her friends. Her own terrifying world occupies her thoughts completely. Though inexperienced, Esther is also observant, poetic, and kind. Plath feels affection toward her protagonist, but she is unswerving in depicting Esther's self-absorption, confusion, and naïveté.

MRS. GREENWOOD

Mrs. Greenwood remains in the background of the novel, for Esther makes little attempt to describe her. However, despite her relative invisibility, Mrs. Greenwood's influence pervades Esther's mind. Mrs. Greenwood subscribes to society's notions about women. She sends Esther an article emphasizing the importance of guarding one's virginity, and while she encourages Esther to pursue her ambition to write, she also encourages her to learn shorthand so that she can find work as a secretary. While Esther worries that her desire to be a poet or a professor will conflict with her probable role as wife and mother, her mother hopes that Esther's ambitions will not interfere with her domestic duties.

Mrs. Greenwood clearly loves Esther and worries about her: she runs through her money paying for Esther's stay in the hospital, and brings Esther roses on her birthday. Still, Esther partly faults her mother for her madness, and Plath represents this assigning of blame as an important breakthrough for Esther. When Esther tells Dr. Nolan that she hates her mother, Nolan reacts with satisfaction, as if this admission explains Esther's condition and marks an important step in her recovery. The doctors decide that Esther should stay in the hospital until winter term at college begins rather than go home to live with her mother. Perhaps Esther hates her mother partly because she feels guilty about inflicting such vast pain on her.

BUDDY WILLARD

A contemporary reviewer of *The Bell Jar* once observed that Buddy Willard is a perfect specimen of the ideal 1950s American male. By the standards of the time, Buddy is nearly flawless. Handsome and athletic, he attends church, loves his parents, thrives in school, and studies to become a doctor. Esther appreciates Buddy's near perfection, and admires him for a long time from afar. But once she gets to know him, she sees his flaws. In what was considered natural behavior in men at that time, Buddy spends a summer sleeping with a waitress while dating Esther, and does not apologize for his behavior. Esther also realizes that while Buddy is intelligent, he is not particularly thoughtful. He does not understand Esther's desire to write poetry, telling her that poems are like dust, and that her passion for poetry will change as soon as she becomes a mother. He accepts his mother's conventional ideas about how he should organize his domestic and emotional life. Buddy's sexuality proves boring—Esther finds his kisses uninspiring, and when he undresses before her, he does so in a clinical way, telling her she should get used to seeing him naked, and explaining that he wears net underwear because his "mother says they wash easily." Finally, he seems unconsciously cruel. He tells Esther he slept with the waitress because she was "free, white, and twenty-one," acts pleased when Esther breaks her leg on a ski slope, and, in their last meeting, wonders out loud who will marry her now that she has been in a mental institution.

In some ways, Buddy and Esther endure similar experiences. They both show great promise at the beginning of the novel, and at the novel's end have become muted and worldly. Buddy's time in the sanitarium during his bout with tuberculosis parallels Esther's time in the mental institution. Both experiment with premarital sex. Still, they share few character traits, and Esther must reject Buddy because she rejects his way of life. She will not become a submissive wife and mother and shelve her artistic ambitions.

CHARACTER ANALYSIS

THEMES, MOTIFS & SYMBOLS

THEMES

Themes are the fundamental and often universal ideas explored in a literary work.

GROWTH THROUGH PAIN AND REBIRTH

The Bell Jar tells the story of a young woman's coming-of-age, but it does not follow the usual trajectory of adolescent development into adulthood. Instead of undergoing a progressive education in the ways of the world, culminating in an entrance into adulthood, Esther regresses into madness. Experiences intended to be life-changing in a positive sense—Esther's first time in New York City, her first marriage proposal, her success in college—are upsetting and disorienting to her. Instead of finding new meaning in living, Esther wants to die. As she slowly recovers from her suicide attempt, she aspires simply to survive.

Esther's struggles and triumphs seem more heroic than conventional achievements. Her desire to die rather than live a false life can be interpreted as noble, and the gradual steps she takes back to sanity seem dignified. Esther does not mark maturity in the traditional way of fictional heroines, by marrying and beginning a family, but by finding the strength to reject the conventional model of womanhood. Esther emerges from her trials with a clear understanding of her own mental health, the strength that she summoned to help her survive, and increased confidence in her skepticism of society's mores. She describes herself, with characteristic humor, as newly "patched, retreaded and approved for the road."

THE EMPTINESS OF CONVENTIONAL EXPECTATIONS

Esther observes a gap between what society says she should experience and what she does experience, and this gap intensifies her madness. Society expects women of Esther's age and station to act cheerful, flexible, and confident, and Esther feels she must repress her natural gloom, cynicism, and dark humor. She feels she cannot discuss or think about the dark spots in life that plague her: personal failure, suffering, and death. She knows the world of fashion she inhabits in New York should make her feel glamorous and happy, but she finds it filled with poison, drunkenness, and violence. Her relationships with men are supposed to be romantic and meaningful, but they are marked by misunderstanding, distrust, and brutality. Esther almost continuously feels that her reactions are wrong, or that she is the only one to view the world as she does, and eventually she begins to feel a sense of unreality. This sense of unreality grows until it becomes unbearable, and attempted suicide and madness follow.

THE RESTRICTED ROLE OF WOMEN IN 1950S AMERICA

Esther's sense of alienation from the world around her comes from the expectations placed upon her as a young woman living in 1950s America. Esther feels pulled between her desire to write and the pressure she feels to settle down and start a family. While Esther's intellectual talents earn her prizes, scholarships, and respect, many people assume that she most wants to become a wife and mother. The girls at her college mock her studiousness and only show her respect when she begins dating a handsome and well-liked boy. Her relationship with Buddy earns her mother's approval, and everyone expects Esther to marry him. Buddy assumes that Esther will drop her poetic ambitions as soon as she becomes a mother, and Esther also assumes that she cannot be both mother and poet.

Esther longs to have adventures that society denies her, particularly sexual adventures. She decides to reject Buddy for good when she realizes he represents a sexual double standard. He has an affair with a waitress while dating Esther, but expects Esther to remain a virgin until she marries him. Esther understands her first sexual experience as a crucial step toward independence and adulthood, but she seeks this experience not for her own pleasure but rather to relieve herself of her burdensome virginity. Esther feels anxiety about her future because she can see only mutually exclusive choices: virgin or whore, submissive married woman or successful but lonely career woman. She dreams of a larger life, but the stress even of dreaming such a thing worsens her madness.

THE PERILS OF PSYCHIATRIC MEDICINE

The Bell Jar takes a critical view of the medical profession, in particular psychiatric medicine. This critique begins with Esther's visit to

Buddy's medical school. There, Esther is troubled by the arrogance of the doctors and their lack of sympathy for the pain suffered by a woman in labor. When Esther meets her first psychiatrist, Dr. Gordon, she finds him self-satisfied and unsympathetic. He does not listen to her, and prescribes a traumatic and unhelpful shock therapy treatment. Joan, Esther's acquaintance in the mental hospital, tells a similar tale of the insensitivity of male psychiatrists. Some of the hospitals in which Esther stays are frighteningly sanitized and authoritarian. The novel does not paint an entirely negative picture of psychiatric care, however. When Esther goes to a more enlightened, luxurious institution, she begins to heal under the care of Dr. Nolan, a progressive female psychiatrist. The three methods of 1950s psychiatric treatment—talk therapy, insulin injections, and electroshock therapy—work for Esther under the proper and attentive care of Dr. Nolan. Even properly administered therapy does not receive unmitigated praise, however. Shock therapy, for example, works by clearing the mind entirely. After one treatment, Esther finds herself unable to think about knives. This inability comes as a relief, but it also suggests that the therapy works by the dubious method of blunting Esther's sharp intelligence.

MOTIFS

Motifs are recurring structures, contrasts, or literary devices that can help to develop and inform the text's major themes.

NEWS AND FASHION MEDIA

Esther frequently reads newspaper headings and thumbs through magazines. The information that she absorbs from these sources tells us what interests her most: the papers fascinate her with their stories of the execution of the Rosenbergs and a man's suicide attempt. Periodicals also reinforce the values of mainstream 1950s America. Esther's mother sends her a pamphlet defending chastity, and in the doctor's waiting room Esther reads magazines about young motherhood. The power of magazine images to distort and alienate is most obvious when Esther sees a picture of herself in a fashion magazine in the mental hospital and feels the distance between her actual life and the image of glamour and happiness she sees in the magazine.

MIRRORS

Esther continually confronts reflections of herself, reflections she often fails to recognize. After her evening with Doreen and Lenny, Esther fails to recognize her own reflection in the elevator doors. After her first shock treatment with Dr. Nolan, she thinks her reflection is another woman in the room. Most dramatically, after her suicide attempt Esther fails to recognize her bruised and discolored face in a mirror, and cannot even tell if the creature she sees is a man or a woman. Esther increasingly struggles to keep the outward self she presents to the world united with the inner self that she experiences. Her failure to recognize her own reflection stands for the difficulty she has understanding herself.

BLOOD

The shedding of blood marks major transitions in Esther's life. When Marco attempts to rape her, she gives him a bloody nose, and he smears his blood on her like war paint. When she decides to kill herself, she slashes her calf to practice slashing her wrists. When she loses her virginity, she bleeds so copiously that she must seek medical attention. The presence of blood suggests a ritual sacrifice: Esther will sacrifice her body for peace of mind, and sacrifice her virginity for the sake of experience. The presence of blood also indicates the frightening violence of Esther's experiences. For her, transformations involve pain and suffering, not joy.

SYMBOLS

Symbols are objects, characters, figures, or colors used to represent abstract ideas or concepts.

THE BELL JAR

The bell jar is an inverted glass jar, generally used to display an object of scientific curiosity, contain a certain kind of gas, or maintain a vacuum. For Esther, the bell jar symbolizes madness. When gripped by insanity, she feels as if she is inside an airless jar that distorts her perspective on the world and prevents her from connecting with the people around her. At the end of the novel, the bell jar has lifted, but she can sense that it still hovers over her, waiting to drop at any moment.

THE FIG TREE

Early in the novel, Esther reads a story about a Jewish man and a nun who meet under a fig tree. Their relationship is doomed, just as she feels her relationship with Buddy is doomed. Later, the tree becomes a symbol of the life choices that face Esther. She imagines that each fig represents a different life. She can only choose one fig, but because she wants all of them, she sits paralyzed with indecision, and the figs rot and fall to the ground.

HEADLINES

Chapter 16 marks one of Esther's most debilitating bouts with her illness. In this chapter, headlines are reprinted in the text of the novel. Joan gives Esther actual headlines from articles reporting Esther's disappearance and attempted suicide. These headlines symbolize Esther's exposure, her effect on others, and the gap between Esther's interpretation of experiences and the world's interpretation of them. First, they show Esther that the public knows about her behavior—she does not act in a vacuum, but in the interested eye of the world. The headlines also demonstrate the power Esther's behavior has on people who are almost strangers to her. Joan, for example, says the headlines inspired her to move to New York and attempt suicide. Finally, the headlines represent the dissonance between Esther's experience of herself and others' experience of her. While Esther sees only pain and swallowing pills in the darkness, the world sees a sensational story of a missing girl, a hunt in the woods, and the shocking discovery of Esther in her own house.

THE BEATING HEART

When Esther tries to kill herself, she finds that her body seems determined to live. Esther remarks that if it were up to her, she could kill herself in no time, but she must outwit the tricks and ruses of her body. The beating heart symbolizes this bodily desire for life. When she tries to drown herself, her heart beats, "I am I am I am." It repeats the same phrase when Esther attends Joan's funeral.

SYMBOLS

Summary & Analysis

Chapters 1–2

Summary: Chapter 1

> *I guess I should have been excited the way most of the
> other girls were, but I couldn't get myself to react. I
> felt very still and very empty.* (See QUOTATIONS, p. 49)

It is the summer of 1953 and Esther Greenwood, a college student, is living in New York and working at a month-long job as guest editor for a fashion magazine. As the novel opens, Esther worries about the electrocution of the Rosenbergs, a husband and wife who were convicted of spying for the Soviet Union and sentenced to death. She also worries about the fact that she cannot enjoy her job, her new clothes, or the parties she attends, despite realizing that most girls would envy her. Esther feels numb and unmoored, and thinks there is something wrong with her. She lives in the Amazon, a women's hotel, with the other eleven girls who work as guest editors and with upper-class girls training to work as secretaries. Esther spends most of her time with the beautiful, sarcastic Doreen, a southerner who shares Esther's cynicism. Betsy, a wholesome girl from the Midwest, persistently offers her friendship to Esther. One day, on her way to a party organized by the magazine, Betsy ask Esther if she wants to share a cab. Esther refuses, catching a cab with Doreen instead. While their cab sits in traffic, a man approaches and persuades them to join him and some friends in a bar. The man's name is Lenny Shepherd, and he exhibits immediate interest in Doreen. He persuades his friend Frankie to keep Esther company, but she treats Frankie coldly because he is short and she towers over him. Esther orders a vodka. She does not know much about drinks, and orders them at random, hoping to stumble on something she likes. She tells the men her name is Elly Higginbottom. Frankie leaves alone, and Esther and Doreen leave with Lenny.

SUMMARY: CHAPTER 2

Esther and Doreen go to Lenny's apartment, which is decorated like a cowboy's ranch. He puts on a tape of his own radio show, saying he enjoys the sound of his voice, and gives the girls drinks. He offers to call a friend for Esther, but Esther refuses. Doreen dances with Lenny while Esther watches, lonely and impassive, growing sleepy. The couple begins fighting playfully, biting one another and screaming, and Esther sees that Doreen's breasts have slipped out of her strapless dress. Esther decides to leave. Although she is drunk, she manages to walk forty-eight blocks by five blocks home. She arrives home sober, her feet slightly swollen from the long walk. In her room, she stares out the window and feels her isolation from New York and from life in general. She takes a hot bath and feels purified. She falls asleep, only to be wakened by a drunken, semi-conscious Doreen pounding on her door with the night maid. Once Esther opens the door, the maid leaves, and Doreen begins mumbling. Esther decides to leave Doreen in the hall. As she lowers her onto the carpet, Doreen vomits and passes out. Esther decides that though she will continue to spend time with and observe Doreen, "deep down" she will have "nothing at all to do with her." She feels that, at heart, she resembles the wholesome Betsy more than she resembles Doreen. When Esther opens the door the following morning, Doreen is gone.

ANALYSIS: CHAPTERS 1–2

Esther narrates *The Bell Jar* in girlish, slangy prose, sounding mature and detached mainly when speaking of her own morbidity and depression. The first sentence of the novel sets the tone: "It was a queer, sultry summer, the summer they electrocuted the Rosenbergs, and I didn't know what I was doing in New York." Esther feels misplaced, sad, and removed from reality. She lacks the cheery good humor that society expects of her, and that she expects of herself. She knows that most girls long to do what she is doing, and she cannot understand her own lack of enthusiasm. It is instructive to read Plath's own letter to her mother during her stint as a guest editor in New York, for in it she presents the chipper front that Esther struggles to maintain: "At first I was disappointed at not being Fiction Ed, but now that I see how all-inclusive my work is, I love it. . . . [A]ll is relatively un-tense now, almost homey, in fact." Plath manages to sound appropriately cheery, flexible, and grateful in this letter, just as Esther manages to pass herself off as suitably happy in front of her employer and sponsors.

Plath paints Esther as not just unhappy, but touchingly inexperienced. When Doreen says that Yale men are stupid, the easily influenced Esther instantly decides that Billy, a Yale man, suffers from stupidity. Esther knows nothing about alcohol, and says, "My dream was someday ordering a drink and finding out it tasted wonderful." Esther has determination that counters her inexperience, however, as she proves when she grits her teeth, looks at her street map, and manages to walk the miles back to her hotel while drunk.

The first two chapters contrast the ideal that life offers a talented and lucky girl like Esther, and her actual experiences of the world. She should feel thrilled by the social whirl of her charmed life in New York, but the death of the Rosenbergs obsesses her. The wealthy girls at her hotel should epitomize glamour, freedom, and happiness, but they seem spoiled and "bored as hell." New York should set the stage for romantic, magical encounters with fascinating men, but Esther gets left with a short older man, and Doreen's encounter with Lenny proves ugly and scary. Lenny plays a song that idealizes faithful love and marriage, but calls Doreen a "bitch" when she bites him, the prelude to their sexual encounter. The beautiful and confident Doreen, whom Esther idealizes, turns herself into a helpless, vomiting heap. The excitement of a big city, material success, romance, and love, get rewritten as an execution, boredom, selfishness, and brutality. Esther's distaste for her life seems in part a reasonable response to her disillusionment at finding her dream summer lacking, but also a harbinger of her impending mental illness.

In the first chapter, the narrator mentions in an aside that she now has a baby. Although we never hear about the baby or Esther's adult life again, this remark tells us that when she narrates them, Esther is likely a few years removed from the experiences the novel describes.

CHAPTERS 3–4

SUMMARY: CHAPTER 3

Esther attends a banquet luncheon given by *Ladies' Day* magazine. Doreen skips the meal in order to spend the day at Coney Island with Lenny. Esther enjoys the rich food at these banquets because her family worries about the cost of food, and because she had never been to a real restaurant before going to New York. Her grandfather used to work as headwaiter at a country club, where he introduced Esther to caviar, which became her favorite delicacy. Esther manages to eat two plates of caviar at the luncheon, along with chicken and avocados stuffed with crabmeat. Betsy asks Esther why she missed the fur show earlier that day, and Esther explains that Jay Cee, her boss, called her into her office. Esther quietly cries as she remembers what happened.

Esther returns to the events leading up to the luncheon. As Esther lies in bed, listening to the girls get ready and feeling depressed, Jay Cee calls and requests she come into the office. When Esther arrives, Jay Cee asks Esther whether she finds her work interesting, and Esther assures her that she does. Jay Cee asks Esther what she wants to do after she graduates, and although she always has a ready answer involving travel, teaching, and writing, Esther says that she does not know. She realizes as she speaks that she truly does not know what she wants to do. She says tentatively that she might go into publishing, and Jay Cee tells her that she must learn foreign languages in order to distinguish herself from the other women who want to go into publishing. Esther has no time in her senior year schedule for a language course. She thinks of a lie she once told to get out of a chemistry course: she asked her dean to permit her to take chemistry without receiving a grade, ostensibly to free up space in her schedule for a Shakespeare course, but actually to avoid the dreaded chemistry class. On the strength of Esther's impeccable grades, the dean and the science teacher, Mr. Manzi, agreed to the plan, believing that Esther's willingness to take the course without credit demonstrated intellectual maturity. She attended the chemistry course and pretended to take notes, but actually wrote poems.

SUMMARY: CHAPTER 4

Esther feels guilty about her deception of Mr. Manzi, who thought her such a dedicated student of chemistry. Although she does not know why, she thinks of Mr. Manzi when Jay Cee talks sternly to her of her future plans. Jay Cee gives Esther some submitted stories to read and comment on, speaks to her gently, and sends her off to the banquet after a few hours of work. Esther wishes her mother were more like Jay Cee, wise and powerful. Her mother wants Esther to learn a practical skill, like shorthand, because she knows how difficult it is for a woman to support herself. Esther's father

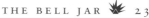

died when Esther was nine, leaving no life insurance, which Esther believes angered her mother.

Esther uses her finger bowl after eating dessert at the banquet. She remembers eating lunch with Philomena Guinea, who provides her scholarship money for college, and, in her confusion, drinking the contents of her finger bowl. Esther leaves the banquet to attend a movie premiere with the other girls. Midway through, she feels ill. Betsy feels sick too, and the girls leave together. They throw up in the cab, in the elevator at their hotel, and in the bathroom at the hotel. Esther vomits until she passes out on the bathroom floor, waking only when someone pounds on the door. She tries to get up and walk, but collapses in the hallway. A nurse puts her to bed and tells her that all the girls have food poisoning. She wakes later to find Doreen trying to feed her soup. Doreen tells her they found ptomaine in the crabmeat from the banquet. Esther feels famished.

Analysis: Chapters 3–4

In the third and fourth chapters, Esther begins to feel inadequate and directionless. She has always been a model student—intelligent, hardworking, and destined for great things—but suddenly her future seems unclear. When she admits to Jay Cee that she does not know what she want to do after college, she shocks herself, realizing that what she says is true. She has always planned on studying abroad, then becoming a professor and writing and editing. Now, however, she has lost her drive. She also worries that her high marks and string of academic honors mask the fact that she is not a good person. When Esther remembers the lie she told the dean, she recognizes that her good academic reputation made it possible for her to avoid an undesirable course. But she feels guilty that she abused her academic success in order to avoid a class, and that she tricked everyone into trusting her and even admiring her.

These chapters detail the financial straits that increase Esther's insecurity. She has grown up poor, understanding the cost of every bite of food she puts in her mouth. Working hard and doing well in school are not merely matters of personal ambition, but matters of survival. The charity of others allows Esther to go to school and to live in New York, and her mother has no money to maintain her at her expensive school should she lose her scholarship. Great pressure to do well weighs on Esther. She does not have the rich girl's luxury of slackening her studies, or taking a few years to decide what she wants to do. Furthermore, Esther feels shaken by getting a taste of the ideal life meant to be the goal and reward of her hard work, and finding it miserable. She begins to wonder, therefore, if she does not even want what hard work will bring her. She cannot continue her hard work, but she also feels she cannot utterly rebel. She lies in bed worrying: "I wondered why I couldn't go the whole way doing what I should any more. This made me sad and tired. Then I wondered why I couldn't go the whole way doing what I shouldn't, the way Doreen did, and this made me even sadder and more tired." Esther feels she can be neither the perfect conscientious student, nor the devil-may-care rebel, and her suspension between the two poles upsets her.

Esther welcomes her illness, as she enjoys allowing other people to take care of her. When her physical health fails, she no longer has to engage actively with the world, and her body mirrors her mental state. When sick, Esther welcomes Doreen's almost maternal comfort. Doreen represents several varieties of freedom for Esther—freedom from fear of convention, from endless pursuit of achievement, and from mandates against sex. While Esther feels she can never behave as Doreen does, she finds comfort in Doreen's freedom from worry, and her brash good humor and self-confidence.

CHAPTERS 5–6

SUMMARY: CHAPTER 5

The morning after her sickness, Esther receives a call from Constantin, a simultaneous interpreter at the United Nations and an acquaintance of Mrs. Willard. Constantin invites Esther to come see the UN and get something to eat. Esther assumes Constantin asked her out as a favor to Mrs. Willard, but she agrees to go nonetheless. Esther thinks about Mrs. Willard's son, Buddy, who is currently in a sanitarium recovering from tuberculosis. Buddy wants to marry Esther, and Esther thinks about how odd it is that she worshipped Buddy from afar before they met, and now that he wants to marry her she loathes him.

Esther recalls her tipping mishaps: upon her arrival in New York, she failed to tip the bellhop who brought her suitcase to her room, and the first time she rode in a cab, the cabdriver sneered at her ten percent tip. Esther opens the book sent by the *Ladies' Day* magazine staff. A cloying get-well card falls out. Esther pages through the books, and finds a story about a fig tree. In the story, a Jewish man and a nun from an adjoining convent meet under a fig tree. One day, as they watch a chick hatch, they touch hands. The next day, the nun does not come out, and in her place comes the kitchen maid. Esther sees parallels between this story and her doomed relationship with Buddy. She thinks about the differences between the two couples: she and Buddy are Unitarian, not Catholic and Jewish, and they saw a baby being born, not a chick hatching.

Esther thinks of Buddy's recent letters, in which he tells her that he has found poems written by a doctor, which encourages him to think that doctors and writers can get along. This comment marks a change from his old way of thinking: he once told Esther that a poem is "a piece of dust." At the time, Esther could think of nothing to say in reply, and now she composes sharp speeches she could have made criticizing his work as meaningless, and his cadavers as dust. She thinks that curing people is no better than writing "poems people would remember and repeat to themselves when they were unhappy or sick or couldn't sleep." Esther recalls the beginning of her relationship with Buddy. She had a crush on him for years, and one day he dropped by her home and said he might like to see her at college. He stopped at her dorm several months later, explaining that he was on campus to take Joan Gilling to a dance. Angry, Esther said she had a date in a few minutes. Buddy departed, displeased, but left Esther a letter inviting her to the Yale Junior Prom. He treated her like a friend at the prom, but afterward kissed her. She felt little besides eagerness to tell the other girls of her adventure.

Summary: Chapter 6

Esther continues to remember the progression of her relationship with Buddy. She went to visit him at Yale Medical School, and since she had been asking to see interesting sights at the hospital, he showed her cadavers and fetuses in jars, which she viewed calmly. They attended a lecture on diseases, and then went to see a baby being born. Buddy and his friend Will joked that Esther should not watch the birth, or she would never want to have a baby. Buddy told her that the woman had been given a drug, and would not remember her pain. Esther thought the drug sounded exactly like something invented by a man. She hated the idea that the drug tricks the woman into forgetting her pain. The woman had to be cut in order to free the baby, and the sight of the blood and the birth upset Esther, although she said nothing to Buddy.

After the birth, they went to Buddy's room, where Buddy asked Esther if she had ever seen a naked man. She said no, and he asked if she would like to see him naked. She agreed, and he took off his pants. The sight of him naked made her think of "turkey neck and turkey gizzards," and she felt depressed. She refused to let him see her naked, and then asked him if he had ever slept with a woman, expecting him to say that he was saving himself for marriage. He confessed to sleeping with a waitress named Gladys at a summer job in Cape Cod. He claimed she seduced him, and admitted that they slept together for ten weeks.

Esther was not bothered by the idea that Buddy slept with someone, but was angry that he hypocritically presented himself as virginal and innocent. Esther asked students at her college what they would think if a boy they had been dating confessed to sleeping with someone, and they said a woman could not be angry unless she were pinned or engaged. When she asked Buddy what his mother thought of the affair, Buddy said he told his mother, "Gladys was free, white, and twenty-one." Esther decided to break up with Buddy, but just as she had made up her mind, Buddy called her long-distance and told her he had TB. She did not feel sorry but relieved, because she knew she would not have to see him very much. She decided to tell the girls in her dorm that she and Bobby were practically engaged, and they left her alone on Saturday nights, admiring her for studying in order to mask her pain at Buddy's illness.

ANALYSIS: CHAPTERS 5–6

Society expects Esther, a well-educated middle-class girl, to find a nice, responsible young man and become his loving wife. As Mrs. Willard explains to Buddy, "What a man is is an arrow into the future, and what a woman is is the place the arrow shoots off from." In her conventional view, a woman must support her husband by creating an attractive and orderly home and by nurturing him and his ambitions. This vision troubles Esther, who has always nurtured ambitions of her own, and has never aspired simply to help a husband. It seems that she cannot have both marriage and a career, and that marrying someone would mean relinquishing her dreams of writing. Failing to marry Buddy would strike most people as lunacy, however. Mrs. Willard and Esther's mother, grandmother, and classmates see Buddy as an ideal match: he is handsome, intelligent, and ambitious. Esther herself thinks him the ideal man before she gets to know him. But she soon understands Buddy's limitations. He cares for Esther, but he cannot understand her passion for literature, he patronizes her with his supposedly superior understanding of the world, and, perhaps worst of all, he is boring. Something of a mama's boy, he seeks a woman who shares his values and does not aspire to anything beyond wifely duties and motherhood.

Buddy separates the pleasures of sex from the pleasures of cozy domesticity. Because he imagines Esther as his future wife, he does not imagine that he could have passionate sex with her. Instead, he removes his clothes in front of her as if their sexual encounters will be a clinical duty. Because he does not associate Esther with sex, he feels only a twinge of guilt at sleeping with Gladys, a passionate girl he does not plan to marry. Examining her own feelings, Esther realizes that she does not object to sex before marriage, but she does object to Buddy's deception. She hates the fact that he presented himself as pure.

CHAPTERS 7–8

SUMMARY: CHAPTER 7

I saw the world divided into people who had slept with somebody and people who hadn't. . . . I thought a spectacular change would come over me the day I crossed the boundary line. (See QUOTATIONS, p. 50)

Constantin picks up Esther and drives her to the UN in his convertible. They discover that neither likes Mrs. Willard. Esther finds Constantin attractive even though he is too short for her, and when he holds her hand she feels happier than she has since she was nine and ran on the beach with her father the summer before his death. While at the UN, Esther thinks it odd that she never before realized that she was only happy until the age of nine. The skills of the interpreters impress Esther, and she thinks about all of the things she cannot do: cook, write in shorthand, dance, sing, ride a horse, ski, or speak foreign languages. She feels that the one thing she is good at, winning scholarships, will end once college is over. She sees her life as a fig tree. The figs represent different life choices—a husband and children, a poet, a professor, an editor, a traveler—but she wants all of them and cannot choose, so the figs rot and drop off the tree uneaten.

Constantin takes Esther to dinner, and she feels better right away, wondering if her fig tree vision came from her empty stomach. The meal is so pleasant that she decides to let Constantin seduce her. Esther has decided she should sleep with someone so that she can get even with Buddy. She recalls a boy named Eric with whom she once discussed having sex. He lost his virginity to a prostitute and was bored and repulsed by the experience. He decided that he would never sleep with a woman he loved, because sex strikes him as animalistic. Esther thought he might be a good person to have sex with because he seemed sensible, but he wrote to tell her he had feelings for her. Because of his views on sex, she knew this confession meant he would never sleep with her, so she wrote to tell him she was engaged.

Constantin invites Esther to come to his apartment and listen to music, and she hopes, as her mother would say, that this invitation "could mean only one thing." She remembers an article her mother sent her listing all of the reasons that a woman should save sex for marriage. She decides that virginity is impractical, because even someone as clean-cut as Buddy is not a virgin, and she rejects a double sexual standard for men and women. To Esther's disappointment, Constantin only holds her hand. Sleepy with wine, she lays down in his bed. He joins her, but the two merely sleep. She wakes, disoriented, at three in the morning and watches Constantin sleep, thinking about what it would be like to be married. She decides marriage consists of washing and cleaning, and that it would endanger her ambitions. She remembers Buddy telling her "in a sinister, knowing way" that she will not want to write poems once she has children, and she worries that marriage brainwashes women. Constantin wakes and drives her home.

SUMMARY: CHAPTER 8

Esther remembers Mr. Willard driving her to visit Buddy in the sanatorium. He stopped along the way and told her that he would like to have her for a daughter. Esther began to cry, and Mr. Willard misinterpreted her tears as tears of joy. To Esther's dismay, Mr. Willard left her alone with Buddy. Buddy had gained weight in the sanatorium. He showed Esther a poem he had published in an esoteric magazine. She thought the poem was awful, although she expressed neutrality. Buddy proposed by saying, "How would you like to be Mrs. Buddy Willard?" Esther told him she would never marry. Buddy laughed at this notion. Esther reminded him that he accused her of being neurotic because she wanted mutually exclusive things, and said she will always want mutually exclusive things. He said he wanted to be with her.

Buddy decided to teach Esther to ski. He borrowed equipment for her from various people. Esther took the rope tow to the top of the mountain and Buddy stood at the bottom beckoning to her to ski down. At first she felt terrified, but then it occurred to her that she might kill herself. She skied straight down at top speed, utterly happy. She felt she was skiing into the past. But suddenly she fell, her mouth filled with ice, and the ordinary world returned. She wanted to ski down the mountain again, but Buddy told her, with strange satisfaction, that she had broken her leg in two places.

ANALYSIS: CHAPTERS 7–8

At the UN, Esther begins to doubt her own worth for the first time. Her identity depends on her success in school. She knows herself, and the world knows her, as the brilliant student who wins piles of scholarships. The end of college looms in the near future, and with it the end of scholarships and prizes, and Esther fears the end of college will erase her identity and success. She feels "like a racehorse without racetracks." Her insecurity mounts when she visualizes her life as a fig tree, using imagery that makes her conundrum clear: she feels she can choose only one profession, only one life, to the exclusion of all others. She cannot decide to be a mother *and* a professor, or a wife *and* a poet. Esther feels enormous pressure from her family and friends to marry and have children, but she also longs to become a poet, so she feels paralyzed with indecision.

The article that Esther's mother sends her reinforces the message she receives from Mrs. Willard and Buddy: women and men have fundamentally different needs and natures, and a woman must discipline her behavior in anticipation of pleasing her future husband. The article also reinforces a sexual double standard: while it is crucial to a woman's happiness to stay "pure" until marriage, purity is optional for men. Esther rejects this double standard, explaining, "I couldn't stand the idea of a woman having to have a single pure life and a man being able to have a double life, one pure and one not."

Esther's conversation with Eric adds a further dimension to the picture of the limiting sexual conventions of her time. Eric, a kind and sensible person, believes that women can be divided into two categories: virgins and whores. He thinks that sex is dirty, something that reduces women to animals, and that nice girls should remain untainted by nasty sexual experience. These categories do not work for Esther, who feels she can have sex without turning herself into an immoral animal. Though she does not explicitly reject Eric's categories, she implicitly seeks a sexual life that will allow her to be adventurous but also to maintain her dignity and sense of self. Her quest to lose her virginity embodies these goals, though it is marked by some confusion. Esther believes that losing her virginity will transform her, because her culture continually sends the message that an immense gap exists between virginity and sexual experience. Plath also suggests that Esther feels comfortable trying to lose her virginity to Constantin partly because he makes her feel happy as her father did. When Constantin holds her hand, the platonic gesture reminds her of her father, and she begins to feel comfortable with him.

Remembering her skiing experience, Esther implies that she liked the thought of killing herself. When she considered that the trip down the mountain might kill her, the thought "formed in [her] mind coolly as a tree or a flower." She understood her plunge down the mountain not as a relinquishment of control, but as an exercise of control. She aimed past the people and things of the ordinary world toward the white sun, "the still, bright point at the end of it, the pebble at the bottom of the well, the white sweet baby cradled in its mother's belly." Moving toward death made Esther happy, and she became distressed only when the ordinary world began reforming itself in her perception. She understands her near-death experience as a rite of purification rather than as self-injury.

CHAPTERS 9–10

SUMMARY: CHAPTER 9

The day of the Rosenbergs' execution, Esther speaks with Hilda, another guest editor, who is glad the Rosenbergs will die. In a photo shoot for the magazine, Esther holds a paper rose meant to represent the inspiration for her poems. When the photographer commands her to smile, she begins to sob uncontrollably. She is left alone to cry, and then Jay Cee brings her some stories to read and critique. Esther fantasizes that one day Jay Cee will accept a manuscript, only to find out it is a story of Esther's.

On Esther's last night in New York, Doreen persuades her to come to a country club dance with Lenny and a blind date, a friend of Lenny's. As they talk, Esther looks around her room at the expensive clothes she bought but could never bring herself to wear. She tells Doreen she cannot face the clothes, and Doreen balls them up and stuffs them under the bed. When the girls arrive for the dance, Esther immediately identifies her date, a Peruvian named Marco, as a "woman-hater." When she first meets him, he gives her a diamond pin that she admires, and tells her he will perform something worthy of a diamond. As he speaks, he grips her arm so hard that he leaves four bruises. At the country club, Esther does not want to dance, but Marco tosses her drink into a plant and forces her to tango. He tells her to pretend she is drowning, and Esther drapes herself against him and thinks, "It doesn't take two to dance, it only takes one." Marco takes her outside, and Esther asks him whom he loves. He tells her that he is in love with his cousin, but she is going to be a nun. Angered, he pushes Esther into the mud and climbs on top of her, ripping off her dress. She tells herself that if she just lies there and does nothing, "it" will happen. After he calls her a slut, however, she begins to fight him. When she punches him in the nose, Marco relents. He is about to let her leave when he remembers his diamond. He smears Esther's cheeks with the blood from his nose, but she refuses to tell him where the diamond is until he threatens to break her neck if she does not tell him. She leaves him searching in the mud for her purse and his diamond. Esther cannot find Doreen, but manages to find a ride home to Manhattan. She climbs to the roof of her hotel, perches precariously on its edge, and throws her entire wardrobe off the roof, piece by piece.

SUMMARY: CHAPTER 10

Esther takes the train back to Massachusetts, wearing Betsy's clothes and still streaked in Marco's blood because she thinks it looks "touching, and rather spectacular." Her mother meets her at the train, and tells her she did not get into the writing course she planned on taking. The prospect of a summer in the suburbs distresses Esther. She thinks about her neighbors: Mrs. Ockenden, a nosy woman she dislikes, and Dodo Conway, a Catholic woman with six children and a seventh on the way. Mrs. Conway has a messy house and feeds her children junk food, and everyone loves her. Esther's friend Jody calls, and Esther tells her she will not be living with her in Cambridge, as planned, because she has been rejected from her writing course. Jody tells her to come anyway and take another course. Esther considers going to Cambridge, but hears a "hollow voice," her own, tell Jody she will not come. She opens a letter from Buddy, which says he thinks he is falling in love with a nurse, but if Esther comes with his mother to visit him in July, she may win back his affections. Esther crosses out his letter, writes on the opposite side that she is engaged to a simultaneous interpreter and never wants to see Buddy again, and mails the letter back to Buddy.

Esther decides to write a novel, but as she begins to type she becomes frustrated by her lack of life experiences. She agrees to let her mother teach her shorthand, but realizes that she does not want a job that requires shorthand. Lying in bed unable to sleep, she considers using the summer to write her thesis, put off college, or go to Germany. She discards all of these plans as soon as she thinks of them. Her mother, who sleeps in the same room with Esther, begins to snore, and Esther thinks of strangling her. The next day she tries to read *Finnegans Wake,* but the words seem to slide and dance all over the page. She considers leaving her school and going to a city college, but rejects this idea. When she asks the family doctor, Teresa, for more sleeping pills, Teresa refers her to a psychiatrist.

ANALYSIS: CHAPTERS 9–10

In these chapters, Esther's behavior becomes increasingly erratic, and her perspective on the world increasingly skewed. Until this point, Esther has been an unconventional but fairly normal young woman: cynical, and sometimes rebellious about the conventions of society, but also eager to behave normally, and guilty about feelings she views as abnormal or ungrateful. Now, however, Esther's healthy skepticism about the absurdities of her world becomes an inability to see the world as real, and she begins to disregard society's expectations.

With Esther's slipping grasp on reality comes an inability to protect herself from danger. Marco bruises her arm within moments of meeting her, speaks to her threateningly, and rips her drink away from her, but she does not detach herself from this clearly dangerous man. She does not grasp that she is taking a risk by putting herself in the hands of this man, instead musing calmly on Marco's likeness to a snake she remembers from the Bronx Zoo. When he throws her to the ground and rips her dress off, initially she seems to consider letting the rape occur, although eventually she reacts. When she returns to the hotel and throws her clothes off the roof, she forgets the practical consideration that she will need something to wear the next day. She throws away the expensive clothes as if throwing away the unhappy remnants of the dream job she ended up despising. While the symbolic gesture is apt, for Esther symbolism has filled the screen, leaving little room for the demands of reality.

Esther begins to disregard people's opinions of her. She wears Marco's blood on the train home to the suburbs as if it is a medal of honor, and cannot understand why people look at her with curiosity. At home, she does not bother to get dressed, and she has trouble sleeping. She starts to feel detached from herself, as evidenced by the fact that she listens with surprise to her own voice telling Jody she will not come to Cambridge. Her uncertainty about her future, understandably intensified after her rejection from the writing class, begins to pummel her. She frantically runs through a list of possible paths, and rejects all of them.

Plath suggests that Esther's troubles originate in her mind, but are exacerbated by the circumstances surrounding her. Marco attempts to rape Esther, a horror she deals with on her own. She bears her pain and shock silently, which surely intensifies these feelings. She must return from New York City, a city that Esther may have found unpleasant, but that forced her to keep busy and keep the company of girls her age. She must now live in isolation in the suburbs. She does not get into her writing course, a staggering blow because writing and prizes and academic laurels have come to seem like the sole achievements defining Esther's character. Events and brain chemistry conspire to loosen Esther's grasp on sanity.

CHAPTERS 11–12

SUMMARY: CHAPTER 11

Esther visits Dr. Gordon, a psychiatrist. She has not changed clothes or washed her hair for three weeks, having decided such chores are silly, and she says she has not slept for seven nights. She hopes that Dr. Gordon will help bring her back to herself, but she immediately distrusts him because he is good-looking and seems conceited. On his desk he keeps a picture of his attractive family, which makes Esther furious. She thinks he keeps the picture there to ward off her advances, and assumes such a handsome man with such a lovely family could never help her. Esther tells Dr. Gordon that she cannot sleep, eat, or read, though she does not tell him of her difficulty writing. That morning, she had attempted to write a letter to Doreen, but could not write legibly. He asks her where she goes to college and comments on how pretty the girls were when he worked there during the war. When Esther tells her mother that Dr. Gordon expects to see her the next week, Esther's mother sighs because Dr. Gordon charges twenty-five dollars an hour.

Esther flirts with a sailor on the Boston Common, pretending she is Elly Higginbottom, an orphan from Chicago. She thinks she sees Mrs. Willard approaching, but is wrong. When the sailor asks what has upset her, she says she thought the woman was from her orphanage in Chicago. The sailor asks if the woman was mean to her. She says yes and cries, momentarily convinced that this horrible woman caused everything unhappy in her life.

During her second visit to Dr. Gordon, Esther tells him that she feels the same and shows him the torn-up letter she tried to write to Doreen. He does not examine the scraps of paper, but asks to see her mother, and tells Mrs. Greenwood that Esther needs shock treatments at his hospital in Walton. Esther starts thinking about suicide while reading a tabloid account of a man prevented from jumping off a ledge. She finds she can read tabloid papers, because their short paragraphs end before the letters start jumping and sliding around. The next day Dodo Conway will drive Esther and her mother to the hospital for the shock treatment. Esther considers running away to Chicago, but realizes the bank will close before she can withdraw bus fare.

Summary: Chapter 12

Esther goes to Dr. Gordon's hospital for her shock treatment. The hospital waiting room looks like part of a summer hotel, but the inhabitants sit listlessly. They remind Esther of store mannequins. On the way to her treatment, Esther encounters a woman who threatens to jump out of the window, which she cannot do because bars across the windows would prevent her. A nurse wearing thick glasses hooks Esther up to the shock machine, and a jolt shakes Esther "like the end of the world." She wonders what awful thing she did to deserve this punishment. The treatment reminds her of the time she accidentally electrocuted herself with her father's lamp. Dr. Gordon again asks her what college she attends, and again remembers the nurses who were stationed there during the war. Esther feels dreadful, and tells her mother she is through with Dr. Gordon. Her mother says that she knew Esther was not like those people at the hospital and feels sure she would decide to get better.

Later, Esther sits in the park, comparing a picture of herself to a newspaper picture of a starlet who has just died after lingering in a coma. She thinks they look the same and imagines that if the starlet's eyes were open, as hers are, they would have the same "dead, black, vacant expression" as her own. She decides to sit on the park bench for five more minutes, and then go and kill herself. She listens to her "little chorus of voices," which repeats critical remarks that people such as Buddy and Jay Cee have made to her. That morning, she had tried to slit her wrists, but could not bring herself to harm the fragile skin of her wrist and practiced on her calf instead. After failing to slit her wrists, she took a bus to Deer Island Prison, near her child-hood home. She talked with a guard and imagined that if she had met him earlier and married him, she could have been living happily with children. She went to the beach and again considered slitting her wrists, but realized she did not have a warm bath to sit in after-ward. She sat on the beach until a small boy told her she should move because the tide was coming in. She considered letting herself drown, but when she put her foot in the water, she could not bear its frigid temperature, and went home.

ANALYSIS: CHAPTERS 11–12

Esther's illness becomes more severe. She cannot read, because the letters appear to literally slide and dance when she focuses her eyes on them. She seems to become delusional, instantly hating her doc-tor and crying about the stranger in the park as if she actually believes the unknown woman caused all of her problems.

Esther increasingly distrusts the medical establishment. This dis-trust first appears in Chapter 6, when she visits Buddy at medical school and watches a woman giving birth. She recoils at the idea that a drug can erase a woman's memory of pain. Now Dr. Gordon and her mother encourage her to forget her pain instead of under-standing or easing it. Dr. Gordon does not seem to hear Esther when she describes her symptoms. He demonstrates that he has not really listened to her when, after her shock treatment, he asks her for the second time where she goes to college and repeats his inane com-ment about the pretty girls stationed there during the war. He does not attempt to understand her suffering—rather, he merely attempts to make her normal again with a shock treatment that increases rather than diminishes her pain. Esther's mother, although well-meaning, also fails to understand her daughter's suffering. Esther says she will not need more shock treatment, and Esther's mother expresses relief, saying she knew Esther would decide to be normal. Esther's mother thinks of her daughter's state as a passing perversity or rebellion, not as a true illness. The numb and inactive patients Esther sees at the hospital reinforce the idea that mental illness is seen as a defect to be hidden, sanitized, and denied, not an illness to be discussed, understood, or cured.

Her mother and doctor having failed her, Esther works on her own cure, suicide. For the most part, she thinks not about *why* she wants to kill herself, but about *how* to kill herself. Her desire to take her life is careful and controlled, not wild or desperate. She thinks rationally about the method, time, and location for her act. In fact, she sounds at her most lucid when thinking about taking her life. Her calm focus on the means of death rather than the reason for death suggests that Esther wants to destroy herself simply because it seems like the only way to stop her pain, not because she irrationally hates herself. Her identification with the dead starlet in the picture suggests she already feels dead, and killing herself will simply bring her body in line with her psyche.

However, Esther realizes on some level that killing her body will not provide satisfaction. After failing to slit her wrists, for example, she explains, "It was as if what I wanted to kill wasn't in that skin or the thin blue pulse that jumped under my thumb, but somewhere else, deeper, more secret, a whole lot harder to get at." Esther understands that her body is not the enemy. The schism between her mind and the world she inhabits is the true enemy, but it is an enemy that Esther cannot reach. She feels that her only choice is to shut down her mind by shutting down her body. We can see the faultiness of this logic—Esther wants to save herself by destroying herself. The novel, however, narrated from Esther's perspective, forces us to understand Esther's point of view and see that, viewed from some angles, her actions seem almost reasonable.

CHAPTERS 13–14

SUMMARY: CHAPTER 13

Esther goes to the beach with her friend Jody, Jody's boyfriend Mark, and a man her age named Cal. She and Cal talk about a play in which a mother considers killing her son because he has gone mad. Esther asks Cal what method he would use if he were going to kill himself, and he says he would shoot himself. This answer disappoints her; she thinks shooting oneself a typically male way of committing suicide, and decides that not only would she have little chance of getting a gun, but she would not know where to shoot herself even if she did get one. She decides to try to drown herself in the ocean. Cal swims out with her, but decides he cannot make it to the rock that is their destination. Esther continues swimming, thinking she will continue until she tires, and then let herself drown. As she swims, the mantra "I am I am I am" thuds in her mind.

She thinks of that morning, when she tried to hang herself. She removed the cord from her mother's bathrobe and walked around the house looking for a place to hang the rope. She could not find a suitable place, however, and tried to kill herself by pulling the rope tightly around her neck, but every time she started to feel woozy, her hands weakened and loosened their hold on the rope. She thought of going to a doctor again instead of killing herself, but then imagined living in a private hospital and impoverishing her family with the cost of her care, and ending up in a state hospital.

Esther decides not to swim to the rock, as she thinks her body will rebel and regain its strength by resting on the rock, and she decides to drown where she is. She pushes herself down through the water, but every time she dives, her body bobs to the surface.

Her mother says that Esther should pull herself out of her depression by thinking of others, so Esther volunteers at the local hospital. On her first day, she must deliver flowers to women who have just given birth. Esther throws out the dead and dying flowers and rearranges the bouquets, which displeases the women. They complain, and Esther runs away from the hospital. Esther considers becoming Catholic, thinking the Catholics could talk her out of suicide, or let her become a nun, but her mother laughs at the idea of a conversion to Catholicism. Esther goes to visit her father's grave for the first time. After some effort, she finds his stone and begins to weep. She realizes she has never cried about her father's death; she did not see his corpse, and she was not allowed to attend his funeral, so his death never seemed real to her. Her mother never cried either, but smiled and said he would rather die than be crippled for life.

Esther decides on her method of suicide. After her mother leaves for work, she writes a note saying she has gone for a long walk. Then she retrieves her sleeping pills from her mother's lockbox. She hides herself in a crawl space in the cellar, takes about fifty pills, and drifts off to sleep.

SUMMARY: CHAPTER 14

Esther wakes, semiconscious, in darkness. She feels wind and hears voices, and light begins to pierce the darkness. She calls out for her mother. She does not realize she is in a hospital, and when she says aloud that she cannot see, a cheerful voice tells her she can marry a blind man. Soon a doctor visits her and says her eyesight is intact and a nurse must have been joking with her—she cannot see because bandages cover her head. Esther's mother and brother come to visit. She wishes her mother would leave, and tells her brother that she feels as she did before she tried to kill herself. She denies calling out for her mother. A young doctor who is an old acquaintance, George Bakewell, visits Esther and she sends him away. She does not really remember him, and thinks he only wants to see how a suicidal girl looks. She asks to see a mirror, and when she sees her bruised face and shaved head, she drops the mirror. The broken mirror angers the nurses, and Esther is moved to a hospital in the city.

In the new hospital, Esther has a bed next to a woman she believes is named Mrs. Tomolillo. When she tells Mrs. Tomollilo that she tried to kill herself, Mrs. Tomollilo asks the doctors to draw the curtain that separates the beds. Esther's mother comes to visit and reproaches Esther for not cooperating with the doctors. Esther thinks she sees Mrs. Tomolillo imitating her mother, and feels certain that the doctors give out false names and write down what she says. She asks her mother to get her out of the hospital, and her mother agrees to try. One day during mealtime, a woman named Mrs. Mole dumps green beans everywhere. The new attendant behaves rudely to Esther when she tells him not to clear the plates yet. She becomes convinced that he has served two kinds of beans in order to test their patience. When the nurse is not watching, Esther kicks him in the calf. Another day, a nurse rests her tray of thermometers on Esther's bed, and Esther kicks it to the floor. The nurses move her to Mrs. Mole's old room, and she pockets a ball of mercury along the way.

ANALYSIS: CHAPTERS 13–14

After many nervous and tentative attempts at suicide, Esther makes a serious attempt to kill herself. This drastic climax seems strangely anticlimactic, however. Esther does not carry through her first suicide attempts because of fear and practical considerations, and we begin to wonder how serious she is about killing herself since she seems so easily dissuaded by small obstacles. When Esther finally makes her nearly successful attempt, nothing in her tone warns us that this attempt will be decisive. Only after the near finality of her attempt do we realize that she has stopped speculating about killing herself, or warming up to do it, and has actually found a practical way of committing suicide. Her matter-of-fact tone as she procures the sleeping pills, pulls herself into the basement crawl space, and takes the pills makes us almost forget that she is doing something momentous in actually trying to take her own life. Again, she focuses not on why she wants to commit suicide, but on how she can achieve this goal, and she coaxes us into thinking in the same way she does.

Plath suggests that despite the many stresses in Esther's life, she attempts suicide because of mental illness, not because of external factors. Those external factors are numerous. Esther cannot be the ideal 1950s woman, chaste, cheerful, and subordinate to her husband. The darkness of life disturbs her—the execution of the Rosenbergs, the suffering and death she witnesses at Buddy's medical school, and the abandonment, distrust, and violence that mark her experience with men. She views the future with apprehension. Family problems exist for Esther too. She lost her father at a young age and, particularly in these chapters, she complains of a cruel mother who laughs at her daughter's desperate desire to become a Catholic, and smiles at the death of her husband. Still, none of these problems seem insurmountable. Esther has mustered the strength to stand up to Buddy. Her mother, although imperfect, clearly loves her, and the adult Esther suggests that the youthful Esther is crazed and misinterprets her mother's actions as sinister. Esther's numerous academic successes seem to outweigh her perfectly normal fears about the future. Therefore, Esther's own mind, not the difficult events of her life, spurs her desire to kill herself. This lack of motive is the most frightening element of Esther's suicide attempt, for her mental illness is mysterious, complex, and completely beyond her control.

After her attempt, nothing changes. She feels equally despairing and begins to feel even more paranoid, worrying that the doctors are giving out false names and recording her conversations.

CHAPTERS 15–16

SUMMARY: CHAPTER 15

> [W]herever I sat—on the deck of a ship or at a street
> café in Paris or Bangkok—I would be sitting under
> the same glass bell jar, stewing in my own sour air.
>
> (See QUOTATIONS, p. 51)

Philomena Guinea, the sponsor of Esther's college scholarship, pays for Esther to go to a private mental hospital. Guinea had once been in an asylum herself. She writes, asking if a boy spurred Esther's attempt on her life, and Esther's mother writes back that Esther worries she will never write again. In response, Guinea flies into Boston and drives Esther to a posh hospital that resembles a country club. Esther's mother tells her she should be grateful, since the family had used up almost all of its money on the hospital bills. Esther knows she should feel grateful, but cannot feel anything. The bell jar of her illness traps her, and everything seems sour. Esther plans to leap from the car and jump from the bridge when they cross the Charles River, but her mother and brother sit on either side of her and grasp the door handles so that she cannot make a move. She admits to herself that even if her family had not been there, she probably would have refrained from jumping.

At the hospital, Esther meets her new psychiatrist, Dr. Nolan. Esther did not know women psychiatrists existed. She finds herself free to wander about the hospital, and encounters a friendly girl named Valerie. During her first visit with Dr. Nolan, Esther explains how much she hated her electroshock treatment. Dr. Nolan says that the treatment was done incorrectly, and that if Esther has to go through electroshock treatment again, it will be different. An older patient, Miss Norris, moves in next door to Esther. Miss Norris never speaks, and Esther watches her carefully. She follows her to the dinner table and sits next to her in silence, enjoying her company.

Three times a day, the nurse injects Esther. Valerie explains that the injections are insulin, and says she may have a reaction one day. Esther has had no reaction; she just grows plump. Valerie shows Esther the scars at her temples and explains that she has had a lobotomy. She says she used to be angry all the time, and now she feels fine. She has no desire to leave the hospital. Esther gets moved into a sun-

nier room, and Miss Norris gets moved to Wymark, a ward considered a move down in the process of recovery. Then the nurse tells
Esther that a recently admitted patient knows her. Esther goes next
door to investigate and sees Joan Gilling, a college acquaintance.

SUMMARY: CHAPTER 16

Joan says she came to the asylum after reading about Esther. Esther
asks her what she means, and Joan explains it started with a terrible
job that gave her painful bunions on her feet. She began wearing
rubber boots to work, a habit that strikes Esther as crazy. Joan says
she stopped going to work, stopped answering the phone, and
began to consider killing herself. Her doctor sent her to a psychiatrist, but the psychiatrist kept her waiting and then decided to allow
his students to observe the appointment. Joan was forced to
describe her symptoms in front of nine people. She left the room
while they discussed her case, and then the doctor informed her that
she needed group therapy. Joan left in disgust, and that day saw an
article about Esther's disappearance.

Joan shows Esther newspaper clippings. The first one reports
Esther missing. The second reports sleeping pills missing along with
Esther, and shows photos of men and dogs searching the woods.
The last article describes how Esther's mother was doing laundry
when she heard moaning, and discovered her daughter. Esther's case
inspired Joan to go to New York and kill herself. She stayed with her
old college roommate, and tried to slit her wrists by shoving her
hands through her roommate's window.

One night, Esther wakes up in the middle of the night to find herself beating on her bedpost with her hands. She has had a reaction to
her insulin treatment, and feels better. To her delight, Dr. Nolan
tells her she will have no more visitors. Esther dislikes the visits she
receives from old teachers and employers, who get nervous or say
her depression is imaginary. She especially dislikes visits from her
mother, because her mother begs to know what she did wrong.
When her mother visits on Esther's birthday she brings a dozen
long-stemmed roses, which Esther throws in the trash. She tells Dr.
Nolan she hates her mother, a statement that pleases the doctor.

ANALYSIS: CHAPTERS 15–16

The treatment Esther receives at the richly appointed asylum contrasts sharply with the treatment she received from Dr. Gordon.

Unlike Dr. Gordon, Dr. Nolan listens to Esther and gains her trust. When Esther admits that she hates her mother, she assumes Dr. Nolan will berate her—instead, Dr. Nolan acts satisfied.

Esther continues to act selfishly, sometimes recognizing her own bad behavior. She realizes that she should feel grateful to Philomena Guinea, but despite this knowledge she plots to hurl herself from the moving car of her patron and commit suicide by jumping off the bridge. This suicidal act would, of course, horrify Guinea. Esther behaves cruelly to her mother, telling her to save the roses for her funeral, and then throwing away the flowers in her mother's presence. This treatment seems particularly heartless because Esther has seen the newspaper clippings that demonstrate the horrible worry her mother endured: Esther went missing, the police searched for her with dogs, and finally she heard her daughter whimpering in the basement. The mother's ordeal strikes us as terrifying, but Esther never seems to consider what her mother suffered. Neither does she consider the fact that her behavior actually inspired Joan to go to New York and attempt suicide.

At the same time, however, some signs point to Esther's improvement. She ceases to focus obsessively on killing herself, even admitting that she would not have jumped over the bridge if given the opportunity. Even if she does not feel grateful to Guinea, she knows she *should* feel grateful. She behaves cruelly to her mother, but in part this cruelty serves a useful purpose in recovery, for Esther has begun to confront her feelings and acknowledge some of the things that exacerbate her desire to kill herself. She shows healthy anger for the first time in Chapter 16, to the delight of Dr. Nolan. Although Esther demonstrates selfishness in her interactions with Joan, at least she finds herself able to listen to Joan's story, and even empathize with Joan's feelings. Such sympathetic responses to another person eluded Esther in the days before her suicide.

Esther mentions the bell jar for the first time in Chapter 15. She says that even if she went on a cruise, or traveled to Europe, "[She] would be sitting under the same glass bell jar, stewing in [her] own sour air." A bell jar is an inverted glass jar used to cover objects, trap certain gases, or contain a vacuum. Esther feels that a bell jar separates her from the world of the living. In it, she breathes "her own sour air," or lives in a vacuum in which she cannot breathe at all. By likening her sickness to a bell jar, Esther suggests that she has no control over its descent. The illness does what it likes, trapping her inside.

CHAPTERS 17–18

SUMMARY: CHAPTER 17

Esther gets moved from Caplan, her current ward, to Belsize, a ward for the women closest to release. She does not feel much improved, but feels relieved that the threat of shock treatments has diminished. The women at Belsize behave fairly normally, playing bridge and gossiping. Esther sits with them, and Joan, who was moved to Belsize earlier, finds a picture of Esther in her fashion magazine. Esther says it is not her.

The next morning, the nurse fails to bring Esther a breakfast tray. Esther thinks a mistake has been made, for only girls who are to have shock treatments miss their morning tray. But the nurse confirms that Esther will not receive her breakfast until later. Esther hides in the hall and weeps, terrified by the prospect of the treatment, but even more upset that Dr. Nolan did not warn her as she promised to do. Dr. Nolan arrives and comforts her, saying she did not tell Esther about the treatment the day before because she did not want her to worry all night, and she will take Esther to the treatment herself. Miss Huey, the nurse who administers the treatment, speaks kindly to Esther. As soon as the treatment begins, Esther falls unconscious.

SUMMARY: CHAPTER 18

Esther wakes from her shock treatment to find Dr. Nolan with her. They go outside, and Esther notices that the metaphorical bell jar has lifted and she can breathe the open air. Dr. Nolan tells her she will have shock treatments three times a week. Later, when Esther cracks an egg open with a knife, she remembers she used to love knives. When she tries to remember why, her mind "slipped from the noose of the thought and swung, like a bird, in the center of empty air."

Both Joan and Esther receive letters from Buddy Willard, who wants to come visit. Joan, who used to date Buddy, explains that she liked Buddy's family more than she liked him—they seemed so normal compared to her own family. Joan wants Buddy to come visit and bring his mother. Earlier Esther hated the idea of his visit, but now she believes that it may allow her to close that part of her life.

Earlier that morning, Esther had come upon Joan and DeeDee, another patient, in bed together. She asks Dr. Nolan what women saw in each other, and Dr. Nolan responds, "Tenderness." Now

Joan tells Esther that she likes her better than she likes Buddy. Esther recalls other lesbians she has known, two college classmates who caused a small scandal, and a professor. She roughly rebukes Joan and walks away.

Esther had told Dr. Nolan that she wants the kind of freedom that men have, but she feels that the threat of pregnancy hangs over her. She told her about the pamphlet on chastity her mother sent her, and Dr. Nolan laughed, called it propaganda, and gave her the name of a doctor who would help her. Esther goes to the doctor to get fitted for a diaphragm. In the waiting room, she observes the women with babies and wonders at her own lack of maternal instinct. The doctor is cheerfully unobtrusive, and as he fits her Esther thinks delightedly that she is gaining freedom from fear and freedom from marrying the wrong person. Her birth control acquired, Esther wants to find the right man with whom to lose her virginity.

ANALYSIS: CHAPTERS 17–18

Esther finds a mother figure in Dr. Nolan. When faced with the prospect of shock treatment, Esther's greatest fear is not the therapy, but the possibility that Dr. Nolan has betrayed her. She explains, "I liked Doctor Nolan, I loved her, I had given her my trust on a platter and told her everything." Dr. Nolan hugs her "like a mother" and regains Esther's trust by explaining her actions. Dr. Nolan is the only character in the novel whom Esther claims to love, and the only person she seems to trust entirely. Esther's ability to form such a loving relationship is an important sign of her healing. She has formed what Freud called a "transference" relationship with her psychiatrist, transferring the feelings that she would normally have for her mother onto her doctor. In Freudian theory, this relationship marks the beginning of healing, because now Esther can explore her feelings about her actual mother in the safe space of a surrogate relationship.

A combination of talk therapy, insulin treatment, and shock therapy (shock therapy was standard treatment for mental illness at the time) helps Esther feel less depressed and causes her to forget her suicidal desires. The contradictory nature of the world she must inhabit has not changed, but Esther is better able to deal with it, both because of her own improved mental health, and because she finds that some authorities support her views. Dr. Nolan confirms Esther's rejection of the sexual role that women are expected to play, dismissing the article on chastity given to her by her mother as "propaganda." The male doctor who gives Esther a diaphragm is kind and does not ask invasive questions about why Esther wants birth control. Esther continues to sort out her feelings about men, recognizing the truth of what Dr. Nolan says: many women lack tenderness in their relationships with men. Esther continues to feel she needs to lose her virginity in order to mark her rejection of the conventional expectation that she will remain "pure" for her husband.

CHAPTERS 19–20

SUMMARY: CHAPTER 19

Joan tells Esther she plans to become a psychiatrist. She will be leaving Belsize to live with a nurse in Cambridge. Even though Esther is due to leave the hospital for winter semester at college, Joan's eminent departure makes her jealous. While on town leave, Esther meets a math professor named Irwin on the steps of the library at Harvard. They have coffee together, and then she goes to his apartment for a beer. A woman named Olga rings the bell. She seems to be a sometime lover of Irwin's, but he sends her away. Esther and Irwin go out for dinner, and she gets permission from Dr. Nolan to spend the night in Cambridge by saying she plans to sleep at Joan's apartment. Esther thinks that Irwin would be a good person to sleep with. He is intelligent, experienced, and unknown. She wants to sleep with an "impersonal, priestlike official, as in the tales of tribal rites." When they return to Irwin's apartment and have sex, she expects to feel transformed, but merely feels sharp pain.

Esther realizes that she is bleeding. She worries, but Irwin reassures her, and she remembers stories about virgins bleeding on their wedding night. The bleeding does not stop, however, and Esther bandages herself with a towel and asks Irwin to drive her to Joan's apartment. Esther shows Joan her problem, telling Joan she is hemorrhaging. Joan does not suspect the real story, and takes her to the hospital emergency room in a taxicab. The doctor examines Esther and expresses surprise, saying that such blood loss after the first sexual encounter is extremely rare. He stops the bleeding. Several nights later, a woman named Dr. Quinn knocks on Esther's door. Joan, who has returned to the asylum, is missing. Esther does not know where she is. She wakes the next morning to the news that Joan hanged herself in the woods.

SUMMARY: CHAPTER 20

> *To the person in the bell jar, blank and stopped as a dead baby, the world itself is the bad dream.*
>
> *How did I know that someday—at college, in Europe, somewhere, anywhere—the bell jar, with its stifling distortions, wouldn't descend again?*
> (See QUOTATIONS, p. 52)

Esther anticipates her return to college in a week. It is snowing, and she thinks of the familiar college landscape that awaits her. Her mother has told her that they will "take up where [they] left off" and act as if Esther's bout with madness has been a bad dream. Esther knows she will not be able to forget what she has gone through. Buddy comes to visit, and Esther helps him dig his car out of the snow. He seems less physically and emotionally self-confident. He asks Esther if she thinks he contributed to her or Joan's madness. Esther thinks of Dr. Nolan's reassurance that no one is to blame for Joan's death, least of all Esther. She reassures Buddy that he did not cause their problems, which seems to hearten him greatly. Thoughtlessly, he wonders out loud who will marry Esther now that she has been in an asylum.

Esther says goodbye to Valerie, and calls Irwin to demand that he pay her doctor's bill from the night they had sex. He agrees and asks when he will see her again. She answers, "Never," and hangs up on him, relieved that he cannot contact or find her. She feels free. Esther attends Joan's funeral and listens to her heart beat its mantra: "I am, I am, I am." Esther waits for her final interview with her doctors. Even though Dr. Nolan has reassured her, she is nervous. She feels ready to leave Belsize, but realizes that the bell jar of her madness may descend again later in her life. She walks into the room of doctors, and the novel ends.

ANALYSIS: CHAPTERS 19–20

Esther finally loses her virginity, and it is not the transformation she expects. Still, the experience pleases her in some ways. Esther feels relieved to relinquish her virginity and its attendant worries; she describes her virginity as "a millstone around my neck." Furthermore, she exercises control by choosing a man who meets her criteria of intelligence and anonymity. These criteria are not conventional. Esther wants not a relationship, but a ritualistic, formal, impersonal first sexual experience. Irwin's involvement with Olga and his admission that he enjoys many women does not dissuade Esther but encourages her, because it suggests Irwin has the kind of experience she needs to offset her own ignorance of sex.

Esther's mental health seems greatly improved in these final chapters. Whereas before she elicited no sympathy for Joan, even after learning that her own suicide attempt inspired Joan to try to take her own life, in Chapter 20 she asks Dr. Nolan if she should feel responsible for Joan's death. Esther can now empathize with others, and think of something other than her own pain. She also demonstrates the maturity and strength that are the rewards of surviving such a harrowing experience. When Buddy visits, his selfish, thoughtless immaturity contrasts with her cool strength. Like someone much older, Esther assures Buddy that she is fine, and generously soothes his fears that he causes women to go mad.

Joan's death elicits quiet reflection in Esther. This quiet suggests Esther's unconventional way of expressing herself. It also suggests that, although Esther does not particularly like Joan, Esther and Joan are two parts of a whole. Esther does not think of Joan as her friend. As she says in Chapter 18, Joan fascinates and disgusts her, for "her thoughts and feelings seemed a wry, black image of [Esther's] own." Because Joan functions partly as Esther's double, her burial symbolizes Esther's burial of the diseased, suicidal part of herself. This rebirth allows the novel to end on a hopeful note, although the symbol of the bell jar returns when Esther asks, "How did I know that someday . . . the bell jar, with its stifling distortions, wouldn't descend again?"

IMPORTANT QUOTATIONS EXPLAINED

1. Look what can happen in this country, they'd say. A
    girl lives in some out-of-the-way town for nineteen
    years, so poor she can't afford a magazine, and then
    she gets a scholarship to college and wins a prize here
    and a prize there and ends up steering New York like
    her own private car. Only I wasn't steering anything,
    not even myself. I just bumped from my hotel to work
    and to parties and from parties to my hotel and back
    to work like a numb trolleybus. I guess I should have
    been excited the way most of the other girls were, but
    I couldn't get myself to react. I felt very still and
    very empty, the way the eye of a tornado must
    feel, moving dully along in the middle of the
    surrounding hullabaloo.

This quotation, which concludes the first section of Chapter 1,
describes the disconnect Esther feels between the way other people
view her life and the way she experiences her life. By all external
measures, Esther should feel happy and excited. She has overcome
her middle-class, small town background with luck, talent, and hard
work, and her reward is a glamorous month in New York. Although
she recognizes these objective facts, Esther feels uncertain both
about her own abilities and about the rewards that these abilities
have garnered her. To her own puzzlement, she does not find New
York thrilling and romantic. Instead, she finds it dizzying and
depressing, and she finds the fashion world she inhabits superficial
and disorienting. The feeling of numbness that Esther describes here
is the kernel of the madness that will soon overtake her. Eventually,
the gap between societal expectations and her own feelings and
experiences becomes so large that she feels she can no longer survive.

2.   When I was nineteen, pureness was the great issue.
      Instead of the world being divided up into Catholics
      and Protestants or Republicans and Democrats or
      white men and black men or even men and women, I
      saw the world divided into people who had slept with
      somebody and people who hadn't, and this seemed
      the only really significant difference between one
      person and another. I thought a spectacular change
      would come over me the day I crossed the
      boundary line.

This quotation from Chapter 7 shows that Esther inhabits a world of limited sexual choices. Convention dictates that she will remain a virgin until she marries. If she chooses to have sex before marriage, she risks pregnancy, displeasing her future husband, and ruining her own name. Esther sets out to defy conventional expectations by losing her virginity with someone she does not expect to marry. Despite this firm goal, she finds it difficult to gain an independent sexual identity. The men in her life provide little help: Buddy has traditional ideas about male and female roles even though he has mildly transgressed by having an affair with a waitress; an acquaintance named Eric thinks sex disgusting, and will not have sex with a woman he loves; and Marco calls Esther a slut as he attempts to rape her. When Esther finally loses her virginity, she does not experience the "spectacular change" that she expects, although the experience does satisfy her in some says. Esther only partially escapes the repressive ideas about sexuality that surround her. By losing her virginity, she frees herself of the oppressive mandate to remain pure, but she fails to find sexual pleasure or independence.

QUOTATIONS

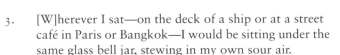

3. [W]herever I sat—on the deck of a ship or at a street café in Paris or Bangkok—I would be sitting under the same glass bell jar, stewing in my own sour air.

This quotation, from the beginning of Chapter 15, introduces the symbol of the bell jar. Esther explains that no matter where she goes, she exists in the hell of her own mind. She is trapped inside herself, and no external stimulation, no matter how new and exciting, can ameliorate this condition. The bell jar of Esther's madness separates her from the people she should care about. Esther's association of her illness with a bell jar suggests her feeling that madness descends on her without her control or assent—it is as if an unseen scientist traps her. Esther's suicidal urges come from this sense of suffocating isolation.

4.   To the person in the bell jar, blank and stopped as a
       dead baby, the world itself is the bad dream.

This quotation comes from the last chapter of the novel, in which
Esther attempts to draw some conclusions about the experiences she
has undergone. Her mother suggests that they treat Esther's madness as if it were a bad dream that can be forgotten. This quotation
records Esther's inward response; she feels that madness is like
being trapped in a bad dream, but it is a bad dream from which one
cannot awake. Esther likens the person who suffers from mental illness to the pickled fetuses she saw at Buddy's medical school, a mor-
bid connection that illustrates the terror of madness.

QUOTATIONS

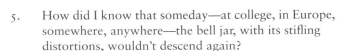

5.   How did I know that someday—at college, in Europe, somewhere, anywhere—the bell jar, with its stifling distortions, wouldn't descend again?

This quotation, also from the last chapter of the novel, provides the final word on Esther's supposed cure. The bell jar has lifted enough that Esther can function more or less normally. She has relinquished her desire to kill herself, and she begins to form tenuous connections with other people and with the outside world. But Esther still feels the bell jar hovering above her, and worries that it will trap her again. Her madness does not obey reason, and though she feels grateful to have escaped from it, she does not believe that this escape represents a fundamental or permanent change in her situation. If we read *The Bell Jar* as partly autobiographical, Plath's own life story confirms that the bell jar can descend again. Just as the pressures that culminated in her late teens drove Plath to attempt suicide, the pressures that culminated in her early thirties drove her to commit suicide.

KEY FACTS

FULL TITLE
The Bell Jar

AUTHOR
Sylvia Plath

TYPE OF WORK
Novel

GENRE
Coming-of-age novel; autobiographical fiction

LANGUAGE
English

TIME AND PLACE WRITTEN
First draft as early as 1957, Cambridge, England; completed in 1962, Devon, England

DATE OF FIRST PUBLICATION
January 1963, under the pseudonym Victoria Lucas

PUBLISHER
William Heinemann Limited (1963); Faber and Faber (first edition under Plath's name, 1966); Harper and Row (first American edition, 1971)

NARRATOR
Esther Greenwood

POINT OF VIEW
First person

TONE
Matter-of-fact; cynical; terse; detached; girlish

TENSE
Past

SETTING (TIME)
June 1953–January 1954

SETTING (PLACE)
New York City; the Boston suburbs; hospitals in and
around Boston

PROTAGONIST
Esther Greenwood

MAJOR CONFLICT
Esther struggles against her oppressive environment and
encroaching madness.

RISING ACTION
Esther spends a month as a guest editor in New York. When she
returns home, she finds herself unable to read, write, or sleep.
She receives her first shock treatment, and contemplates
methods of suicide.

CLIMAX
Esther almost succeeds in killing herself.

FALLING ACTION
Esther recovers in a city hospital and then in a private mental
hospital, where she finds a psychiatrist whom she can trust.
After losing her virginity, she prepares to leave the hospital.

THEMES
Growth through pain and rebirth; the emptiness of
conventional expectations; the restricted role of women in
1950s America; the perils of psychiatric medicine

MOTIFS
News and fashion media; mirrors; blood

SYMBOLS
The bell jar; the fig tree; headlines; the beating heart

FORESHADOWING
Esther's semi-suicidal plunge down the ski slopes foreshadows
her later, more systematic suicide attempts.

KEY FACTS

STUDY QUESTIONS & ESSAY TOPICS

STUDY QUESTIONS

1. *What is the significance of the Rosenbergs' execution in the novel?*

Esther's summer in New York is supposed to be one of carefree pleasure, but newspaper headlines and radio broadcasts keep the execution of the Rosenbergs at the forefront of her mind. Esther does not see 1950s America as a reasonable, moral place, but a façade hiding darkness and suffering such as the impending execution of the Rosenbergs. The Rosenberg case was controversial for political reasons. Some felt that the Rosenbergs' guilt was questionable and their sentence too harsh, others that in order to combat Communism, spies must receive harsh punishment. However, Esther does not mention the politics of their case. Instead, the machinery and physical process of their deaths fascinates and horrifies her. Esther's obsession with the Rosenbergs represents her general obsession with death.

2.   *What reasons does the novel give for Esther's madness?*

The novel avoids attributing Esther's mental illness to external factors, and blames it on a mysterious and powerful inward force. A number of factors exacerbate Esther's condition: she lost her father when she was a child, her mother fails to understand her, she comes from a poor family, and she feels great and crushing pressure to succeed. Contradictions in the culture that surrounds her also aggravate Esther's madness. As a young, talented woman in 1950s America, she is encouraged to be independent and self-sufficient, but is also expected to become a submissive wife and mother. Along with identifying marriage and motherhood as signs of achievement, society also defines female success by physical attractiveness and a home filled with lovely possessions, but Esther feels the emptiness of the fashion magazine world she inhabits in New York. Both personal difficulties and the problems of being an intelligent, sensitive woman plague Esther and fan the flames of her mental illness.

QUESTIONS & ESSAYS

3.   *In what way is* The Bell Jar *a coming-of-age story?*

The Bell Jar revolves around Esther's journey of self-discovery. She experiences some of the typical milestones of young womanhood: her first wedding proposal, her first sexual experience, and her first time in a big city. Esther becomes acutely aware that the college phase of her life is about to end and that she must make decisions about her future lifestyle and career. But Esther's journey does not smoothly progress toward positive self-knowledge and a growing exercise of her own abilities. Instead, she suffers a breakdown, and madness disrupts her coming-of-age. By the end of the novel, Esther feels as if she has been put back together to face the world, but she must live from now on with the memory of her insanity, and with the threat of its return. In this sense, *The Bell Jar* could be understood as an anti-coming-of-age story.

QUESTIONS & ESSAYS

Suggested Essay Topics

1. What role does Esther's memory of her father play in the story?

2. Choose a poem by Sylvia Plath and relate its imagery to the imagery of *The Bell Jar*.

3. *The Bell Jar* is both a true story and a novel. Describe the ways in which Plath selects and presents the episodes that she describes to give her narrative dramatic shape.

4. There are several recurring images in the novel, such as the bell jar, the dead baby, and the fig tree. Select one of these images and trace its occurrence from the beginning of the novel to the end, describing how its meaning evolves.

5. How does Esther's attitude toward men change over the course of the novel? What role does this attitude play in her madness and recovery?

6. When Esther tells Dr. Nolan that she hates her mother, Dr. Nolan interprets this statement as a breakthrough in Esther's recovery. What role does Esther's mother play in her insanity? What does Esther's attitude toward her mother tell us about Esther herself?

REVIEW & RESOURCES

QUIZ

1. To what does the title of *The Bell Jar* refer?

   A. The jars containing fetuses at Buddy Willard's medical school

   B. The jar containing the sleeping pills with which Esther tries to kill herself

   C. Esther's feeling that her madness distorts and separates her from the outside world

   D. The private mental hospital where Esther resides

2. Which of the following is *not* a method of suicide tried by Esther?

   A. Hanging

   B. Shooting

   C. Drowning

   D. Overdosing on pills

3. What is the subject of the article that Esther's mother sends her?

   A. A defense of chastity

   B. How to be a good wife

   C. How to use birth control

   D. How to maintain a positive attitude

4. During the magazine photo shoot, what occupation does Esther claim to desire?

   A. Editor at a publishing house

   B. Poet

   C. College professor

   D. Cape Cod waitress

5. How does Esther know Joan before they meet again at the mental hospital?

    A. Joan was one of Esther's friends in New York
    B. Esther was supposed to live with Joan while taking a writing course
    C. Joan was Esther's lover
    D. Joan was from Esther's hometown and a year ahead of her in college

6. Who pays for Esther's treatment at the private mental hospital?

    A. Jay Cee
    B. Philomena Guinea
    C. Her mother
    D. Mrs. Willard

7. To whom does Esther lose her virginity?

    A. Buddy
    B. Irwin
    C. Marco
    D. Constantin

8. Why does Esther become violently ill after the magazine banquet?

    A. She suffers from food poisoning
    B. She ate too much caviar
    C. She is disgusted at the life she is living
    D. She is upset by the Rosenbergs' execution

9. During what era does *The Bell Jar* take place?

    A. The late 1940s
    B. The early 1970s
    C. The early 1950s
    D. The early 1960s

10. What disappointment greets Esther when she returns to suburban Boston?

    A.   Buddy Willard is engaged to a nurse
    B.   She has been rejected from a summer writing course
    C.   Her brother has not come back home, as she had hoped
    D.   Her room has been rented to a boarder

11. What does the fig tree symbolize for Esther?

    A.   The tree of knowledge
    B.   All of life's bewildering choices
    C.   Her desire to become a nun
    D.   A fantasy wedding with Buddy

12. Why does Esther fail to drown herself?

    A.   Her friends come to her rescue
    B.   She climbs out and rests on the rock
    C.   The water is too shallow
    D.   Her body keeps floating to the surface

13. Whose grave does Esther visit?

    A.   Joan's
    B.   Her grandmother's
    C.   Her father's
    D.   Her grandfather's

14. Which family member does Esther claim to hate?

    A.   Her father
    B.   Her mother
    C.   Her brother
    D.   Her grandmother

15. What is in Esther's suitcase when she returns home from New York?

    A.   Avocados and a book of short stories
    B.   Her clothing
    C.   Nectarines and Marco's diamond
    D.   Doreen's clothing

16. What is Esther's attitude toward the Rosenbergs' execution?

    A.   She is glad that they will die
    B.   She is indifferent
    C.   She thinks their death will be horrible
    D.   She supports the U.S. government

17. Why is Buddy in a sanitarium?

    A.   He is a ski instructor
    B.   He has tuberculosis
    C.   He is going insane
    D.   He has pneumonia

18. What is Esther's mother's attitude toward Esther's
    mental illness?

    A.   Her mother is furious and unresponsive
    B.   Her mother finds Esther's illness understandable
    C.   Her mother cannot bear to visit her
    D.   Her mother is worried and tries to help

19. What happens to Esther at the end of the novel?

    A.   She successfully kills herself
    B.   She plans to leave the institution
    C.   She marries Buddy
    D.   She goes home to live with her mother

20. Which treatment does Esther *not* undergo?

    A.   Shock therapy
    B.   Group therapy
    C.   Insulin treatment
    D.   Psychotherapy

21. Who visits Esther just before the end of the novel?

    A.   Jay Cee
    B.   Irwin
    C.   Her mother
    D.   Buddy

REVIEW & RESOURCES

22. How does Joan kill herself?

    A. She hangs herself
    B. She jumps from a window
    C. She overdoses on pills
    D. She slits her wrists

23. How does Esther behave at the city hospital?

    A. She is sleepy and unresponsive
    B. She is trusting and cooperative
    C. She is paranoid and difficult
    D. She tries to escape

24. What form of birth control does Esther use?

    A. A diaphragm
    B. The pill
    C. An IUD
    D. Condoms

25. What happens to Esther after she loses her virginity?

    A. She runs away from the mental hospital
    B. She realizes she has felt sexual pleasure for the first time
    C. She bleeds uncontrollably
    D. She confides in Joan

ANSWER KEY:
1: C; 2: B; 3: A; 4: B; 5: D; 6: B; 7: B; 8: A; 9: C; 10: B;
11: B; 12: D; 13: C; 14: B; 15: A; 16: C; 17: B; 18: D; 19: B;
20: B; 21: D; 22: A; 23: C; 24: A; 25: C

SUGGESTIONS FOR FURTHER READING

DAVIS, GARY. *Existential and Pathological Anxiety in* THE BELL JAR. Maryville: Northwest Missouri State University, 1979.

PLATH, SYLVIA. *The Collected Poems.* New York: HarperPerennial, 1992.

———. *Letters Home.* Edited by Aurelia Schober Plath. New York: Harper & Row, 1975.

———. *The Unabridged Journals of Sylvia Plath.* Edited by Karen V. Kukil. New York: Anchor Books, 2000.

ROSE, JACQUELINE. *The Haunting of Sylvia Plath.* Cambridge, Massachusetts: Harvard University Press, 1992.

STEVENSON, ANNE. *Bitter Fame: A Life of Sylvia Plath.* Boston: Houghton Mifflin, 1989.

WAGNER, LINDA, ed. *Sylvia Plath: The Critical Heritage.* New York: Routledge, 1988.

WAGNER-MARTIN, LINDA. THE BELL JAR: *A Novel of the Fifties.* New York: Twayne Publishers, 1992.

REVIEW & RESOURCES

SPARKNOTES STUDY GUIDES:

Learning to Research, Researching to Learn

Learning to Research, Researching to Learn

Cally Guerin, Paul Bartholomew
and Claus Nygaard

THE LEARNING IN HIGHER EDUCATION SERIES

LIBRI
PUBLISHING

First published in 2015 by Libri Publishing

Copyright © Libri Publishing

Authors retain copyright of individual chapters.

The right of Cally Guerin, Paul Bartholomew and Claus Nygaard to be identified as the editors of this work has been asserted in accordance with the Copyright, Designs and Patents Act, 1988.

ISBN 978-1-909818-66-8

A CIP catalogue record for this book is available from The British Library

Cover design by Helen Taylor

Design by Carnegie Publishing

Printed in the UK by Short Run Press Ltd

Libri Publishing
Brunel House
Volunteer Way
Faringdon
Oxfordshire
SN7 7YR

Tel: +44 (0)845 873 3837

www.libripublishing.co.uk

Contents

Foreword

Research is central to contemporary democratic society. The complexity and uncertainty that characterise daily life in the twenty-first century demands that citizens are able to investigate situations and phenomena, weigh and judge evidence, make critical judgments and present ideas clearly and unambiguously in democratic discussions. The ability to carry out research is thus a key characteristic of any citizen. It is absolutely essential for effective professional engagement. So learning to research at university is vital.

It is through research that society learns. There is not a single aspect of contemporary life that has not been affected by research, much of which has been conducted in universities. This is most obviously seen in the technology we use on a daily basis but it is also evident in how we think — about the environment we inhabit, about ourselves, and about each other.

It is therefore perhaps surprising that research appears to have been peripheral to university pedagogy. Until now. In this book we witness a variety of ways in which students are learning about research and learning to do research. Indeed, here, research becomes central to higher education learning and teaching. Through students' engagement, teaching and research are brought together.

The relationship between teaching and research has for a long time been viewed as central to the idea of a university. In the late twentieth century, many efforts were made to understand and to strengthen this relationship. Debates about how to do this tended to focus on what academics could do to bring their research into their teaching, for example, by talking about their own research, discussing research ideas and so on.

However, understanding more about the nature of the relationship between teaching and research, at that time, went hand in hand with a strong tide of change that was serving to divorce it. On the research side, national funding priorities designed to check and then enhance research output transformed research into a political endeavour. So talk of research carries political overtones. This has the effect of separating research from teaching. It denies that research is a process of learning and focuses academics' attention on publications, outputs and impacts. On the teaching side, pressure on university funding for teaching and growth in student numbers has endorsed the dominance of lecture-based pedagogies. Technological innovation, in particular social networking, has offered the opportunity for pedagogical innovation in what is now a mass higher education system, but all too often it maintains the lecture ethos as course material is 'delivered' through the internet for students' passive reception. This too means separating teaching from research. Disciplinary content knowledge is divorced from the processes of discovery and is sanitised for mass consumption.

Thus, different facets of the changing nature of higher education have served to divide research and teaching rather than bring them closer together. Efforts to challenge these trends have been hampered by a lack of specific strategies to do it in many cases. If the relationship between teaching and research is central to the idea of a university, then new strategies were needed.

This has happened through a change in the focus of attention away from viewing the relationship between teaching and research as being a question about what academics do in their teaching, to emphasise the ways in which students engage with research in their learning. A number of studies around the world had shown that students were generally distanced from the research enterprise of the institution in which they were enrolled but that they would have liked to have been more involved. This is now happening and on a global scale too.

Opportunities for undergraduates to engage in research have been a feature of academic life in the USA for over 40 years and are growing in many other countries. Although in Australia many universities now have special programmes for undergraduates to pursue research and it is clear that the number of students in these programmes is growing, such developments are relatively recent. Commitment to student research training right from the start of their university careers is evident in the existence of a significant number of nationally funded projects to develop research-based learning pedagogy, in the introduction and spread of research degrees at the undergraduate level, and in numerous attempts to introduce experiences within the curriculum. Such activities see research engagement as starting in the early undergraduate years and continuing through to postgraduate and doctoral study. There have also been a growing number of ways that undergraduates can disseminate their research through national and local research conferences and journals.

These developments are not surprising since such practices are known to have high impact in engaging students (Kuh, 2008). The benefits to students of engaging in research have also been well known for some time. They include: personal and professional gains such as increased confidence; and intellectual development, including critical thinking and problem solving skills and a more advanced understanding of how scientific knowledge is built (see for example, John & Creighton, 2011; Laursen, Hunter, Seymour, Thiry & Melton, 2010; Lopatto, 2009). It is worth noting that many Nobel prize-winners engaged in research during their undergraduate years.

In this context, this book is timely. There is a huge need for pedagogies of research engagement that see learning to research and researching to learn as processes that begin when the student enters university and continue until they leave either after bachelors, masters or doctoral degrees. The examples of research-based learning pedagogies provided in this book will be helpful to many who are keen to find ways to engage their students in research.

If, in the future, all students are going to be adequately prepared for the professional lives that they will lead after they graduate, then they will need to learn to research and research to learn during their university education. Academics will need to extend their knowledge to enable them to do this in a variety of different settings. So this book should become essential reading as they prepare themselves for the important task of educating the next generation of professional democratic citizens.

Angela Brew
Associate Professor
University of Sydney

Bibliography

John, J. & J. Creighton (2011). Researcher Development: The Impact of Undergraduate Research Opportunity Programmes on Students in the UK. *Studies in Higher Education*, Vol. 36, No. 7, pp. 781-797.

Kuh, G. (2008). *High-Impact Educational Practices: What They Are, Who Has Access to Them, and Why They Matter.* Washington, DC: Association of American Colleges and Universities.

Laursen, S.; A.-B. Hunter; E. Seymour; H. Thiry & G. Melton (Eds). (2010). *Undergraduate Research in the Sciences: Engaging Students in Real Science.* New York: Jossey-Bass.

Lopatto, D. (2009). *Science in Solution: The Impact of Undergraduate Research on Student Learning.* Tucson, AZ: Research Corporation for Science Advancement.

Chapter One
Learning to research, researching to learn

Cally Guerin, Paul Bartholomew & Claus Nygaard

Introduction

Increasingly in the knowledge-based economy, universities are encouraged to move beyond the simple transmission of content to a pedagogy that enables deeper learning through active engagement with the world. A promising approach to this kind of pedagogy involves the integration of research into teaching and learning at all levels of higher education. This book includes chapters that showcase innovative ways of *learning to research*: How is research integrated into coursework teaching? How do students learn the processes of research? And how are universities preparing students to engage with the world? The chapters also showcase innovative ways of *researching to learn*, exploring how students learn through doing research, how they conceptualise the knowledge of their fields of study through the processes of doing research, and how students experiment and reflect on the results produced.

In considering the kind of education demanded by today's society, our starting point needs to be a serious questioning of the role of the university—and of a university education—in the twenty-first century. It is important to think carefully about the work we want our universities to do for us as individuals, and for our broader society; after all, "*Universities have a responsibility to prepare students for professional life*" (Brew, 2013:603). Now is the time to implement strategies that will produce graduates who are appropriately skilled to play a useful role in their professions and as citizens of a broader community. The stakeholders whose interests are served by this education stretch from those individuals enrolled in university degrees, their families and local communities, through to the professional bodies seeking to employ these graduates, and on to the higher education sector, government and industry more generally. That is, every member of society has a stake in higher education being delivered effectively. Given the enormous personal and state investment in higher education, these are serious issues that require ongoing re-evaluation and updating as society's needs change over time, shifting the emphasis not only in terms of the kinds of graduates we desire, but also the pedagogies used to produce those graduates.

These are the key questions addressed by the chapters in this anthology, as they bring together analyses of the ways in which university teachers are developing research skills in their students, creating enquiry-based approaches to teaching, and engaging in education research themselves as they examine different aspects of "*student engagement, participation and inquiry*" (Brew, 2013:604). The studies reported here explore the links between teaching, learning and research in a range of contexts, from pre-enrolment through to academic staff development, in Australia, the UK, the US, Singapore and Denmark. Through a rich array of theoretical and methodological approaches, the collection seeks to further our understanding of how universities can play an effective role in educating graduates suited to the twenty-first century.

Links between teaching and research

In thinking about learning to research and researching to learn, the chapters in this anthology draw on the long and ongoing debate about the teaching–research nexus in universities. Although the vast majority of academics believe that there is an important and valuable link between teaching and research (Verburgh *et al.*, 2007), the precise nature of this relationship continues to be contested. The primary aim of Humboldt's nineteenth-century vision of the purpose of the university was to create a place where research and teaching were united, and this concept still has currency today. Many of those engaged in contemporary university teaching recognise the validity of Humboldt's ideal of teacher and student working together as they critically examine disciplinary knowledge in order to advance learning in the particular field (Healey & Jenkins, 2006; Simons & Elen, 2007); that is, the purpose of university study in this vision is to add to knowledge in the field, not simply to transmit the existing state of knowledge.

More recently, Boyer (1990) opened up the concept of university research to include not only "discovery scholarship", but also "applied" and "integrative" scholarship alongside the scholarship of teaching. Following from this, the Boyer Commission (1998:5) strongly recommended that opportunities for research, collaborative learning and inquiry-based learning be built into undergraduate degrees: "*Undergraduate education in research universities requires renewed emphasis on a point strongly made by John Dewey almost a century ago: learning is based on discovery guided by mentoring rather than on the transmission of information. Inherent in inquiry-based learning is an element of reciprocity: faculty can learn from students as students are learning from faculty*".

One strand of the debates surrounding the relationship between teaching and research explores the precise nature of "research" as it is understood in different disciplines. At the centre of this discussion is Angela Brew, who distinguishes between research in the external environment (e.g., presentations at conferences and seminars, publications) and in the internal environment (e.g., developing skills of data analysis, understanding of methodologies) (Brew, 2003, 2007). Trowler and Wareham (2008) have added to the complexities encountered in defining what constitutes "research" across disciplines in their comparison of creative disciplines with other disciplines. While scholars in the Humanities might regard locating relevant literature, reading critically, synthesising the information and structuring an argument for an essay as the key research approach, those in Sciences may consider experimental design and data collection from work in the laboratory to be the most important part of "doing research".

Further, what is regarded as "knowledge" and "research" may have specific constructions in the digital age. Many of today's students expect vastly different styles of communication and instruction from what they might have only a few years ago. The explosion of uptake of new social technologies (such as Facebook, MySpace, YouTube, Instagram) means that these learners are in the habit of constructing knowledge for themselves in their own terms. Consequently, their understanding of what constitutes "research" is also vastly different from their peers of ten years ago. Interactions with the research–teaching nexus that speak meaningfully to such undergraduates may well be quite different from what influenced and excited those of an earlier cohort. In this regard, "connectivist" theories of learning (Cormier & Siemens, 2010; Downes, 2012; Siemens & Matheos, 2010) take account of the places students seek knowledge and the ways in which they see themselves as active contributors to knowledge. This approach to learning recognises that *"knowledge is distributed across a network of connections, and therefore that learning consists of the ability to construct and traverse those networks"* (Downes, 2012:9). Linking items of information and bodies of knowledge, and understanding the relationships between them, is the essence of learning in this recent development of constructivism. For students in the twenty-first century, connectivism describes their processes of gathering information from a wide variety of sources, mostly in digital forms, and actively contributing to the creation of new knowledge—in other words, how they research their topic or discipline, and advance the state of knowledge in that field. Lecturers and academics charged with the responsibility for developing appropriate pedagogies for these students must understand how to tap into this existing mindset if they are to engage undergraduates with the value of rigorous research as a way of approaching the world—and also, perhaps, to demonstrate the potential excitement of advanced research at doctoral level and beyond.

A number of models for organising the kinds of research experiences students might have as undergraduates have been put forward. Griffiths (2004) outlines three main forms of the research–teaching nexus in universities: research-led; research-oriented; and research-based. Healey (2005) adds "research-tutored" to this list, and organises the approaches into a useful framework that relates these methods to the extent to which they are focused on the student or lecturer, and to the extent to which they are focused on research content or research processes and problems. The result is a structure that encourages us to notice pedagogies that actively engage students as participants in research (i.e., research-tutored and research-based learning strategies), and those in which lecturers are teaching the knowledge that is the outcome of disciplinary research (research-led strategies) or teaching the processes and skills needed to undertake rigorous research projects.

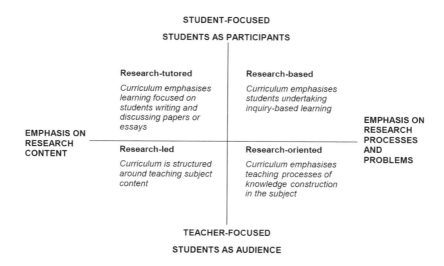

STUDENT-FOCUSED

STUDENTS AS PARTICIPANTS

Research-tutored

Curriculum emphasises learning focused on students writing and discussing papers or essays

Research-based

Curriculum emphasises students undertaking inquiry-based learning

EMPHASIS ON RESEARCH CONTENT

EMPHASIS ON RESEARCH PROCESSES AND PROBLEMS

Research-led

Curriculum is structured around teaching subject content

Research-oriented

Curriculum emphasises teaching processes of knowledge construction in the subject

TEACHER-FOCUSED

STUDENTS AS AUDIENCE

Figure 1: Curriculum design and the research-teaching nexus (Healey & Jenkins, 2009:7).

The point, however, is not that one pedagogy is necessarily better than the others; rather, appropriate strategies must be adopted according to the specific learning outcomes required by the curriculum. In some situations, the direct teaching of specific skills and techniques is clearly more useful than allowing students to flounder without enough knowledge to make progress in their research projects. Disciplines vary in what and when research can be undertaken at different points in a student's development, as the chapters in this anthology demonstrate.

Levy and Petrulis (2012) conducted an investigation into the research experiences of first-year students in arts, humanities and social sciences disciplines. From this study they developed a framework for conceptualising inquiry-based learning that frames four basic modes of student activity: authoring, producing, pursuing, and identifying. As in Healey's (2005) model, this model takes into account the roles of the lecturer/tutor and the student, and the activities of learning about existing content and how to do research. However, Levy and Petrulis (2012) shift the emphasis away from teaching to a focus on learning, and are therefore concerned here with what the student does; the teaching role is conceived only in terms of the degree of support offered to the student.

Authoring: Inquiry tasks are designed to encourage students to explore their own open questions, problems, scenarios or lines of inquiry, in interaction with a knowledge base ('how can I answer my open question?').

Producing: Inquiry tasks are designed to encourage students to explore open questions, problems, scenarios or lines of inquiry, framed by teachers, or others such as an external 'client', in interaction with a knowledge base ('how can I answer this open question?').

Pursuing: Inquiry tasks are designed to encourage students to explore a knowledge base actively by pursuing their own questions, problems, scenarios or lines of inquiry ('what is the existing answer/response to my question?').

Identifying: Inquiry tasks are designed to encourage students to explore a knowledge base actively in response to questions, problems, scenarios or lines of inquiry framed by teachers ('what is the existing answer/response to this question?').

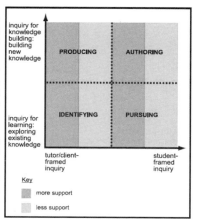

Figure 2: *Modes of inquiry-based learning (Levy & Petrulis, 2012:97).*

Brew (2013) offers a third framework in response to what she sees as the limitation of the previous models put forward by Healey (2005) Healy and Jenkins (2009) and Levy and Petrulis (2012), which fail to distinguish between curriculum and pedagogy. Instead, a wheel-shaped model is proposed that places students at the centre and *"integrates decisions about the curriculum context including the nature, number and type of students, learning outcomes including disciplinary knowledge acquisition and attributes, capabilities and skills to be developed as well as the nature of knowledge and the nature of the tasks to be completed and how they are to be assessed"* (Brew, 2013:613).

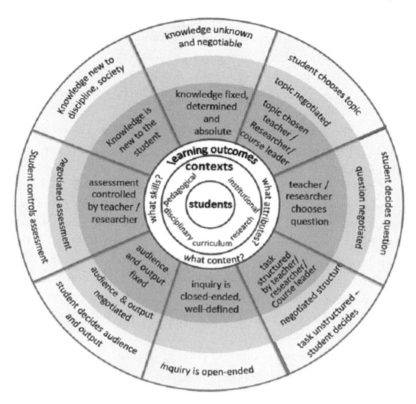

Figure 3: A holistic model for research-based learning decision-making (Brew, 2013:613).

The chapters that follow encompass many of these understandings of research and pedagogy in their various explorations of different disciplines and different degree levels. They are united by their concerns with the identities of the graduates produced through research experiences, and also with the pedagogies that can be harnessed to maximise those graduates' research-related learning.

Identity

Central to discussions about contemporary university education is a consideration of the identities of university graduates. There appear to be several key qualities that emerge from the studies presented in the chapters here: a shared aim is to develop forms of university education that develop lifelong learners who are autonomous practitioners in their profession and who regard themselves as members of a community of enquiry. This transformation of identity is achieved through active experiences of research—both of learning to research, and researching to learn.

In describing these graduates as "lifelong learners", we draw on Billett's (2010) explanation that "*lifelong learning is a socio-personal process as we negotiate our thinking, acting and doing across activities and interactions*" (403). Thus, lifelong learning implies an approach to being in the world, an ontological position, in which one expects to continually seek new information, not only through the formal avenues of accredited higher education institutions, but often through informal learning opportunities too. For many universities, these qualities are included in the graduate attributes, capacities or competencies they aim to inculcate in those passing through their programmes and degrees preparing them for the future. Lawson *et al.* (2006:7) identify the following attributes possessed by lifelong learners:

+ *literacies required for different parts of life (e.g., literacy in language, number and technology);*
+ *facility with processes that can be applied to many tasks in different domains (e.g., problem solving and critical thinking);*
+ *personal qualities that contribute to the development of agency in the learner (e.g., self-efficacy and interests); and*
+ *interpersonal skills that facilitate social interaction (e.g., empathy and ethics).*

Together, these attributes provide a solid foundation for the capacity to continue learning and to behave as engaged employees and citizens on a path towards economic progress, personal fulfilment and a socially inclusive democracy (Aspin & Chapman, 2000).

These lifelong learners are also expected to become autonomous practitioners, well trained to work independently and to continue developing not only their professional selves, but also their professions more generally. They require a range of research skills in order to perform in this way, including the ability to investigate perceived problems in their workplace, and to reliably assess and evaluate the findings of those investigations. In this sense, they become not only members of a community of practice (Wenger, 1998), but also members of a community of enquiry. Many of the chapters here present a close relationship between the research skills and their deployment in professional practice. Rather than regarding "research" as something that occurs in a rarified atmosphere of scholarly pursuit, the ability to conduct rigorous, reliable research is seen as central to the professional skill set of graduates. Importantly, this research capacity is a desirable quality that leads directly to graduates' employability. In her call for a renewed understanding of the relationship between teaching and research, Brew (2012:112) explains the value of imbuing students with good research skills: *"for all students, no matter what their ability or study motivation, the pursuit of professionalism embodied in the quality conception of scholarship can be a useful foundation for whatever the student engages in when they graduate. The ability to carry out a rigorous systematic process of inquiry and the capacity to apply the skills so acquired in a range of different contexts needs to be developed".*

Clearly, "research" is not an activity reserved solely for those Masters and doctoral students who have earned the "right" or the authority to add to knowledge in the discipline on completion of undergraduate studies; rather, research is a way of being in the world, a way of approaching tasks and problems, and a way of conceiving the self. Hence, the chapters in this anthology explore the research needs and experiences of university learners from pre-enrolment (those preparing to enter university through English language programmes and foundation skills programmes), through all levels of undergraduate and Masters degrees, to doctoral candidates, early career researchers and academic staff.

Pedagogy

Running alongside an understanding of the kinds of graduates we might wish to produce is a parallel discussion of the kinds of pedagogies that will help to produce these graduates. Lifelong learners need to develop a sense of how they go about doing that learning beyond their formal coursework; an effective way of doing this is to design curricula that explicitly engage with the necessary skills. Deliberate learning design can ensure that students not only develop the required skills, but also make it clear to students that this is what they are learning by articulating both the learning outcomes of courses and the rationale for the pedagogical approach.

For some learning designers and lecturers, the principles of critical pedagogy offer a useful way into the transformative power of a curriculum. Foundational to this teaching approach is Paulo Freire's *Pedagogy of the Oppressed* (1968/1970). This approach to education sees a central role for the teacher in leading students towards a capacity to perceive systemic oppression and marginalisation in society—and how it might relate to their own situation. Obviously not all university lecturers will seek to radicalise their students, but most would want to see students learn to think critically about the world around them. For other lecturers, a university education might be regarded as providing "transformative learning"; that is, *"learning is understood as the process of using a prior interpretation to construe a new or revised interpretation of the meaning of one's experience in order to guide future action"* (Mezirow, 1996:162). Again, a capacity for critical reflection is key to unlocking such learning (Taylor, 2007). Clearly, there is an important role for developing the skills of critical thinking, and the ability to question received knowledge and scrutinise one's own values and assumptions. Indeed, for many, this capacity for critical thinking is the cornerstone of a university education.

Another aspect of developing lifelong learners is to inculcate in these students the ability to find out about the world independently. That is, they benefit from a curriculum that allows them to be actively engaged in their own learning, and one that encourages autonomy in managing that learning. To this end, the range of discovery-based, enquiry-based pedagogies are invaluable for their student-centred approaches to pedagogy. These pedagogies are used in very structured programmes (see, for example, problem-based learning (PBL) and Process Oriented Guided Inquiry Learning (POGIL)), while others are much more loosely organised around project-based learning. In all these approaches the focus is on actively engaging students in undertaking different methods of research to find answers to the problems and questions posed.

However, the skills required for learning in these kinds of pedagogies generally need to be explicitly articulated: many students cannot simply be thrown into such "research" and be expected to succeed without any kind of instruction or guidance. Rather, environments that are conducive to learning through research often provide a scaffolded approach to research tasks, breaking down the processes and drawing students' attention to the what, how and why of their actions. Another way of explicating the principles of research is to provide students with frameworks for research skills, for example, Willison and O'Regan's *Research Skills Development Framework* (Willison & O'Regan, 2006/2012). Such frameworks aid students in identifying the specific skills they are developing, and help them understand how different elements of the research process fit together in order to produce reliable results.

The Chapters

As we explored our theme from a variety of theoretical and empirical perspectives, it became clear that authors had conceived of the teaching–research nexus as a continuum from learning to research <=> researching to learn. Some chapters are more focused on the "learning to research" side of the equation or on the "researching to learn" part, while others are set squarely in the middle and benefit from the oscillations between the two poles. For all, a dynamic relationship exists between learning about how to do robust, reliable research, and using research as the pathway into learning disciplinary knowledge.

1. Learning to research

In the first section we present three chapters that focus on the preparation of students to undertake rigorous research. Here we see innovative approaches to how lecturers have designed curricula to enable their students to learn the skills of research processes. This is aimed at building students' capacity for lifelong learning, and for them to become independent researchers not only in the academic context, but also in their professional lives beyond university. Research here is seen as central to the way in which students will conceive of themselves as learners, and as professionals.

Chapter 2, "Embedding Research Skills in the Curriculum Design of a Pathway Programme for International Students" by Richard Warner and Kayoko Enomoto, explores the experiences of international students preparing for entry to an Australian university. The programme provides a scaffolded approach to support students as they engage in research projects and develop the skills to become independent learners ready to tackle their degree programmes.

In Chapter 3, Jesper Piihl, Jens Smed Rasmussen and Jennifer Rowley also provide a scaffolded approach to developing research skills in "A Multi-disciplinary Framework for Building Students' Capacity as Practitioner Researchers" for those engaged in business education and music education. Concerned with the transformative power of learning to research, their focus is on preparing undergraduate students to become research-oriented, reflexive practitioners.

Linda Kalejs and Robbie Napper are also interested in exploring how learning to research can benefit undergraduates preparing for professional practice, in this case in the context of industrial design. In Chapter 4, "Research, Learn, Design: Project-Based Learning and Research Skill Development in Industrial Design", Kalejs and Napper document how they have used the Research Skill Development Framework to scaffold research training in order to develop confidence in students and improving employability outcomes.

2. Learning to research/researching to learn

The chapters in this section explore pedagogies that move in both directions along the continuum. These studies engage with the cyclical, mutually reinforcing processes of developing research skills and using those skills to research the discipline. Here, the students' learning is seen to benefit from the lived experience of doing research. Crucially, that research curriculum is designed to be appropriate to the level of study and the discipline.

The first chapter in this section, Chapter 5, explores the experience of non-traditional students preparing to enter university. In "Learning to Research with Pre-Undergraduate Students: Curriculum as Support in the First-Year Experience", Phyllida Coombes explicates a curriculum designed to transform learners into students ready for the unfamiliar demands of a university education. Key to this is a programme that provides opportunities to learn about research, and to learn by doing research.

Next is Chapter 6 by Michelle Picard and Cally Guerin that focuses on the experiences of first-year students at a university seeking to infuse a research-based pedagogy into all levels of undergraduate degrees.

"Learning to Research in the Professions: Possibilities of Discovery Learning" evaluates the benefits and challenges of introducing research to first-year students enrolled in degrees aimed at producing graduates who also meet the requirements of accrediting bodies in the professions.

The focus shifts to final year students of Sociology in Sarah Hayes's Chapter 7, "Encouraging the Intellectual Craft of *Living* Research: Tattoos, Theory and Time". Hayes argues that the modularised approach to some university degrees works against students' understanding the ways in which the research skills they learn in one context apply in other parts of their study—and in their own lives. She takes the example of "time" as a lens through which students can learn to move back and forth between practice and theory. Moving further out into the broader community, "Developing Deeper Learning in Adult Learners: A Research-oriented Curriculum in Leadership for School–Family and Community Engagement" takes us into the realm of educational management and leadership. Here in Chapter 8, Lana Yiu Lan Khong demonstrates how research experiences can be used to transform learners' understanding of their roles and potential as leaders actively engaged with real-world situations.

3. Researching to learn

The final group of chapters explores the further end of the continuum where research provides the pathway to learning, particularly in terms of the informal learning that occurs for more experienced researchers. Here the active doing of research is closely linked to becoming a member of the research community, through the process of establishing credibility in a community of peers. At the forefront of these studies is the transformative power of the learning that occurs through research and the identities it shapes in the process.

First up we have Chapter 9, Michelle McGinn's study, "Postgraduate Research Assistantships as Spaces for Researching, Learning, and Teaching". Interviews and observations are used here to explore the ways in which postgraduate students learn the skills of research through their work as research assistants, in the process transforming their own identities into researchers rather than students.

In Chapter 10 Helen Benzie then explores the ongoing experiences of doctoral students and early career researchers in "Reflecting on Feedback in a Peer-led Research Writing Group". In supporting each others' development in learning to write about research, the participants in this study also recognise the transformative power of this research as they experience their own becoming as legitimate, validated researchers.

Continuing the discussion of a group of researchers at a similar stage in their careers is Chapter 11, "Forms of Capital and Transition Pedagogies: Researching to Learn Among Postgraduate Students and Early Career Academics at an Australian University". In this chapter, Patrick Danaher conducts a case study to explore the tensions experienced by those teaching and researching inside the context of universities, articulating the competing demands of the individual as agent and the socialisation required by the institution.

Finally, Paul Bartholomew interrogates his own learning in Chapter 12, "Learning Through Auto-Ethnographic Case Study Research". With a focus on professional development, academics are encouraged to draw on their own experiences in order to advance their understandings of what research can achieve. The insights developed here then lead to a new typology of case study research.

Together, these chapters provide wide-ranging explorations of what it means to engage in learning to research and researching to learn at all levels of study within the university system. While the majority of chapters investigate Australian attempts to push pedagogical possibilities in this area, we also see how these ideas are played out in the UK, the US, Singapore and Denmark. The chapters take as their subjects students who are aspiring to enter university, undergraduates and postgraduates, right through to early career academics and established researchers. We trust that our readers will find much of value here that will inspire them to experiment with even more ways of "learning to research and researching to learn" in universities.

About the authors

Dr Cally Guerin is a lecturer in the Researcher Education and Development Unit at the University of Adelaide. She can be contacted at this email: cally.guerin@adelaide.edu.au

Professor Dr. Paul Bartholomew is Director of Learning Innovation and Professional Practice at Aston University, Birmingham, England. He can be contacted at this email: p.bartholomew@aston.ac.uk

Professor Dr. Claus Nygaard is Executive Director of the Institute for Learning in Higher Education and CEO of cph:learning. He can be contacted at this email: info@lihe.info

Bibliography

Aspin, D. N. & J. D. Chapman (2000). Lifelong Learning: Concepts and Conceptions, *International Journal of Lifelong Education*, Vol. 19, No. 1, pp. 2-19.

Billett, S. (2010). The Perils of Confusing Lifelong Learning with Lifelong Education. *International Journal of Lifelong Education*, Vol. 29, No. 4, pp. 401-413.

Boyer, E. L. (1990). *Scholarship Reconsidered: Priorities of the Professoriate.* Princeton, N.J: Carnegie Foundation for the Advancement of Teaching.

The Boyer Commission on Educating Undergraduates in the Research University (1998). *Reinventing Undergraduate Education: A blueprint for America's Research Universities.* Stony Brook, State University of New York.

Brew, A. (2001). Conceptions of Research: A Phenomenographic Study. *Studies in Higher Education*, Vol. 26, No. 3, pp. 271–285.

Brew, A. (2003). Understanding research-led teaching. *HERDSA News*, Vol. 25, No. 1, pp. 1–3.

Brew, A. (2007). Research and Teaching from the Students' Perspective. Keynote address presented at International Policies and Practices for Academic Enquiry. An International Colloquium, Marwell Conference Centre, Winchester, UK, 19-21 April, 2007.

Brew, A. (2012). Teaching and Research: New Relationships and Their Implications for Inquiry-Based Teaching and Learning in Higher Education. *Higher Education Research & Development*, Vol. 31, No. 1, pp. 101-114.

Brew, A. (2013). Understanding the Scope of Undergraduate Research: A Framework for Curricular and Pedagogical Decision-Making. *Higher Education*, Vol. 66, No. 5, pp. 603-618.

Cormier, D. & G. Siemens (2010). Through the Open Door: Open Courses as Research, Learning and Engagement. *Educause Review*, Vol. 45, No. 4, pp. 31–39.

Downes, S. (2012). *Connectivism and Connective Knowledge: Essays on Meaning and Learning Networks*. National Research Council.

Friere, P. (1970). *Pedagogy of the Oppressed*. New York: Herder and Herder.

Griffiths, R. (2004). Knowledge Production and the Research–Teaching Nexus: The Case of the Built Environment Disciplines. *Studies in Higher Education*, Vol. 29, No. 6, pp. 709–726.

Healey, M. (2005). Linking Research and Teaching: Exploring Disciplinary Spaces and the Role of Inquiry-Based Learning. In R. Barnett (Ed.). *Reshaping the University: New Relationships Between Research, Scholarship and Teaching*, Buckingham: Open University Press, pp. 67-78.

Healey, M. & A. Jenkins (2006). Strengthening the Teaching–Research Linkage in Undergraduate Courses and Programs. *New Directions for Teaching and Learning*, Vol. 107, pp. 45–55.

Healey, M. and A. Jenkins (2009). *Developing Undergraduate Research and Inquiry*. York: Higher Education Academy.

Lawson, M. J.; H. Askell-William & R. Murray-Harvey (2006). *The Attributes of the Lifelong Learner: A Report Prepared for the Queensland Studies Authority*. School of Education, Flinders University, Adelaide, Australia.

Levy, P. & R. Petrulis (2012). How Do First-Year University Students Experience Inquiry and Research, and What are the Implications for the Practice of Inquiry-Based Learning? *Studies in Higher Education*, Vol. 37, No. 1, pp. 85-101.

Mezirow, J. (1991). *Transformative Dimensions of Adult Learning*, San Francisco, CA: Jossey-Bass.

Mezirow, J. (1996). Contemporary Paradigms of Learning. *Adult Education Quarterly*, Vol. 46, pp. 158–172.

Siemens, G. & K. Matheos (2010). Systemic Changes in Higher Education. *Studies in Higher education*, Vol. 16, No. 1, pp. 3–18.

Simons, M. & J. Elen (2007). The 'Research-Teaching Nexus' and 'Education Through Research': An Exploration of Ambivalences. *Studies in Higher Education*, Vol. 32, No. 5, pp. 617–631.

Taylor, E. W. (2007). An Update of Transformative Learning Theory: A Critical Review of the Empirical Research (1999–2005). *International Journal of Lifelong Education*, Vol. 26, No. 2, pp. 173-191.

Trowler, P. & T. Wareham (2008). *Tribes, Territories, Research and Teaching: Enhancing the Teaching–Research Nexus*. The Higher Education Academy.

Verburgh, A.; J. Elen & S. Lindblom-Ylanne (2007). Investigating the Myth of the Relationship Between Teaching and Research in Higher Education: A Review of Empirical Research. *Studies in the Philosophy of Education*, Vol. 26, pp. 449–465.

Wenger, E. (1998). *Communities of Practice: Learning, Meaning and Identity*. Cambridge: Cambridge University Press.

Willison, J. & K. O'Regan (2006/2012) *Research Skill Development (RSD), A Conceptual Framework for Primary School to PhD*. The University of Adelaide, Australia.

Chapter Two

Embedding Research Skills in the Curriculum Design of a Pathway Programme for International Students

Richard Warner and Kayoko Enomoto

Introduction

This chapter contributes to the anthology by presenting how to embed research skills in the curriculum design of a pathway programme for international students with English as an Additional Language (EAL). We consider the Pre-enrolment English Programme (PEP), a direct-entry pathway programme to a research-intensive Australian university, the University of Adelaide, as one practical example of research skills capacity building within a learning-to-research paradigm. The PEP curriculum is designed to develop EAL students as independent researchers by building their capacity for learning to research. The PEP curriculum comprises four components: 1) Reading and Writing Skills, 2) Speaking Skills, 3) Listening Skills and 4) Independent Learning Skills. Our focus is on the fourth component, namely, the Independent Learning Skills component consisting of a range of tasks and activities, including the Independent Research Paper and the associated Research Portfolio, both of which we discuss later in some detail.

The curriculum presented in this chapter is underpinned by the Control Wedge Model (Cadman & Grey, 2000) and the Experiential Learning Model (Kolb, 1984). We discuss how learning to research is realised through the process of engaging in the tasks and activities embedded in the aforementioned Independent Learning Skills component. Such tasks and activities are systematically scaffolded, mirroring the control wedge model and carefully designed to enable students to undergo experiential learning cycles. Reading this chapter, you will:

1. gain insights into why it is crucial for EAL international students to "learn to research", prior to university entry, for enhancing their own chances of success once they enter their chosen university degree programmes;

2. learn how to systematically scaffold and manage the process of developing "learning to research" skills in such a pathway programme; and

3. be provided with six key recommendations for realising capacity building for "learning to research", through the design of pathway programme curricula in similar institutional contexts.

The concept of research presupposes the occurrence of some form of learning. Specifically, two types of learning can be brought about as a result of research; one is that learning can occur in the process of researching itself at an individual level, and the other is that learning can also occur through the output of the research. In short, learning can be distinguished as both process and product of research. This chapter specifically focuses on the process of research rather than the product, in order to explore the individualised process of capacity-building, whilst learning to research.

This capacity-building is pivotal to those EAL international students aiming to begin a university degree, be it undergraduate or postgraduate. The term "capacity-building" we use here does not just refer to developing their English "language skills", as examined by such agencies as IELTS (International English Language Testing System). Rather, we go beyond the IELTS four skills-based capabilities (reading, writing, listening, speaking) and use "capacity-building" to encapsulate a much wider range of skills including the "independent learning skills" required for "learning to research", which enables *concomitant growth in student independence and control*" (Pre-enrolment English Program Curriculum, 2011:II 5). To become independent researchers, students must develop capacities as independent learners in order to exercise meta-cognition, reflection and self-regulation (Schunk, 2008). Therefore, as we show later, within the PEP curriculum, the Independent Learning Skills component is designed to enable students to build such capacities through tasks and activities which facilitate the practice of their meta-cognition, reflection and self-regulation in the process of learning to research.

In the literature, there is a paucity of research investigations made into the role that "learning to research" plays in EAL pathway programmes — those programmes which provide direct entry into both undergraduate and postgraduate studies. In contrast to such scant attention to pathway programmes, i.e., prior to university entry, past studies abound on learning to research "during" studying in undergraduate (Maunder *et al.*, 2013, Walkington, 2014; Willison & O'Regan, 2007) and postgraduate degree programmes (Atley & Lawrence, 2011; Picard *et al.*, 2011). In particular, transition pedagogy in the context of first-year experience has been widely disseminated (Kift *et al.*, 2010). Yet, we propose that the notion of transition pedagogy (see Coombe, this volume; Piihl *et al.*, this volume) is equally relevant to pathway programmes for EAL international students.

Whilst not diminishing their importance, such post-entry "learning to research" programmes are part of a bigger picture which should include pre-entry pathway programmes. To fill this gap, this chapter discusses how a direct-entry pathway programme, the PEP, can best facilitate EAL international students' capacity building for learning to research, a crucial aspect of their preparation for success in undergraduate and postgraduate degree programmes.

This chapter begins with an overview of the context and rationale behind the direct-entry PEP curriculum, tied to the entry criteria set by the university itself. This is followed by the theoretical underpinnings of its curriculum — we interrogate the critical issue of learning to research through the perspectives of two theoretical models. We describe how the PEP curriculum mirrors the Control Wedge Model (Cadman & Grey, 2000). This is followed by the description of how each task under the "independent learning skills" component purposefully utilises the Experiential Learning Model (Kolb, 1984) to scaffold the capacity building of the student as an independent researcher. In so doing, we demonstrate how the learning to research element is showcased through specific research-based tasks and activities, which are subject-based and pertinent to each student's own future study areas and disciplines. We conclude this chapter by presenting key recommendations for realising capacity-building, in order to both enable and enhance learning to research in a pathway programme.

Context and Rationale behind the PEP Curriculum

The design of the PEP, a direct-entry pathway programme, means that its successful completion allows EAL international students to enter their chosen undergraduate or postgraduate degree programme, without the need to take an IELTS examination or equivalent. Such pathway programmes are equivalent to International Foundation Courses overseen by U.K. universities and to Academic Preparation Programmes run by U.S. universities. At the University of Adelaide, the PEP was first established in 1999, as a pathway programme for EAL international students. Since then, the PEP curriculum has been developed with necessary revisions made to meet the changing needs of EAL student cohorts, including their need to build capacity for learning to research. One indication of the enabling success of the PEP pathway programme can be seen in the growth of student enrolments (Figure 1).

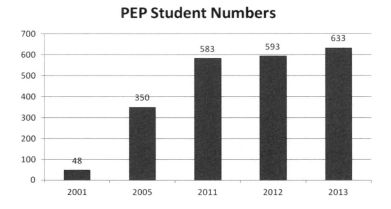

Figure 1: Growth in student enrolment numbers since 2001.

At present, Australian universities are legally required to ensure, through their admissions process, that prospective students are adequately equipped with the knowledge and skills necessary to successfully undertake university studies (Kemp & Norton, 2014:19). It was in this higher education context that Kemp and Norton (2014) notably highlighted the role that pathway programmes can play in the future of Australian higher education. In their recent review of the demand-driven funding system, Kemp and Norton (2014:x) report that *"a key to success"* at university is *"academic preparation"* before students commence university studies, and that outcomes for less-prepared students improve substantially if they first take a 'pathway' programme. Indeed, the rationale behind the PEP curriculum is tightly grounded by this view – it is designed to enhance EAL international students' future success.

As Table 1 shows, the PEP curriculum has three different entry points for EAL students, with each entry point resulting in different lengths of PEP: 20 week, 15 week and 10 week. Each student's existing IELTS score (< 6.0) determines the length of the PEP that they have to undertake. When EAL students complete their required length of the PEP study, their PEP overall "pass" grade is deemed equivalent within the University of Adelaide, to an IELTS 6, an overall "credit" grade to an IELTS 6.5, and an overall "distinction" grade to an IELTS 7. These equivalents are vindicated by the statistics we present later in this chapter. Currently, PEP class size is capped at 16 students – smaller than usual tutorial or seminar sizes in a first-year course at the University. Each class has one or two assigned homeroom teacher(s) responsible for teaching, marking, academic guidance and pastoral care. The class meets four hours five days a week (20 contact hours per week).

Learner-centredness is one of the defining characteristics of the PEP curriculum, responding to both perceived student needs, and the demands and expectations of the university environment (Warner, 2007). To bring about *"learning to function within a new culture while maintaining your own identity"* (Schumann, 1978:7), learner-centred curriculum design must incorporate an adequate amount of appropriate scaffolds for facilitating student academic acculturation. Scaffolds are defined here as *"the support that a teacher can give learners so that they can work at a much higher level than on their own"* (Rose et al., 2003:42). There are two types of scaffolds. Hard scaffolds are devised support structures embedded in advance by anticipating student difficulties in relation to specific tasks, whilst soft scaffolds are teacher or peer support to be offered as necessary in response to situation-specific student needs (Brush & Saye, 2002). It is through the sufficient provision of appropriate hard and soft scaffolds that the PEP learner-centred curriculum encourages EAL students to "*make critical pedagogical decisions…about what they want to learn and how they want to learn…to move towards the fully autonomous end of the pedagogical continuum*" (Nunan, 2013:53), preparing them to meet the post-PEP demands and expectations.

A curriculum should not only be a statement of intent, rather it should also reflect institutional responsibility, involving objectives, content, methodology and evaluation (Cannon & Newble, 2000). In the case of PEP, as its learner-centred curriculum develops, both the student control and responsibility gradually increase when engaging with tasks. The teacher's role in the PEP is not to act as merely a purveyor of knowledge as consumable data, but rather to act as a facilitator for each student's reflective transformational learning (Enomoto & Warner, 2013). This form of learning regards learning as an issue of personal growth and development, in which experience is a driver for conscious processing via reflection. Knowledge is thus gained through the understanding and transformation of such experience (Kolb, 1984). The element of reflection is one key component of the Experiential Learning Model (Kolb, 1984) which underpins the independent learning skills component tasks embedded within the PEP curriculum, mirroring the Control Wedge Model of Curriculum Design (Cadman & Grey, 2000). We will now discuss these two models with specific reference to learning to research.

Scaffolding Learning to Research through a Control Wedge Based Curriculum Design

As mentioned above, the notion of a learner-centred curriculum is central to the PEP, as it places a substantial focus upon developing student capacity-building to become an independent learner, ready for the academic rigours of university. Lying within the process of such development is the crucial issue of learning to research. One way to realise student capacity building for learning to research is through a gradual transfer of control and responsibility from teacher to student.

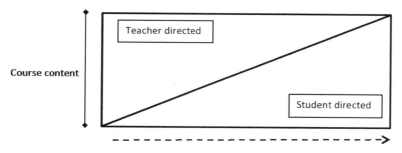

Figure 2: The control wedge model of curriculum design (adapted from Cadman & Grey, 2000:24).

The Control Wedge Model of Curriculum Design (Cadman & Grey, 2000) allows such a gradual shift of control and responsibility as a course develops (Figure 2). The PEP curriculum is designed to mirror the control wedge model whereby, *"embedded scaffolds are gradually withdrawn, as students gain their active position in their learning processes, allowing a gradual shift of control"* (Enomoto, 2012:350). Indeed, as Table 1 indicates, the PEP curriculum is devised in such a way that, as the programme progresses over time, the less scaffolds are given, the more students gain control. It is significant to note that such a control wedge based curriculum can systematically allow students to experience a series of (small) successes during the process of learning, whilst enabling them to build both the necessary skills and confidence to progress to the next task (see Kalejs & Napper, this volume).

We argue that this gradual gain of student control and responsibility accompanied by their experiences of small successes and confidence is central to maximising learning to research. However, its effectiveness depends upon how systematically and carefully tasks are embedded.

Programme length

Reading & Writing Skills			
Diagnostic Writing Task (x1) (optional – set by teacher for new students)	Diagnostic Writing Task (x1) (optional – set by teacher for new students)	Diagnostic Writing Task (x1) (optional – set by teacher for new students)	Final Integrated Reading & Writing Task (x2) (in class – timed)
Integrated Reading & Writing Task (x2) (in class – can be used as a diagnostic task)	Integrated Reading & Writing Task (x2) (in class – can be used as a diagnostic task)	Integrated Reading & Writing Task (x2) (in class – can be used as a diagnostic task)	
Academic Poster (x1) (with issue analysis document)	Group Project (x1) (cultural information report)	Group Project (x1) (case study analysis)	Final Essay (x1)
	Essay (x1) (one draft only)	Essay (x1)	Final Essay Exam (no feedback provided)
	Essay Exam (x1)	Practice Essay Exam (set by teacher in class)	
Speaking Skills			
Seminar Participation – lead one seminar; participate in all (schedule negotiated in class)	Seminar Participation – lead one seminar; participate in all (schedule negotiated in class)	Seminar Participation – lead one seminar; participate in all (schedule negotiated in class)	Seminar Participation – lead one seminar; participate in all (schedule negotiated in class)
Individual Oral Presentation (x1-2) (set by teacher)	Individual Oral Presentation (x1-2) (set by teacher)	Individual Oral Presentation (x1-2) (set by teacher)	Individual Oral Presentation (x2-3) (set by teacher) – independent research paper (IRP) work-in-progress (x1); set by teacher (x1) (optional); final IRP oral presentation (x1) (no feedback)
Academic Poster Interactive Presentation (x1)	Group Oral Presentation (x1) (cultural information report)	Group Oral Presentation (x1) (case study analysis)	

Programme length

Listening Skills			
Diagnostic Listening Task (x1) (optional – set by teacher for new students)	Diagnostic Listening Task (x1) (optional – set by teacher for new students)	Diagnostic Listening Task (x1) (optional – set by teacher for new students)	Listening & Note-taking Test (x1) (no feedback provided)
Listening & Note-taking Test (x1)	Listening & Note-taking Test (x1)	Listening & Note-taking Test (x1)	

Independent Learning Skills			
Reflective Blog (x2)	Reflective Blog (x2)	Reflective Blog (x2)	Reflective Blog (x1)
Report Review (x2) (in class)	Report Review (x2) (in class)	Report Review (x2) (in class)	Report Review (x2) (in class)
Academic Poster Self-evaluation (x1)	Group Project Self-evaluation (x1) (cultural information report)	Independent Research Paper (Draft x1)	Independent Research Paper (x1)
		Research Portfolio (Draft x1)	Research Portfolio (x1)
		Group Project Self-evaluation (x1) (case study analysis)	

Table 1: Embedded tasks in the PEP curriculum mirroring the Control Wedge Model (Adapted from PEP Curriculum, 2011:IV 11-12).

Facilitating Learning to Research through the Experiential Learning Cycle

As Table 1 shows, the PEP curriculum consists of four major skills components: 1) reading and writing skills, 2) speaking skills, 3) listening skills and 4) independent learning skills. To interrogate the issue of learning to research, we now place our focus on the tasks under the independent learning skills component, requisite for becoming an independent researcher. Such tasks as reflective blogs, report reviews, the independent research paper and associated research portfolio, are systematically and carefully set to enable students to undergo Kolb's (1984) experiential learning cycle (Figure 3) in the process of task engagement. In his model of experiential learning, Kolb contends that reflection by the learners needs to happen prior to the testing of new hypotheses. As such, learning represents a recycling of previous experiences at increasingly deeper levels of understanding (Warner & Smith, 2006; Kalejs & Napper, this volume).

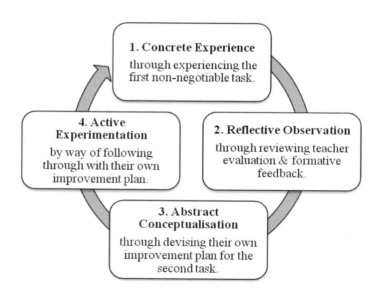

Figure 3: The experiential learning cycle brought about in the process of engaging with the independent learning skills component tasks.

We propose that undergoing the cycles of experiential learning will facilitate students to actively engage in and focus on the process of learning to research. After the student experiences the first non-negotiable task as concrete experience (Stage 1), reflective observation (Stage 2) through reviewing teacher evaluation and formative feedback, facilitates a shift away from dependency. Then, abstract conceptualisation (Stage 3), through devising their own improvement plan for the second task, promotes more student control and independence away from traditional knowledge transmission-based learning. Finally, active experimentation (Stage 4) by way of following through with their own improvement plan prepares them to more independently engage in the next task.

However, staged and balanced scaffolding is essential to avoid students slipping back into dependency on teacher-imposed directions. Therefore, we now demonstrate how the control wedge based PEP curriculum allows for a staged and balanced shift of control and responsibility from teacher to student, in order to realise learning to research, by particularly addressing the three aforementioned "independent learning skills" component tasks, namely, i) reflective blogs, ii) report reviews and iii) the (major) independent research paper and associated research portfolio.

Independent Learning Skills Component Tasks

This section discusses the first two component tasks, the first task being written and the second task oral.

i) Reflective Blogs (written): Independent of disciplinary domain, core to realising learning to research is the use of reflection to develop reflective capacity. In this task, students write about their own learning experiences and performance (Stage 1). They are required to use both teacher feedback and comments left by peers to identify their learning needs, whilst reading and commenting on other students' blogs (Stage 2) in order to devise their own independent action plan (Stage 3). Then, they follow through with the devised action plan (Stage 4) by demonstrating initiative in learning. Students will write a minimum of three cycles of reflective blogs depending on their entry point.

ii) Report Reviews (oral): To reflect upon and evaluate students' own learning experiences, it is vital to facilitate the use of critical thinking and logical argumentation. The capacity-building of such skills is also central to realising learning to research. Students orally report to group members about their learning experiences describing what, where, who, why and how (Stage 1). This is followed by evaluation feedback by the group members and the teacher who together provide constructive suggestions and queries (Stage 2). Then, they create their own action plan utilising new knowledge and insights gained from the feedback and present it to the group (Stage 3). Finally, they are encouraged to follow through with the action plan by writing it down (Stage 4). Students will conduct report reviews for a minimum of four cycles depending on their entry point.

We will now discuss the third component task, iii) the independent research paper and associated research portfolio, in more detail, as it is a major final assessment task in the PEP curriculum.

Independent Research Paper and Associated Research Portfolio

Crucial to the development of the PEP student, primed for the rigours of undergraduate or postgraduate life, is experience-based understanding of the importance of research processes in such academic environments. To that end, an important strand of the PEP, since its inception, has been a designated and scaffolded "learning to research" element – in the form of the Independent Research Paper (IRP) and the associated Research Portfolio. All PEP students are required to submit both IRP and the portfolio twice as part of their double-marked overall assessment. For both components, the students first submit a draft in order to begin the experiential learning cycle with concrete experience of submitting their IRP (Stage 1). With teacher feedback, they then move onto reflective observation (Stage 2) of the cycle through reviewing teacher comments and evaluation. This is followed by their abstract conceptualisation (Stage 3) to devise an improvement plan for their final version. They then actively experiment and follow through with such a plan to improve and submit the final version (Stage 4).

The IRP is a written task which involves pre-undergraduate PEP students submitting a 1000-1500 word paper and pre-postgraduate PEP students submitting a 2000 word paper. Negotiation of the topic of each student's IRP is done in conjunction with the class teacher(s) and relates to the student's proposed field of study in their future degree programme.

Making their topic pertinent to their own future study areas and disciplines is more likely to maximise their engagement with the IRP task. All sources to be used by the students are academic sources which are published in English. We provide the specific hard scaffolds below for the process of researching and writing the IRP:

+ a research paper task list, which includes such elements as scheduled work hours for each stage of the process, whether or not the task needs to be submitted, and deadline and completion dates;

+ a step-by-step guide for writing a research paper, including such elements as reader expectations, brainstorming, narrowing down the topic, drafting the question, beginning research and note-taking, refining the question, drafting and responding to feedback and final submission;

+ a checklist of the final IRP, to ensure that the final document matches the expectations of the academic (non-specialist) readers.

The students are given an assessment/marking rubric in advance so they can see how their IRP will be assessed, by explicitly presenting the expectations of the IRP contents. During the IRP process, each student has two in-class opportunities whereby their individual progress made so far, is shared with their peers and the teacher(s) in order to receive both peer and teacher feedback.

The IRP is complemented by the associated Research Portfolio, which forms hard documentary evidence of the "research processes" of evidence collection and evaluation. As a hard scaffold to the portfolio, students are given a task sheet which both outlines the purpose of the portfolio and details the organisational structure and contents of a portfolio, including the presentation of evidence, both written and oral, with the latter requiring two (PowerPoint) presentations about the topic, both work-in-progress and a final assessed presentation. Another scaffold takes the form of a "portfolio checklist" which guides the students through the considerations for completion of an appropriate portfolio including:

+ a contents page;

+ evidence of brainstorming/developing the question/interpreting notes/cross-referencing;

+ a reading log of collected sources and evaluation thereof/complete with reference list/bibliography;

+ a plan for oral presentation complete with PowerPoint slides and draft of the IRP.

The students are given an assessment/marking rubric in advance so they can see how their research portfolio will be assessed, by clarifying the expectations of the portfolio contents. The rubric includes such criteria as:

+ evidence of brainstorming and developing a topic/question
+ list of source texts used thus far
+ reading log of collected sources to date with notes and summaries
+ evidence of evaluation, interpretation and critical analysis
+ writing plans/outline
+ draft(s) of IRP

As an adjunct to the portfolio, students are required to submit a reflective conclusion of 200-300 words, which includes both an evaluation of their own learning processes – what they learnt from doing the assignment and an evaluation of the research processes, reasons for choosing the readings, any difficulties they had and the strategies they used to deal with them and how they monitored their progress. They submit this reflective conclusion through Turnitin for two reasons: 1) to get used to using the Turnitin portal, which is a requirement for assignment submissions across the University, and 2) to ensure their reflective conclusion writing is original work and not something plagiarised from previous students' submissions.

Throughout all the above-mentioned "learning to research" experiential learning cycles, students are provided, through embedded induction sessions, with full and scaffolded access to university research librarians and library databases. In addition, students are also provided with one formal individual "course progress consultation" every five weeks in the process of learning to research. So, depending on student entry point into the programme (Table 1), students have between four (for 20 week PEP) and two (for 10 week PEP) consultations to formally meet with the homeroom teacher to discuss their learning progress made so far. In each consultation, teachers provide feedback on the areas of weakness to work upon and improve for the following five-week period, general speaking and listening competence, and demonstrated independent learning skills. Complementing such planned consultations, informal individual consultations are also available at any time to those who need them by appointment. These formal and informal consultations provide crucial hard and soft scaffolds for identifying and helping in a timely manner, those who are struggling to develop their capacity for learning to research.

Discussion and Key Recommendations

The PEP curriculum has had positive impact on student performance in the long term. As shown in Table 2, this impact is reflected in the longitudinal data. These data show that the Grade Point Average (GPA out of 7 [high distinction]) results of former PEP students compares very favourably with students following the IELTS pathway of entry.

UG & PG students commencing degree programme in 2007 across the University	Percentage of students achieving GPA of 4 (Pass) and above
Direct entry with IELTS 6.0	47%
Direct entry with IELTS 6.0 to 8.5	61%
Direct entry through PEP	68%

Table 2: PEP entry students' GPA in comparison with other direct-entry students (The University of Adelaide, 2012: Appendix IX).

The success of the PEP can be seen to lie in its ability to help students prepare themselves for the academic demands of on-campus life. The PEP moves beyond the language-skills focus base of IELTS (and other examination based) entry pathways and allows students to build capacity through its scaffolded learner-centred movement of the locus of control from teacher to student, in order to develop independent learning skills, that lead to learning to research capacity building. Such skills are vital for students to function effectively within their chosen degree programmes.

As discussed previously, the PEP curriculum consists of four components. One of them is the Independent Learning Skills component for promoting learning to research which comprises the Independent Learning Paper and the associated Research Portfolio. These sub-components allow the students to undergo the scaffolded experiential learning cycles of the research processes – capacity-building for learning to research, whilst supporting them to complete their final research products.

Learning to research has not been a focus for IELTS style examinations, which have been extensively used as the entry pathway of choice for many EAL students into universities. As we have demonstrated, using the PEP curriculum as a practical example of learning to research, embedding experience of learning to research itself in a pathway programme curriculum, is indeed crucial for achieving its programme success and long-term effectiveness. That is, learning to research is not just to be promoted for those EAL students who are already enrolled in undergraduate and postgraduate programmes. Rather, that learning to research experience could, and indeed should involve direct-entry programmes such as PEP.

Likewise, our finding concurs with the afore-mentioned Kemp and Norton's (2014:x) recent review finding that *"students who successfully complete pathway programs often do as well as, or out-perform, students with better original school results"*. However, here, they largely refer to "students" as those Australian high school graduates with an Australian Tertiary Admission Rank below 50 (out of 99.95). That is, the review report (2014:65) suggests that less well-prepared *local* students would have a better chance of future success if they first studied in pathway programmes, than to make direct entry to university. In this respect, our finding extends Kemp and Norton's scope, to include the positive impact of pathway programmes on EAL international students' future success, by way of development of their capacity for learning to research.

The following are key recommendations for realising student capacity building for learning to research in the curriculum design of such pathway programmes:

- embed a control wedge model-based gradual increase of student control and responsibility as a programme progresses to maximise student capacity-building for learning to research;
- scaffold appropriately and adequately any learning to research component tasks in such a way that students undergo experiential learning cycles.
- use tasks themselves as scaffolds (e.g. a reflective blog, report-review) so that students can recognise that learning to research is a developmental process, not just an end product;

- make the topic/s of their learning to research component task pertinent to their future study areas so that their task engagement is maximised in the process;
- enable students to have full access to university research support staff and services (e.g. research librarians), and to all available information and learning management systems (e.g. university library databases, online learning platforms) in the process of learning to research;
- bear in mind that a curriculum like PEP could prove difficult for some students who would need extra personal support both within and beyond the classroom to help them develop their capacity for learning to research.

Conclusion

The focus of this chapter is upon the PEP curriculum design as a practical example of building student capacity for learning to research, prior to their university entry in a particular Australian university context. The PEP curriculum allows students to develop the necessary skills required for becoming an independent researcher through the process of learning to research, and to build their identity and confidence as independent researchers, before they commence university studies. This learning to research facet differentiates the PEP, an EAL student pathway programme, from the English language skills based IELTS route currently followed by many prospective international students.

We believe that our key recommendations, presented in the discussion section, can be applied to other higher education institutions. Following these recommendations, "learning to research" can be systematically embedded within theory-grounded curriculum design and incorporated in pathway programmes, as part of transformative, transition pedagogy for international students to enhance their future success. This is one way of promoting the "learning to research" experiences of EAL international students enrolled in a direct-entry pathway programme.

Acknowledgements

The authors wish to thank Erica Smith, Grant Packer and Beth Hutton for their invaluable support and input into the development of this chapter.

About the Authors

Richard Warner is a Lecturer in the School of Education at the University of Adelaide, Australia. He can be contacted at this email: richard.warner@adelaide.edu.au

Kayoko Enomoto is a Senior Lecturer in the School of Social Sciences at the University of Adelaide, Australia. She can be contacted at this email: kayoko.enomoto@adelaide.edu.au

Bibliography

Atley, M. & L. Lawrence (2011). Taking the Mystery out of Mastery: Unpacking the Taught Postgraduate Experience. In C. Nygaard; N. Courtney & L. Frick (Eds.), *Postgraduate Education – Form and Function.* Oxfordshire: Libri Publishing Ltd., pp. 27-42.

Brush, T. & J. Saye (2002). A Summary of Research Exploring Hard and Soft scaffolding for Teachers and Students Using a Multimedia Supported Learning Environment. *The Journal of Interactive Online Learning*, Vol. 1, No. 2, pp. 1-12.

Cadman, K. & M. Grey (2000). The 'Action Teaching' Model of Curriculum Design: EAP Students Managing their own Learning in an Academic Conference Course. *EA Journal*, Vol. 18, No. 2, pp. 21-36.

Cannon R. & N. Dewble (2000). *A Handbook for Teachers in Universities and Colleges.* London: Kogan Page.

Enomoto, K. (2012). Promoting Deeper Learning through a Scaffolded Language Curriculum: Double Tasking Language-specific and Research-skills Development. In J. Hajek; C. Nettelbeck & A. Woods (Eds.), *The proceedings of LCNAU's Inaugural Colloquium.* Melbourne: University of Melbourne, pp. 347-360.

Enomoto, K. & R. Warner (2013). Building Student Capacity for Reflective Learning. In C. Nygaard; J. Branch & C. Holtham (Eds.), *Learning in*

Higher Education: Contemporary Standpoints. Oxfordshire: Libri Publishing Ltd., pp. 183-201.

Kemp, D. & A. Norton (2014). *Review of the Demand Driven Funding System*. Canberra: Department of Education.

Kift, S.; K. Nelson & J. Clarke (2010). Transition Pedagogy: A Third Generation Approach to FYE – A Case Study of Policy and Practice for the Higher Education Sector. *The International Journal of the First Year in Higher Education*, Vol. 1, No. 1, pp. 1-20.

Kolb, D. A. (1984). *Experiential Learning: Experience as the Source of Learning and Development*. Englewood Cliffs: Prentice Hall.

Maunder, R. E.; M. Cunliffe; J. Galvin; S. Mjali & J. Rogers (2013). Listening to Student Voices: Student Researchers Exploring Undergraduate Experiences of University Transition. *Higher Education*, Vol. 66, pp. 139-152.

Nunan, D. (2013). *Learner-Centered English Language Education: The Selected Works of David Nunan*. New York: Routledge.

Pre-enrolment English Program Curriculum (2011). *An Academic Program for University Entrance in Australia*. Adelaide: University of Adelaide.

Picard, M.; R. Warner & L. Velautham (2011). Enabling Postgraduate Students to Become Autonomous Ethnographers of their Disciplines. In C. Nygaard; N. Courtney & L. Frick (Eds.), *Postgraduate Education – Form and Function*. Oxfordshire: Libri Publishing Ltd., pp. 149-166.

Rose, D.; L. Lui-Chivizhe & A. Smith (2003). Scaffolding Academic Reading and Writing at the Koori Centre. *Australian Journal of Indigenous Education*, Vol. 32, pp. 41-49.

Schumann, J. H. (1978). *The Pidgination Process: A Model for Second Language Acquisition*. Rowley, MA: Newbury House.

Schunk, D. H. (2008). Metacognition, Self-regulation, and Self-Regulated Learning: Research Recommendations. *Educational Psychology Review*, Vol. 20, pp. 463-467.

University of Adelaide (2012). *Review of English Language Admission Requirements & English Language Services & Support Report*. Adelaide: University of Adelaide.

Walkington, H. (2014). GEOverse: An Undergraduate Research Journal: Research Dissemination Within and Beyond the Curriculum. *Geoscience Research and Education Innovations in Science Education and Technology*, Vol. 20, pp 189-197.

Warner. R. (2007). The Pre–enrolment English Program – integrating experiential learning with language development to acculturate Japanese students studying at an Australian university, *KASELE Bulletin*, No. 35, pp. 189-201.

Warner, R. & E. Smith (2006). The Pre-enrolment English Program (PEP): a reality of learner-centredness'. *The Proceedings of the Second CLS International Conference: CLaSIC 2006 – Processes and Process-Orientation in Foreign Language Teaching and Learning [CD-ROM]*. Singapore: National University of Singapore, pp. 884-897.

Willison, J. & K. O'Regan (2007). Commonly Known, Commonly not Known, Totally Unknown: A Framework for Students Becoming Researchers. *Higher Education Research & Development*, Vol. 26, No. 4, pp. 393-409.

Chapter Three

A Multi-disciplinary Framework for Building Students' Capacity as Practitioner Researchers

Jesper Piihl, Jens Smed Rasmussen and Jennifer Rowley

Introduction

This chapter contributes to the anthology by proposing a framework that explains pedagogies for learning to research to encourage the transition from student to professional practitioner. The framework is aimed at students across disciplines.

Research and professional practice embrace different concepts across a range of measurable attributes – in particular, valid knowledge, working procedures, authenticity and evidence. In this chapter we discuss how the process of learning to research can develop skills and competencies for future professional practice across the disciplines. A multi-disciplinary incremental framework for higher education teachers is presented in three stages throughout the chapter that emphasises potential tensions that could emerge during the often-fluid movement from student to professional. The tensions between the different roles serve as a source of transformation and motivation for students as they move into the role of professional and are required to act reflexively with stakeholders (e.g. employers, peers, academics etc.). The proposed theoretical frame-work describes two movements – the first movement *becoming a reflexive researcher* and the second presenting evidence for *becoming a research-based professional practitioner.*

Specifically, the chapter analyses different pedagogical concepts applied in higher education teaching within business education in Denmark and music education in Australia that have both been purposely designed to engage students with their future professional practice through research-based teaching. These two very different disciplines are a good comparison as they mirror pedagogic practice that embraces student autonomy and creativity. The pedagogies presented here differ in respect to the types of research performed by students, yet also share common-alities in well-known methods such as case-based teaching, collaborative peer knowledge production and action research. The exploration of these pedagogies enables an analysis of experiences and observations in regard to learning processes related to the research activity required for developing future work-ready practitioners. A result of the pedagogical processes is a research-engaged participant who demonstrates profes-sional competence as an outcome of their learning experience.

The first section relates the chapter's contribution to established literature on Research-enhanced Learning and Teaching (ReLT) and student-engaged pedagogies. We construct evidence for the proposed theoretical framework by demonstrating how learning to research qualifies students for professional life. The framework, built around Bourdieu's (1990) notion of *habitus*, argues that research and profes-sional practice potentially hold different aspects of the accepted meaning of valid knowledge, working procedures, authenticity and evidence. The evidence as such is seen as a continuum for positioning pedagogies related to a student's commitment to learning how to be a practitioner and the issues that emerge in specific environments, such as higher education internship programmes. Analysis in this section informs the proposed conceptual framework and suggests ways to improve pedagogies that show a relationship between learning to research and the development of competencies for skilful professional practice. In fact, the preparation of students as researchers for their future real world experience (e.g. as university students, industrial technicians and professional practitioners across disciplines) is a common thread in chapters in this anthology (see Warner & Enomoto; Kalejs & Napper, this volume).

All authors have been engaged – as practitioners – in developing peda-gogies related to practice in research-based higher education teaching. The process of researching for this chapter enabled us to reflect on practices we are engaged in. Therefore, we propose that the process contains three steps: 1) developing a theoretical framework for understanding teaching research practices; 2) reflecting on our practices in the light of the proposed theoretical framework; and 3) subsequently refining the framework and our future professional practice. Both reflection and refinement of this process are emerging in a continuous interactive process between past experiences, theoretical undertakings, and on-going engagement in learning and teaching in higher education. The second section therefore presents the theory of the practice and, in itself, the collaboration between authors illustrates the process of practitioner research proposed in the chapter. The examples of pedagogy in business and music education are presented in such a way that encourages the reader to replicate the process and adapt components of it to their own discipline. The final discussion summarises how the proposed framework has legitimacy in assisting students to develop the habit of research practice and why this is vital for developing future professional reflective practitioners. Reading this chapter you will:

1. learn how research-based curriculum models can support preparation for professional practice;
2. learn how Bourdieu's notion of habitus is key to understanding practice;
3. learn how tensions between *research habitus* and *habitus as professional practice* can be exploited as a context that supports learning.

Research based teaching and student engaging pedagogies

Healey (2005) discusses the nexus between teaching and research and how it varies across disciplines based on two dimensions. One dimension distinguishes between considering the student as *participants* in learning activities and considering the student as *audience* to teaching. The other dimension of Healey's (2005) model, focuses on the role of research in curriculum design. So, is the emphasis on research *content* or is the emphasis on research *processes* and problems? In Healey's (2005) model, our chapter considers the student as an *active* participant in learning and has a focus on *processes* of research. Healey (2005) labels this type of design *research-based*, and links it with students undertaking Inquiry-Based Learning (IBL).

Savery (2006) compares the concepts of IBL and Problem-Based Learning (PBL) and suggests that both pedagogical strategies share the idea of beginning with a question which is ill-structured to allow students open inquiry. Savery (2006) does, however, consider the role of the instructor to be the most important distinguishing feature of PBL and IBL and compares these pedagogical concepts to Case-Based Learning (CBL) and PBL. The two latter concepts are narrower in the way they define problems and set clearer goals for learning outcomes and possible solutions. Savery (2006) argues that in the real world the ability to both define problems and develop solutions is important.

Both IBL and PBL have an interest in real-world problems and apply research-based knowledge and research procedures to address the problems. However, the pedagogies discussed in this chapter commit to taking the development of good professional practices a step further. The approaches take the context of professional practice explicitly into consideration by gradually moving from researching practices to take research-based ways of thinking out of the university context into practices outside the university. In these practices, outside university, research is not necessarily a legitimate way of framing problems and the traditional research process is not necessarily considered a legitimate process leading towards solutions.

PBL and IBL start with (ill-defined) problems. However, in practical settings, routines sometimes act as automatic responses to stimuli (Pentland & Rueter, 1994). In such settings, the very act of pronouncing and defining situations as problematic may not be straightforward. The pedagogies gradually relate the act of learning to research to the act of becoming a professional practitioner, by showing the students how research can act as a source of continuous development in professional practice.

The importance of learning the processes of research compared to learning the content of research-based knowledge is highlighted in Jarvis' (1999) discussion of practitioner-researchers. In professional settings, practitioners are not simply applying general theory into well-defined and recognisable situations. Instead, he argues, each situation is unique and ephemeral. Therefore, the practitioner cannot rely on theoretical knowledge and must bring their own experience to the situations, which he or she needs to create unique practical knowledge. *"Fundamentally, they are not applying theory to practice, since any theory they learnt in the university reflected a previous situation – so that the theory with which they are presented is information not knowledge. It is information to be tried out in practice, to recognize that valid knowledge is learnt in practice and this demands that universities rethink their role and also the way in which they validate learning"* (Jarvis, 2001:13).

Therefore, being a practitioner involves knowledge creation in unique, ephemeral situations with an ability to recognise when established routines are no longer valid and need to be rebuilt. Therefore, preparing the students for the role of *practitioner-researcher* is an outcome for pedagogical development that links the goal of learning to research with an ambition of developing skilful practitioners. Thus, we argue that a framework for relating learning to research with competency, and for skilful practice, needs to incorporate a perspective of knowledge as context dependent.

What is practice?

As discussed above, the focus in this chapter contributes to established perspectives by discussing the relationship between learning to research and subsequent professional practice by emphasising: 1) gradually taking research procedures and ways of thinking into the flow of professional practices; 2) gradually avoiding taking problems as points of departure, since problems are not necessarily acknowledged in the flow of practice; and 3) gradually training the students in local knowledge creation within the professional settings they engage in.

To qualify the discussion this section explains the theory of practice that the chapter is built upon. The section concludes by integrating these ideas into a framework for analysing the three pedagogies we discuss in this chapter.

Habitus as a key to understand practice

Following Özbilgin and Tatli (2005), Bourdieu's framework operates on three levels; a micro level with focus on the individual agent's capital and dispositions; the meso level with a focus on *habitus* amongst collectives of agents; and the macro level termed the field, emphasising the structures and systems within which the micro and meso level phenomena occur. Agency evolves in a dynamic interplay between these levels. In this chapter, we draw our attention to the meso level: *habitus* (for another example of applying concepts from Bourdieu into the theme of research and learning, see Danaher, this volume).

In the words of Bourdieu: *"[..]habitus, [is] a product of history, produces individual and collective practices—more history— in accordance with the schemes generated by history. It ensures the active presence of past experiences, which, deposited in each organism in the form of schemes of perception, thought and action, tend to guarantee the 'correctness' of practices and their constancy over time, more reliably than all formal rules and explicit norms"* (Bourdieu, 1990:54).

That is, *habitus* produces practices based on history. *Habitus* can be conceptualised as a set of schemes that are present and evolving in a collective of individuals. These schemes contain rationales that guide perceptions, thoughts and actions and are important in defining the correctness of practices as they maintain constancy over time.

Özbilgin and Tatli (2005) argue that the concept of *habitus* resembles ideas of culture within organisational research. The concept emphasises the dynamic nature of practices as a result of *"continuous power struggle/ game between different agents in the organization"* (Özbilgin & Tatli, 2005:864) Therefore the mechanism for development of practices in this chapter, is a dialectic perspective, beginning with the *"[..]assumption that the organizational entity exists in a pluralistic world of colliding events, forces, or contradictory values that compete with each other for domination and control"* (Van de Ven & Poole, 1995:517). In other words, organisational *habitus* is the site of tension and negotiation among different organisational members. It is the tension and competition among the organisational actors that become a source of what Özbilgin & Tatli (2005) call *reproductive transformation* in the organisational culture.

Research and professional practice as distinct habitus

Within this perspective, conducting research and being an advanced practitioner are not two inherently different endeavours. Both endeavours are seen as distinct *habitus* with distinct sets of schemes of perception, thought and action. Furthermore, both endeavours encourage knowledge creation. The *habitus* of research may involve other schemes guiding action and defining knowledge than otherwise present in a specific professional practice (Jarvis, 1999). For example a *habitus* of research may contain requirements of certain methods, reason, theory and transparency.

Since *habitus* of research and *habitus* in a professional practice may hold different schemes regarding rationales guiding perceptions, thoughts and actions it might be expected that working across these *habitus* are a potential source for creating tensions and negotiations amongst members. The tensions and negotiations created can potentially be sources for the *reproductive transformation* in professional practice (as well as research). However, due to the risk of unquestioned routines when working within one of these *habitus*, the act of creating tensions is not necessarily straight-forward, but requires reflexivity. This chapter argues that reflexivity is the element from research that can develop skilful practitioners. Jarvis (1999) points to Schön's (1995) reflective practitioner who artfully develops his practise by reflecting upon it.

Figure 1 illustrates how the ideas in the framework are linked, and prepares for setting up a continuum for differentiating pedagogies related to these issues in the following section. The figure has an area illustrating a research *habitus* and another area illustrating a *habitus* in professional practice. The diagonal line between them illustrates that tensions created between the rationale, thoughts and action in these *habitus* can be a potential source for *reproductive transformation*.

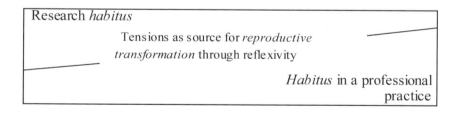

Figure 1: Confronting a habitus of research and professional practice.

In the following section, 1) the distinction between a *habitus* of research and *habitus* in professional practice, 2) the tensions potentially emerging between these, and 3) reflexivity as source of *reproductive transformation*, are translated into a framework for analysing three specific pedagogies used for training research practitioners.

Pedagogies for creating learning tensions between habitus

Figure 1 shows the two *habitus* where students are moving into and across; the *habitus* of research and the *habitus* of professional practice. Figure 2, below, translates this model into a continuum for distinguishing pedagogies working with the intersections between research and professional practices. Pedagogies on the left-hand side of the continuum have to let the students enter into the special *habitus* of research, whereas pedagogies on the right-hand side have a primary focus on the *habitus* of professional practices. The specific pedagogies are elaborated in the following section.

	Moving into research		Moving into practitioner research
Primary commitment	Commitment to research *habitus* Tensions as source for *reproductive transformation* through reflexivity		Commitment to *habitus* in a professional practice
Research Pedagogies	Case-research researching a practice	Action research on a predefined issue	Practitioner research related to practical tasks in specific practices

Figure 2: Overview of pedagogies, courses and focus points for research.

In all pedagogies explored in this chapter, there is a dual focus on both research and a commitment to practice. However, the closeness and commitment to each of the research *habitus* or *habitus* in professional practice is different. In the models the diagonal line, separating the two *habitus*, does not touch the corners. This is to illustrate that this dual focus is also prevailing in the pedagogies on the extremes of the continuum. On the left-hand side, the point of departure for students' learning is the issues and rationales prevailing in research. The approach to practice is through the lens of research and with a goal of contributing to research and research training. In the right-hand extreme, the point of departure is a specific professional practice and issues experienced by stakeholders. The goal pedagogy in this side of the framework is contributing to the development of a specific practice.

The diagonal line between the *habitus* illustrates the area of tensions emerging in working across or confronting the rationales in these *habitus*.

To develop skilful practitioners through learning to research, different pedagogies can be designed to encourage students to work in and across these two areas. We emphasise that the students' movements into and between *habitus* are not by chance, but designed through specific pedagogies. The pedagogies presented share a focus on the role of research in learning, and they differ regarding the closeness and commitment to interaction with practice. The pedagogies share a focus on developing a *habitus* of research with the students, while they differ in their commitment to create and negotiate tensions with the profession as they work toward creating reproductive transformations in the practices the students engage with.

In the overall curriculum where these three pedagogies and courses are embedded, specific teaching of research methodology is included in the students' programme of learning. A common thread amongst the three pedagogies investigated in this chapter is developing students' skills to undertake research and engage in dialogues with research fellows – staff, students and potential employers. The three pedagogies share a common goal of researching practice and developing professional practitioners. However, due to the focus in this chapter we are not detailing the scaffolding of the learning experiences in the different pedagogies as are other authors in this anthology (see Hayes; Khong, this volume).

Pedagogies for relating learning to research to skilful practice

This section elaborates on specific courses representing the three pedagogies in Figure 2. Courses illustrating the overall pedagogies are from both music education in Australia and business education in Scandinavia. The pedagogies are briefly described with specific consideration of course designs and how tensions are built into their structure. The descriptions are informed by the ideas in the theoretical framework to develop insights in how these pedagogies apply research in a way that gradually changes the commitments from *habitus* of research to *habitus* in professional practices.

The descriptions are followed by elaborations on tensions experienced by students, and conclude by exploring similarities and differences amongst the courses.

Case-research – researching a practice

This pedagogy allows students to enter into the *habitus* of research with the distinct procedures, ethics and criteria for developing knowledge within a research logic, and is therefore placed on the left-hand side of the continuum. In learning to research, the students are asked to conduct a case study of a professional practice related to the specific topic of study. In both music and business education, the specific courses illustrating this pedagogy require the student researcher to conduct case studies autonomously but under supervision in a Community of Practice (CoP) where student researchers engage in scaffolded peer review processes during one semester.

The Business course on Modern Management Concepts trains students in reflexivity through working with competing theoretical explanations to an empirical phenomena and working with an empirical study of a rationale in a professional practice with this theoretical knowledge. In this course the students are required to conduct case studies *of* practice. The course aims at learning to research through learning about different theoretical and empirical positions taken by different research traditions. Two overall positions on modern management concepts are juxtaposed in the course: 1) an instrumental rational perspective and 2) a critical theoretical and mainly new institutional perspective.

Groups of students are asked to formulate research questions from different theoretical positions to make qualitative case studies. Students must go into the field to observe and study the use of modern concepts in real management practices. Besides supervision and ordinary teaching in class, students learn from giving and receiving peer review and feedback three times on each other's research reports. The last of these is also the final exam.

The pedagogy in this course is to form a research context of peer researchers studying real management practices. Students are invited to do empirical research on the question: What is the nature of management concepts when seen in real management practices? This question is intended to challenge the *taken for granted* knowledge held by students, which is often dominated by instrumental perspectives, which emphasises formalised structures in organisations and normative models to be implemented into practices.

In music education, the case study research task is set for students in the final subject of the music education degree programme. Students are placed in schools for a 10-week period during which they research one school student *in the field* and write a case study on that student's *individual difference*. University students engage in the standard research protocols (ethical, professional, policy, etc.) and determine appropriate research practices to gather their data. The systematic approach to this task is scaffolded through weekly meetings with tutors over the 10 weeks where they receive feedback and interact with peers in a CoP. Their only instructions are to follow all procedures determined by the state education policies surrounding a professional teacher and that the school student for the case study is diagnosed with an *individual difference* according to legislation.

Taking university practices into the *field* through the weekly seminars, supports the students' developmental processes as researchers and enables students to apply theoretical research knowledge developed over the previous three years of their degree. Students are asked to learn in the university and then apply that knowledge to the field where they assess the specific individual needs and employ strategies taught for gathering research in a sensitive and professional manner. In preparing the case study, students are encouraged to interview all relevant parties (student, parent/carer; other teachers; peers; professional service staff etc.) and to build their case through ethical practices. The outcome is that the case study provides information that the school can use to enhance learning experiences of the specific student (e.g. a modification of their individual learning plan or future plan for intervention).

In this pedagogy, exemplified through two courses, we observe at least two movements creating tensions: 1) when students question their *taken for granted* preconceptions and have to work with their research question regarding the distinct practice they study; and 2) when students must act as peer reviewers and in this process practice reflexivity in collaboration with fellow researchers. As one student phrased it: "*Now I see that I have learned more about the relation between theory and reality during this course, than ever before in my entire study*".

Action research on a predefined issue

This pedagogy is placed in the middle of the continuum, as it requires the students to conduct action research *in* a professional practice context. It has an emphasis on meeting criteria and procedures of research and contributing toward changes in actual practices. The courses from business and music education exemplify this pedagogy slightly differently due to differences in the changes they are aiming for in actual professional practice.

Within business education, the course titled Controlling and Management Processes uses this pedagogy and has a commitment to actually create new insights for the participants in the practice under investigation. The point of departure in the course is a change in the role of business controllers in companies going from *bean counters*, who register past events, to *strategic partners* who contribute to decision making on strategic issues in companies. Students are required to research controlling practices as they are performed by a controller in a company. Action research is undertaken as the students enter into an interactive production of knowledge in collaboration with research practitioners by applying the interactive analytical interview technique (Kreiner & Mouritsen, 2005). The research methodology focuses on dilemmas as constituent elements in organisational practices. Through this technique, students are asked to develop insights into dilemmas as observed in the practice together with the practitioner they are interviewing. This experience aims to develop new insights for the students about contemporary controlling practices and at the same time create changes in practice through developing new insights for the practitioner controller participating in the interview where unrecognised subtleties of his or her own practice are exposed.

The students are prepared for participating in this type of interview through both reading seminal work in the issues on accounting and organisational improvement and practising this interview form through role playing before entering the field. Furthermore, in the framing of the course, this special interview technique is considered to be a relevant competency for a practising controller as it potentially reveals new insights into the *habitus* the practitioner becomes a participant in. Hence, learning to research is an element in developing real world practice.

In the music education degree, pre-service music teachers are expected to undertake an action research project in their final professional experience placement in a school. The rationale for action research is that they unpack an issue that exists at their placement. Issues might include the use of mobile technologies for engaging school students in learning practice; understanding the music of other worlds in a culturally sensitive manner; or adapting QR codes for identifying elements of musical understanding.

The research is broadly classified as action research because students have to apply the research specifically to the context of a work environment and the student must collect data in the *action* of implementing the research. Before the student goes into the field, they are supported by weekly seminar meetings where *experts* from the field are invited to share their knowledge and experiences. This approach to learning assists the university student in their transition from student/learner to research practitioner. The action research is delivered to the lecturer as a proposal where traditional research components are identified (i.e. outlining the problem/issue to be investigated; developing research questions; critiquing the existing literature; gathering data and analysing it in a meaningful manner and discussing and concluding the outcome of the data collected in a discussion paper). The results of the action research are presented to the CoP peers and experts, where students have to convince the audience of the importance and the impact of the research in providing *new* information to the teaching profession. This is peer reviewed and when assessed as excellent, students are encouraged to publish their results to the wider community.

Practitioner research in specific practices

This pedagogy has the closest connection to practice and an explicit commitment regarding producing changes in one's practice. Therefore, it is placed on the right-hand side of the theoretical framework.

Whereas the specific issues described in the two earlier pedagogies are 'pushed' by the university, the issues here are 'pulled' from the practice in which the student is involved. The goal for students is to practise applying research skills to engage in mutually beneficial interactions with stakeholders in actual practices (i.e., the organisations they are researching in). Based on the framework developed earlier in this chapter, these stakeholders potentially hold other *schemes of perception, thought and action* as compared to the schemes known from the *habitus* of research.

The Internship in both music and management education is an example of this pedagogy as it requires undergraduate and graduate students to learn to become academics in practice. This is achieved by pushing students to engage in complex interactions with multiple stakeholders from an organisation where they solve problems and develop knowledge about the process of solving problems in practice. The student's role in this resembles the concept of the *practitioner researcher* as described by Jarvis (1999). The courses aim at developing perspectives and knowledge in unique situations while building on research-based knowledge, research procedures and to see the university peers and staff as peer researchers. For a more detailed description and discussion of this pedagogy, see Piihl *et al.* (2014). The process of translating and applying research knowledge and procedures within real-life settings and work-rhythms is the focus of the research in the internship. Furthermore, the students have to work closely with stakeholders to legitimise and create value through research-based approaches to knowledge construction. Students create a portfolio of their experience where they are encouraged to justify and provide evidence of the transition from student-researcher to research-practitioner.

Several tensions are experienced by students undertaking these research-based internships; some students find that they are reluctant to ask questions in the practical setting, which are based on theoretical frameworks; others experience tensions in following the procedures learned in their research practice and applying it in a professional practice setting. One reason is that the amount of time for following these procedures cannot be assigned to the task, given the logistics of professional practice. Another reason is that arguments put forward by research theory and procedures are not necessarily relevant to the criteria for *correctness* held amongst the stakeholders in the professional practice.

These tensions experienced by the students make them vulnerable to the criteria and work procedures existing in the professional practice. In the pedagogical design of the internships, research-seminars are organised so that students practise research-based reflexivity amongst peer researchers and the tutor (expert).

The aim of the internship and supporting seminars is to move students into actively working within and across the potentially conflicting *habitus* of research and professional practice. The goal is to let the students experience how a research-based approach can act as a source for reproductive transformation in the practices they are embedded in. It is important that the students have sufficient research training before the internship so as to be able to avoid the pitfall of simply performing the tasks within the mind-set of the practitioners – and thereby failing to fulfil their potential to offer constructive *reproductive transformation* and learning.

Discussion

Through the lens of the theoretical framework we observe in each of the pedagogies that they are designed to let students develop a capability to reflect on the relationship between theory and practice. Learning to research in this reflective way (Bourdieu, 1977, 1990) is considered a potential source to becoming a competent practitioner-researcher (Jarvis, 1999). These pedagogies allow students to build capacity for developing professional practises, through the ability to research and understand reflectively (Schön, 1995), and to act as a source for *reproductive transformation* of practises (see also Hayes, this volume, for a discussion of research as lived experience). Therefore we encourage students to actively experience research as a constant thread they can retain, develop and reflect upon.

Figure 3 summarises the insights from pedagogical cases according to the theoretical framework. First it shows the difference in balance between moving the students into a *habitus* of research and moving them into practitioner research for each of the other pedagogies. Next the figure focuses on the extremes in summarising the pitfalls and tensions. In the last part, the figure suggests future refinements of the pedagogies.

	Moving into research		**Moving into practitioner research**
Primary commitment	Commitment to research *habitus* Tensions as source for *reproductive transformation* through reflexivity		Commitment to *habitus* in a professional practice
Pedagogies	Case-research researching a practice	Action research on a predefined issue	Practitioner research related to practical tasks in specific practices
Courses exemplifying the pedagogy	Business: Modern Management concepts Music: Professional and Social Issues	Business: Controlling and management processes Music: Professional and Social Issues	Business and Music: Internships
Differences — Closeness and commitment in interaction with practice	Qualitative research *of* a practice.	Qualitative research *in* a practice.	Qualitative research *in* a practice.
		Knowledge creation in collaboration with practitioners on *theoretically defined* issues.	Knowledge creation in collaboration with practitioner on evolving *issues emerging in the practice.*
			Development of practice and learning through research-based interaction with stakeholders. Reproductive transformations of practice.
Pitfalls to be avoided	Reading theoretical concepts into interpretation of practice.		Un-reflexively entering the logics and schemes in the professional practice.
Tensions the students experienced between:	Alternative theoretical frameworks. Theoretical grounded expectations and *habitus* in the field.		Tensions between criteria for "truth claims" in research and criteria for "truth claims" in professional practice.
Future refinements in courses	Being more explicit on *habitus* as a way of describing practice.		More explicit focus on how work across *habitus* can be a source for creating tensions that potentially can lead to reproductive transformations in the professional practice

Figure 3: Comparison of pedagogies for researching practice.

The courses balance differently between commitment to research rationales and the rationales in professional practice. This is done by elaborating on the special relationship each of the pedagogies has to researching practice. The case study pedagogy has an emphasis on research *of* a specific professional practice. This moves the students into the *habitus* of research, with its distinct rationales, procedures and ethics. Simultaneously, it introduces the students to the intricacies of professional practices that can be unravelled through deliberate application of research methodologies. The action research methodology balances differently between the two *habitus*, since it introduces a commitment to create knowledge *in* a professional practice in relation to the issues at hand defined by the curriculum. The practitioner research pedagogy tips the balance towards creating value in a specific professional practice by applying research skills to act as a source for *reproductive transformation* of the practices students are invited into.

Second, typical methodological pitfalls are highlighted. In the pedagogy on the left-hand side – with strongest commitment to moving the students into the rationales of research – our experiences highlight the risk of students reading the theoretical concepts into the practices they are studying. When this happens the students find what the theory suggests without reflexively considering if it is found due to their empirical work or due to their theoretical preconceptions. In the other extreme, in pedagogies with *habitus* in a professional practice, the students risk forgetting their theoretical and methodological background and simply uncritically adopting the rationales and schemes prevalent in the existing *habitus* and miss the opportunity for transforming the practices.

In these extremes, the tensions between the *habitus* of research and professional practice differ. In the left-hand side, the tensions relate to the ability to work with alternative theoretical frameworks and relating this to the experiences they gain from empirical investigations in the field. In the other extreme, students are confronted with tensions regarding how knowledge is produced in research and in professional practices and how valid knowledge is defined.

Conclusion and contributions

Through development of a theoretical framework based on the notion of *habitus* and analysis of three different pedagogies, this chapter has discussed how the process of learning to research can develop skills and competencies for professional practice. The key mechanism emphasised is that research and professional practice, when analysed as distinct *habitus*, hold different conceptions of knowledge, procedures, truth claims etc. Tensions between these differences can serve as a source for *reproductive transformation* in professional practices, when research-based practitioners act reflexively with stakeholders in specific practices. The chapter has discussed three pedagogies, which can gradually move students into research and professional practices.

The notion of *habitus* emphasises how deep the differences are between rationales guiding perceptions, thoughts and actions within research and within professional practice. The work on internships exemplifies the differences and shows how students develop competency to translate and apply values, knowledge definitions and procedures from research to critically and constructively question and develop *habitus* of research practice. In this way, learning to research has a potential to develop skilful practitioners.

Methodological reflexivity is a skill seen in the competent researcher who is capable of acting as a practitioner-researcher. Reflexivity is one major achievement from learning to do research – that enhances the ability to act as a skilful practitioner. This chapter takes the perspective that these competencies can be learned from pedagogies that invite the students to step into certain kinds of research practices through carefully planned teaching and learning activities.

In essence, the chapter develops insights into two themes. At the most immediate level, insights are developed on designs of courses aimed at introducing students' ways of learning from doing research into practice. At a more advanced level, we suggest new intricate links between research methods, procedures and professional practice, and therefore contribute to the evolving discussion on research-based learning for professional practice. The chapter provides input into the debate on the role of research within teaching and learning in higher education emphasising a process perspective linking research closely to learning.

Compared to research-based learning, which Healey (2005) exemplifies with problem or inquiry-based learning, the ideas proposed here go a step further in involving direct interaction with stakeholders in specific practices. Secondly, where PBL/IBL starts with a problem, the ideas proposed here demonstrate a capacity of applying research methodology reflexively to suggest and develop new issues in distinct practices, which stakeholders in the practice do not necessarily consider as issues that, through being addressed, could potentially create new value.

The right context of research-based teaching communicates the concept that researching professional practices can enhance learning about how to do research and provide links between theory and practice and is an important prerequisite to become a practitioner-researcher in work-life. Learning how to do research is a way to become a better and more advanced practitioner.

About the Authors

Jesper Piihl is Associate Professor at the Faculty of social sciences, Department of Entrepreneurship and Relationship management, University of Southern Denmark. He can be contacted at this email: jpi@sam.sdu.dk

Jens Smed Rasmussen is Teaching Assistant Professor at the Faculty of social sciences, Department of Entrepreneurship and Relationship management, University of Southern Denmark. He can be contacted at this email: jsr@sam.sdu.dk

Jennifer Rowley is a Senior Lecturer in Music Education at the Sydney Conservatorium of Music, The University of Sydney, Australia. She can be contacted at this email: jennifer.rowley@sydney.edu.au

Bibliography

Bourdieu, P. (1977). *Outline of Theory of Practice*. Cambridge: Cambridge University Press.

Bourdieu, P. (1990). *The Logic of Practice*. Stanford, CA: Stanford University Press.

Healey, M. (2005). Linking Research and Teaching: Exploring Disciplinary Spaces and the Role of Inquiry-Based Learning. In R. Barnett (Ed.), *Reshaping the University: New Relationships between Research, Scholarship and Teaching*, Berkshire, GBR: McGraw-Hill Education, pp. 67-78.

Jarvis, P. (1999). *The Practitioner-Researcher: Developing Theory from Practice*. San Francisco: Jossey-Bass Publishers.

Jarvis, P. (2001). *Universities and Corporate Universities – The Higher Learning Industry in Global Society*. London: Kogan Page Limited.

Kreiner, K. & J. Mouritsen (2005). The Analytical Interview: Relevance Beyond Reflexivity. In S. Tengblad; R. Solli & B. Czarniawska (Eds.), *The Art of Science*, Liber & Copenhagen Business School Press, pp. 153-176.

Özbilgin, M. & A. Tatli (2005). Book Review Essay: Understanding Bourdieu's Contribution to Organization and Management Studies. *Academy of Management Review*, Vol. 30, No. 4, pp. 855-869.

Pentland, B. T. & H. H. Rueter (1994). Organizational Routines as Grammars of Action. *Administrative Science Quarterly*. Vol. 39, No. 3, pp. 484-510.

Piihl, J.; J. S. Rasmussen, & J. Rowley (2014). Internships as case-based learning for professional practice. In C. Nygaard; J. Branch & P. Bartholomew (Eds.), *Case-Based Learning in Higher Education*, Oxfordshire: Libri Publishing Ltd., pp. 177-196.

Savery, J. R. (2006). Overview of Problem-Based Learning: Definitions and Distinctions. *Interdisciplinary Journal of Problem-based Learning*, Vol. 1, No. 1, pp. 9-20.

Schön, D. A. (1995). The New Scholarship Requires a New Epistemology. *Change*, Vol. 27, No. 6, pp. 27-34.

Van de Ven, A. H. & M. S. Poole (1995). Explaining Development and Change in Organizations. *Academy of Management Review*, Vol. 20, No. 3, pp. 510-541.

Chapter Four

Research, Learn, Design: Project-Based Learning and Research Skill Development in Industrial Design

Linda Kalejs and Robbie Napper

Introduction

"This project helped me to understand how to do structured and professional research" (Student A, 2013). Research begins with a problem or question. By undertaking research, students augment their knowledge (Candy, 2011) – they are researching to learn. By learning to research, students build skills for further research and employability. This chapter discusses the design pedagogy employed to embed research skill development into an undergraduate Project-Based Learning curriculum, and its effectiveness as a method of learning. The chapter reveals data to support that this method leads to an improved level of student engagement, higher quality project outcomes, and development of skills relevant to the course of study and ultimately, transferable to the workplace. The value of the Library/Faculty partnership is clearly articulated, alongside evidence of the value of building a research skills development learning sequence into the curriculum.

The research design draws upon a review of literature outlining the benefits of integrating Project-Based Learning and research skill development pedagogical models into an undergraduate curriculum. This chapter introduces a case study involving a third year cohort of Monash

University Industrial Design students undertaking a major project in Semester 2, 2013- *'Travel Light'*, highlighting the positive outcomes of augmenting and scaffolding student research capabilities through the introduction of the Research Skill Development Framework (RSDF) (Willison & O'Regan, 2012). Qualitative and quantitative research methodologies were utilised to gather data about the programme's impact, including a survey, with student pre and post tutorial self- assess-ments, triangulated with observational and assessment based outcomes. Comparisons are drawn between the students' reflection of their skills before and after the training, and against the control group of the same cohort from 2012. Findings revealed increased confidence levels after completing research skill instruction, with students clearly recognising the transferability of these research techniques to future research topics as well as the workplace. The implementation of scaffolded research skill instruction was found to have a positive effect on the quality of research, and design work produced by the student sample. An assessment of the students' learning outcomes witnessed a marked increase in project depth and quality compared to the previous cohort.

This chapter contributes to the Learning to Research strand of the anthology by illustrating the practical implementation of an integrated and embedded designed pedagogy within the curriculum. Reading this chapter will give the following three insights:

1. how an established research framework was taught in an applied setting;
2. the impact of research skill instruction on undergraduate Project-Based Learning; and
3. why and how students are motivated to learn through project based research tasks, linking these skills to future projects and the workplace.

Researching and designing: literature review

Project-Based Learning is based on the constructivist method of teaching, organising learning around a realistic project – investigating, researching, designing and problem-solving to find a solution (Frank *et al.*, 2003; Thomas, 2000). Project-Based Learning, as a strategy for student moti-vation and invigorating the undergraduate curriculum, requires two essential components – a question or problem that directs their activities, with a final product that addresses the initial problem (Blumenfeld *et al.*, 1991). Project-Based Learning encourages student autonomy in research and project development, learning by thinking and doing in social contexts (Vygotsky, 1986), with the educator taking on the role of facilitator, yet providing feedback, monitoring educational goals and boundaries (Bell, 2010; Moursund, 1999). Rios *et al.* (2010:1368) refer to Project-Based Learning as cooperative and collaborative learning, facilitated through reflection, research and teaching whilst providing an opportunity to master technical, personal and contextual competencies.

The work of an industrial designer is historically founded in object design, however it has since expanded to include services, experiences, interactions and systems; with design outcomes exhibiting several of these. Design practice is concerned with the creation of *"that which does not exist"* (Nelson & Stolterman, 2003:9), and a principal means of building skills for such creation is the heuristic of Project-Based Learning. Like many professions, Industrial Design is practised, managed, and taught through a project model. The notion of a project, as distinct from a strategy or a task (Cleland & Ireland, 2006) is a useful compartmentalisation of design work and leads naturally to the foundation of design education in a Project-Based Learning framework for units such as Industrial Design Studio. Researching to learn, and extending one's knowledge across multi-disciplinary fields to inform the design outcome, is a key skill for design students. The link between disciplines associated with a profession and the scholarship of discovery versus integration and application (Boyer, 1990) is clearly demonstrated by Picard and Guerin (this volume), through a case study into the application of a new pedagogy using Small Group Discovery Experience.

Learning to research extends far beyond merely searching for resources. The strong partnerships built between Faculty and the Library provide a solid grounding for research skill development, shifting the emphasis from generic training to an embedded, tailored and scaffolded approach. Educators have developed various research cycle models and taxonomies, including the Vitae Researcher Development Framework (CRAC, 2014), which provides four domains of development including: knowledge and intellectual abilities; personal effectiveness; research governance and organisation; and engagement, influence and impact. These frameworks stress the importance of students becoming active participants in the research process, evolving from gatherers to producers of information and moving through distinct stages of the research cycle: *"questioning, planning, gathering, sorting and sifting, synthesizing, evaluating and reporting"* (McKenzie, 2000:143).

The Research Skill Development Framework (Willison & O'Regan, 2012), moves students beyond information production and retrieval, towards becoming *"critical, analytical and integrative thinkers"* (Webster & Kenney, 2011), clearly defining the necessary skills to be developed, and providing measures (levels of autonomy) to assess these skills. The RSDF relates and maps facets of research to the extent of student autonomy. Students move through the research cycle or process *"spiralling through the facets, adding degrees of rigour and discernment as they dig and delve"* (Willison & O'Regan, 2012). As shown in Figure 1, Willison and O'Regan (2012) classify facets of research as:

[a] embark and clarify;

[b] find and generate;

[c] evaluate and reflect;

[d] organise and manage;

[e] analyse and synthesise;

[f] communicate and apply.

RESEARCH SKILL DEVELOPMENT FRAMEWORK:
SUMMARY OF FACETS AND AUTONOMY

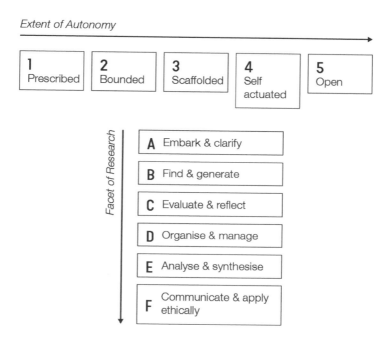

Figure 1: RSDF summary of facets and autonomy (adapted from Willison & O'Regan, 2012).

The progression or level of student autonomy in the skill building process is assessed by five levels: *"Level 1 Prescribed Research, giving highly structured directions and modelling from the educator, through to Level 5 Open Research, witnessing student determined and discipline specific guidelines"* (Willison & O'Regan, 2012), as shown in Figure 1. Parallels can be drawn between these levels of student autonomy and Warner and Enomoto's (this volume) research which states that *"learning represents a recycling of previous experiences at increasingly deeper levels of understanding"*.

Learning to research, that is, the development of research skills, provides students with skills that can be transferred to the workplace and future learning. Our research adopts the definition of employability skills as outlined by Monash University —*"hard skills gained from technical and discipline specific work, and soft skills that enable an employee to perform in a constantly changing environment: communication, teamwork, problem solving, initiative and enterprise, planning and organisation, self-management, learning, technology*" (Monash University, 2013:np). Employers and strategic leaders in Higher Educational institutions concur that successful and employable graduates require particular skill sets, seven of which have been coined by Moylan (2008:287) as: *"critical thinking and problem solving skills; creativity and innovation; collaboration, teamwork and leadership; cross-cultural understanding; communications and information fluency; computing and information & communication technology fluency; and career and learning self-reliance".* Baker and Henson (2010:70) acknowledge employability skills within research-intensive universities, as a means of advancing post-graduation career opportunities, addressing development in the following as key generic skills: *"team work; project management; leadership; problem solving; presentation skills; self-directed learning; networking and developing links with employers; information interviewing; researching and the ability to use technology".* Monash University recognises the soft skills attained through research activities that have relevance to employment, for instance development of communication skills gained through composing a literature review, or presenting at conferences (Monash University, 2012). A major finding from our research established a link between embedded research skill development in the Industrial Design curriculum using a Project-Based Learning approach, and employability skills.

Project-Based Learning and the Travel Light project

In semester two 2013 the unit, Industrial Design Studio 6, was undertaken by 38 third year students. The "Travel Light Project" provides students with the *"opportunity to demonstrate their capability to integrate all aspects of industrial design project work in a holistic design that demonstrates professional competence. … Project work is presented in a folio format, documented for production and final design proposals are also undertaken in detailed model form"* (Monash University Art Design and Architecture, 2013). This third year design project amalgamates all studies undertaken in the first three years of a four year Bachelor of Industrial Design honours degree.

Excerpts from the project brief: *"Your client … has determined that the niche of lightweight travel represents an exciting opportunity. … The client wants to offer a product more in tune with contemporary values of materiality, sustainability, quality and affordability."* (Monash University Art Design and Architecture, 2013:np).

Two examples of student work are used throughout the discussion to illustrate the nature of the Travel Light project, and to explain observations of RSDF implementation. "TranSit" is an urban furniture product that links users into their local amenities while providing the core functionality of seating, shown in Figures 2 and 3. The physical product is installed in the urban environment, with each seat including information about local landmarks such as transport nodes and distances to them. "Mirror" is a project which provides an innovative approach to videoconferencing and collaboration, shown in Figures 4 and 5. The product is an electronically mediated mirror and window, affording users at either end of a connection the ability to see and talk to one another, while at the same time collaborating on a document or virtual whiteboard. Both student projects are indicative of a successful product intervention backed by the development of system attributes for a thorough final result.

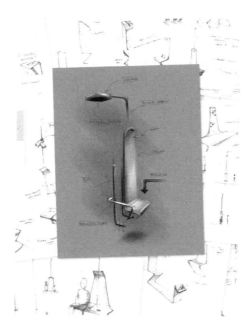

Figure 2: TranSit concept sketch.

TRANSIT
WALKING WAYPOINTS FOR URBAN ENVIRONMENTS

Figure 3: TranSit final design, designer's rendering.

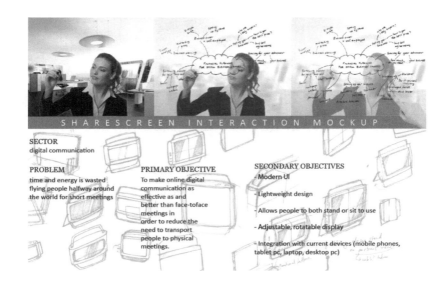

SHARESCREEN INTERACTION MOCKUP

SECTOR
digital communication

PROBLEM
time and energy is wasted
flying people halfway around
the world for short meetings

PRIMARY OBJECTIVE
To make online digital
communication as
effective as and
better than face-toface
meetings in
order to reduce the
need to transport
people to physical
meetings.

SECONDARY OBJECTIVES
- Modern UI

- Lightweight design

- Allows people to both stand or sit to use

- Adjustable, rotatable display

- Integration with current devices (mobile phones,
tablet pc, laptop, desktop pc)

Figure 4: Mirror design objectives.

Figure 5: Mirror final design, designer's rendering.

Students were encouraged to enter this project with a view to solving a problem. By the end of the semester, students had produced a resolved physical product, communicated by means of a poster, a lifelike physical model, technical drawing pack, and a professionally finished eBook, all presented by exhibition. Throughout the journey, students gathered their reflections, development work, and research reports within the eBook, and presented their researched concept and project proposal to peers through 'PechaKucha style' presentations, an intensive method of distilled communication, followed by valuable feedback from peers and educators. A critical part of design education and Project-Based Learning is the combined use of a formative assessment, providing qualitative feedback, and summative assessment, monitoring educational outcomes through the provision of a final grade.

Implementation of the RSDF in a Project-Based Learning setting: practical steps

The Bachelor of Industrial Design (Honours) course outcomes are rigorously aligned with the Australian Qualifications Framework Level 8, the Bologna Cycle 1 and Monash Graduate Attributes. To achieve the course outcomes, the RSDF provided an ideal basis to develop student research skills. Monash University is one of five Australian universities leading and embracing the framework as a tool to embed research skill development within the curriculum.

Research formed a major part of the Travel Light project, as students were required to source relevant data to inform their design, from a wide range of specialised industry and University Library resources. Combining the two pedagogical approaches as shown in Figure 6 witnessed significant improvements to student learning, and project quality outcomes. Students developed their research capabilities into a scholarly skill set by attending a face-to-face Library tutorial. These skills were then used to research their chosen design field of enquiry which led to a design intervention. Guiding students through the facets articulated in the RSDF in the face-to-face session, as well as providing supporting materials for post-session support, was a critical component of the constructivist approach. Students began to understand that the research process involved more than just "looking for information" to complete their literature review. Student motivation in learning to research was high, as they could see the relevance of sharpening these skills for their future careers.

Research is an embedded component of the design process and as such students in their third year of Industrial Design education are comfortable with the concept of 'doing' research and basing their decisions on research findings. Industrial designers undertake research through a variety of means, for example building and evaluating physical prototypes, critique sessions with peers, and literature review. These approaches can be somewhat introspective, in that they evaluate what a student has already created. One of the educational aims of the Travel Light project is to increase students' ability to draw on external information sources and synthesise them into their project. The students' engagement with the RSDF and the research cycle is discussed with reference to the facets of research below.

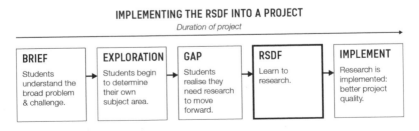

Figure 6: Implementing the RSDF into a Project-Based Learning environment.

Embark and clarify...

When embarking on research, the first step for students is task clarification (Green & Bonollo, 2002), interpretation and formulation of the research topic, setting parameters, and thinking about requirements and expectations of the project (Willison & O'Regan, 2012) – RSDF facet [a]. This provides a foundation to the problem-solving approach and initiative fostered in design education. When faced with the increasing difficulty of projects throughout their undergraduate studies the shift can be observed from a challenge of answering, to asking questions, as the Travel Light project requires, and as student autonomy levels 4 and 5 of the RSDF suggest. At this stage, criteria for the project might be negotiated and discussed with the educator, providing some expert guidance. Students begin querying the types of information they may require, where it might be available, and how they might augment their current knowledge. The face to face tutorial and provided resources, based on facets on research, assisted the students in clarifying these questions, and articulating their research topic, by providing relevant prompts.

Find and generate...

Students then began a systematic process of locating relevant resources and generating required information/data using the prescribed methodology – i.e. RSDF facet [b] (Willison & O'Regan, 2012). Structure was provided within an information research planning document: identifying keywords and concepts of potential use when formulating a search strategy for online searching. Once the keywords were identified and search strategies formulated, students collected and recorded information from self-selected sources, utilising methods of expanding and restricting search results- a successful process taught by specialist library and information professionals. A comprehensive collection of scholarly journal articles, trade publications, patents, standards, and innovative materials and technical databases were available through the University Library collection. The generalist nature of Industrial Design and diversity of chosen topics required consideration of multi-disciplinary content and discipline specific terminology. For example, beyond expected research themes of materials, usability and a market survey of existing products, the "Mirror" project was founded in business practices, information communications technology and user experience; "TranSit" was concerned with the intersection of ageing, public health, transport, and urban form. These projects required students to search across information resources outside their expertise, and learn to use unfamiliar discipline-specific technical terminology. In some cases, students initially struggled to locate information due to the complex or very specific nature of their chosen topic. Learning to weave available information together to provide solutions to problems is a key skill in learning to research. Students had the opportunity to ask for assistance in the face-to-face tutorial, providing some guidance to alternative sources, or evaluation and re-calibration of their search techniques.

Evaluate and reflect...

A process of evaluation and reflection involved students reviewing and determining the credibility of gathered information, identifying gaps, reflecting on the effectiveness of their search methodology and chosen research processes – RSDF facet [c] (Willison & O'Regan, 2012). The face-to-face tutorial provided the opportunity for students to ask questions and receive guidance, before launching into further information retrieval. Students learnt to discriminate between scholarly peer-reviewed sources, trade publications, and industry resources – and how to discerningly use information found through broader web searching.

Organise and manage...

As the students began searching for resources, they were shown how to effectively organise and manage information and data – RSDF facet [d] (Willison & O'Regan, 2012). It was recommended that students systematically record their search strategy, the online resources that were utilised and the achieved results, in an electronic or print logbook. Students were informed about bibliographic management tools, and how to create search alerts.

Analyse and synthesise…

Analysing and synthesising – RSDF facet [e] (Willison & O'Regan, 2012), was a critical component to the research process. Scrutinising information research results critically, asking questions, and synthesising existing and new knowledge (Willison & O'Regan, 2012) meant that students were constructing a sound understanding of their area of research, providing them with the necessary basis to embark on the creative processes involved in answering the Travel Light brief. As outlined in Khong (this volume), building skills in critical thinking, and interrogating information and concepts through engagement in the research process can *"lead to higher-quality and higher-order learning outcomes"* (Khong, this volume).

Communicate and apply…

Communication and application (Willison & O'Regan, 2012) of research findings is the final step of the research process – RSDF facet [f]; interestingly, these elements were visible at each step from concepts onwards. The research assessment task required that students write a concise document and accompany this with a single summary page for presentation and discussion in class. Following from this milestone, students undertook the main design and development task of the project, which challenged them to apply their findings in the generation of considered design responses. Students engaged with discipline-specific technical language, marketing techniques, technical drawing and building processes, presentation skills, and problem solving processes, working towards the exhibition to industry, peers and the wider University community. The opportunity to engage with industry gave the students a "real-life" experience, discussing and promoting their project results using a professional approach.

Survey results: autonomy, confidence, quality and employability

Students voluntarily opted into an anonymous survey, in which they self-assessed and scored their pre and post tutorial levels of confidence in undertaking various facets of research using a five point Likert scale. The self-perception survey questions were informed by the facets of research outlined in the RSDF and results scaled according to extent of student autonomy i.e. Level 1 being highly structured prescribed research, through to Level 5 requiring students to research openly within self-determined guidelines that are in accord with discipline or context (Willison & O'Regan, 2012). It was anticipated that this student cohort, in their third year of study, would be assessed as requiring a scaffolded approach, with prompts placed by the educators to allow the student to independently pursue their research – RSDF Level 3 (Willison & O'Regan, 2012). The results of the student self-perception survey revealed that introducing the RSDF and utilising a scaffolded approach to skill development produced high levels of confidence and engagement with the research cycle.

Engaging with facet [a] "embark and clarify" was observed to provide students with the prompts required to clarify their topic and generate research questions. Firstly, students were asked to indicate on a five point Likert scale whether they required structured directions, through to no guidance required, when embarking on a research topic and clarifying required tasks (Question 1, Figure 7). It is noteworthy that while the levels of autonomy are spread, only a few students regarded themselves as being at the lowest level of autonomy. Students were then asked to indicate their level of comfort in initiating a research question of their own, with 63% rating their comfort level in the two highest levels of student autonomy (Question 2, Figure 7).

SURVEY RESULTS

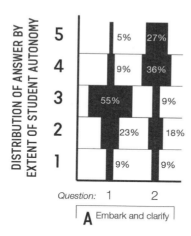

Figure 7: Student survey results: RSDF facet [a].

Using a five point Likert scale students were asked to indicate their levels of confidence in gathering required information for the Travel Light project pre- and post-workshop (Question 1Pre and Question 1Post, Figure 8). Survey results for RSDF facet [b] 'find and generate' show that student autonomy levels shifted from levels 2 and 3 pre-workshop (only 27% rated themselves at levels 4 and 5), to levels 4 and 5 (82%) after the workshop, indicating significant growth in research confidence. As third year students, it is observed that confidence in research skills will prepare them well for honours-level study; will likely transfer to other projects, and be transferable to the workplace. Creating a successful search strategy is paramount to information research, providing accurate results, saving time and recording/tracking results for future reference. As indicated in survey results, 68% of students indicated that they strongly agreed or agreed that they had gained skills in search strategy creation (Question 2, Figure 8). Scaffolded research explicitly highlighted the difference between a formal research approach and merely "Googling"; this enabled a cultural shift in the research process, as evidenced by a greater proportion of peer reviewed references than previous years, and a shift towards insights rather than just information. The complex nature of chosen topics, and the need to engage with higher level information research skills to locate multidisciplinary and sometimes "non-existent" resources, anecdotally accounts for the 18% who indicated that they require further assistance (Question 3, Figure 8). Student results were spread across the levels of autonomy for Question 3, which required students to establish their rate of success versus their need for assistance in locating required information for a topic (Question 3, Figure 8). This is an area flagged for future development and due to the complex nature of project topics across multiple disciplines, students may still require individual consultations with specialist Subject Librarians to give direction in locating obscure resources.

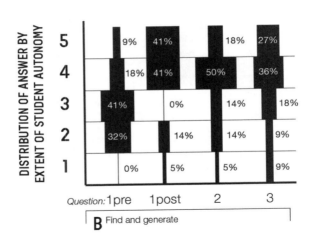

Figure 8: Student survey results: RSDF facet [b].

Students self-reported high levels of ability in critiquing and analysing the credibility of selected information (Question 1, Figure 9) for RSDF facet [c] 'evaluate and reflect'. This was evidenced by the students' new found ability to check credibility and be critical of selected sources, particularly Internet sources. Student autonomy levels were mapped at levels 4 and 5 post-workshop. A tendency to favour peer reviewed research was observed after the workshop, a finding that is in line with the increased effectiveness of student time spent researching – that they have become more discerning.

SURVEY RESULTS

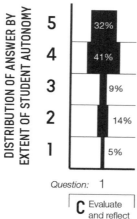

Figure 9: Student survey results: RSDF facet [c].

The structuring of thoughts and ideas, organisation of search strategies and collected resources provided a strong intervention into RSDF facet [d] 'organise and manage'. Students were asked to indicate whether they strongly agreed or disagreed, using a five point Likert scale, with the statement: I am able to organise and manage collected information and data (Question 1, Figure 10). Survey results here corroborate with the observation that once students realised that they were entering into a world of peer reviewed, and referenced research work, they embraced the idea of organising literature in preparation for a reference list, with some students beginning to utilise alerts and more advanced database features.

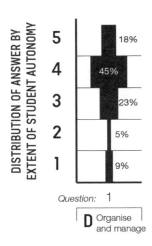

Figure 10: Student survey results: RSDF facet [d].

Analysis and synthesis as described in RSDF facet [e] had the lowest results for student autonomy across the survey with some 36% of responses being at or below level 3 autonomy. Students were asked to rate their confidence in analysing and synthesising collected information for the research project (Question 1, Figure 11). These results may indicate that the core cognitive research task is still the most difficult to learn, teach or feel confident in. Student work shows that the adoption of specific data into the project was successfully achieved, but that there was some room for growth in the synthesis of higher-order information. This identifies an area for focus of future work and student tuition.

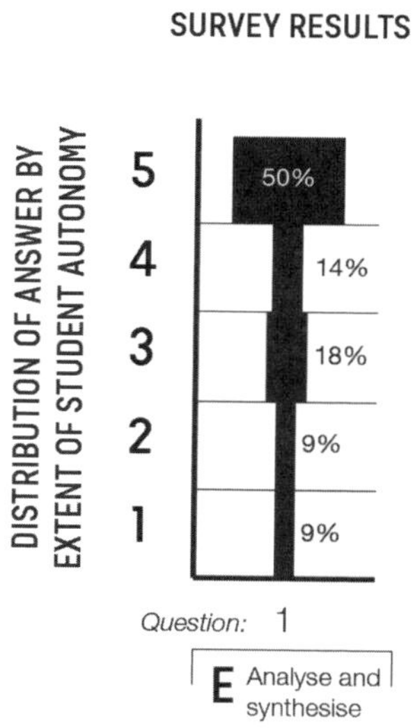

SURVEY RESULTS

Figure 11: Student survey results: RSDF facet [e].

Communication and application in RSDF facet [f] was achieved successfully through the workshop and a scaffolded approach employed. It is
observed that the nature of Industrial Design education and Project-
Based Learning may have a role to play in this strong self-perception
of autonomy. Communication of results is specifically taught in Design
education, with students required to illustrate, annotate, technically
document and speak publicly about their work. In a similar sense, the
nature of Project-Based Learning leads to a strong visible link between
doing a project and how it may be applied in the workplace. Students
were asked to indicate their level of confidence in communicating and
presenting their research findings, with 73% indicating high levels of
confidence (Question 1, Figure 12). Mapping survey results to RSDF
student autonomy levels 4 and 5 was consistent with use of discipline-
specific technical language and genres, and articulation of ethical, social
or cultural issues relevant to chosen topics.

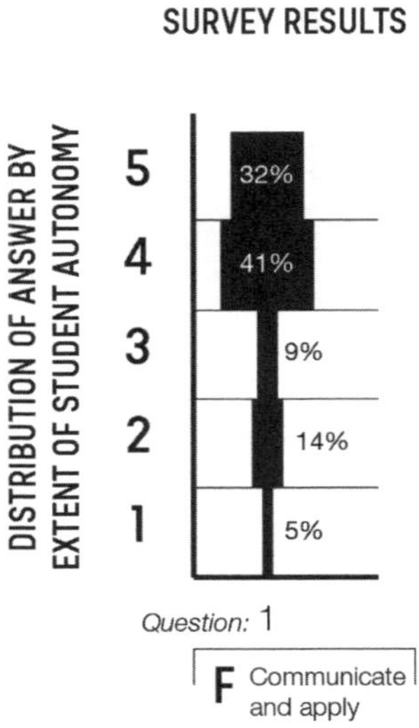

SURVEY RESULTS

Figure 12: Student survey results: RSDF facet [f].

A key finding from this research, was a clear three-pronged link between researching to learn (through the application of Project-Based Learning); and learning to research (through research skill development informed by the RSDF); and employability skills. Of those surveyed, 81% indicated high levels of confidence in applying newly learned research techniques to other assignments and research topics (Question 1, Figure 13). Eighty-two percent strongly agreed or agreed that their improved research skills were directly transferable to a workplace research project (Question 2, Figure 13). These were major research findings and established the link between Project-Based learning, research skills and employability skills. The combined use of a Project-Based Learning model and the introduction of the RSDF into the curriculum to scaffold research skill development, make a significant contribution to attainment of course and graduate attributes, particularly the provision of innovative solutions to problems; explicitly embedding research skill development into the project; building critical thinking skills and written and oral communication skills.

SURVEY RESULTS

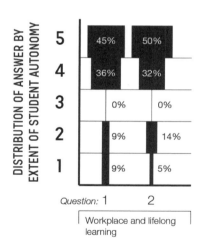

Figure 13: Student survey results: application of research skills to other assignments, research topics and the workplace.

Outcomes: depth and discovery

Educator observations, as well as student survey responses observed various improvements as a result of the implementation of research skill development into the Project-Based Learning curriculum (Figure 14). The first and most important breakthrough was the level of engagement exhibited by the students with scholarly literature, and resultant knowledge in their field of research. A scaffolded research approach enabled students to reach beyond the one or two scholarly articles they have typically referred to in previous cohorts' approaches to this project. Students listed in the order of 20 references per project and showed, through their own writing, how different pieces of knowledge had been acquired to build up relevant information. Of particular note was where students grasped conflicts of emerging knowledge and were able to make a balanced assessment. The positive outcome for this increased depth in research as evidenced in the design outcomes was that the designs were less hypothetical than in previous years.

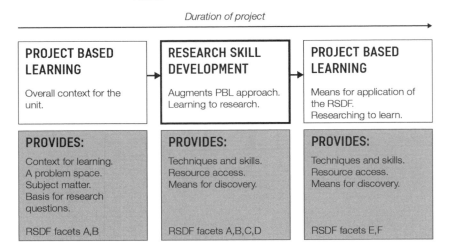

COMBINING PROJECT-BASED LEARNING AND RESEARCH SKILL DEVELOPMENT

Duration of project

PROJECT BASED LEARNING	RESEARCH SKILL DEVELOPMENT	PROJECT BASED LEARNING
Overall context for the unit.	Augments PBL approach. Learning to research.	Means for application of the RSDF. Researching to learn.

PROVIDES:	PROVIDES:	PROVIDES:
Context for learning. A problem space. Subject matter. Basis for research questions.	Techniques and skills. Resource access. Means for discovery.	Techniques and skills. Resource access. Means for discovery.
RSDF facets A,B	RSDF facets A,B,C,D	RSDF facets E,F

Figure 14: Outcomes: combining Project-Based Learning and RSDF.

Industrial Design practice and education are characterised by a preponderance of project constraints in technical, stylistic, material and functional forms. A reluctance to document project constraints early-on is often observed in Industrial Design education as these become part of the assessment process once the project is complete and therefore a liability to a student's grade. Part of the scaffolded approach to research applied in this study was asking the students to determine, from their reading, a single main objective for their project, and up to three secondary objectives they'd like to achieve. This gave the research undertaking a tangible aim, and a clear link with the act of designing. In identifying a main objective for their project, the students showed evidence of their ability to identify a knowledge gap (although this terminology was deliberately not used in order to avoid going beyond their threshold for new terms and processes). For example the "Mirror" project identified a knowledge gap in human interactions using videoconference tools, where it is difficult to simultaneously see a document and discuss it with people who are visible, in order to replicate a group task around a whiteboard. In this case the primary objective was to develop a product which could actually improve the effectiveness of communication by making a collaborative working environment work over long distances.

The determination of knowledge gaps – albeit by another name – is an important step in the education of a designer. The majority of students enter their Industrial Design education with a product-based mentality about the role of design. While this is correct in a market sense, it is also incomplete. A designer may well be asked to create a product in order for a company to enter a particular market, and while profitable in the short term this rarely leads to innovation. The identification of knowledge gaps, through research as project objectives, empowers students and designers to create anew where there was nothing previously, grounded in the surrounding knowledge of a particular "problem space".

Following on from the above points, and returning to the observation that students working in a scaffolded research setting found a greater volume of scholarly work, a follow on effect is one of depth. The "TranSit" example shows increased depth of enquiry compared to previous years, with the concept offering responses to issues beyond basic physicality. "TranSit", achieves innovation in the areas of urban way-finding, public health and multi-modal transport. This tangible example of depth provides one further benefit; students can create and observe first hand a response to the common belief that "everything has been designed before". A deep approach to research at the project outset shows that innovation, and new territory in which to design, can be found with the right methods and a diligent approach to information.

A corollary to the above depth, discovery and thoroughness in research is an observable increase in student ownership and care for their own work. While there are many other methods, to achieve a material increase in project quality, it was observed that including the RSDF motivated student ownership of their projects and, compared to the previous year's cohort, increased levels of detail in product execution as evidenced primarily in the sophistication of functional characteristics and physical geometry. The eBook submission encouraged and documented student awareness of research, both existing and their own. When compared to the previous cohort, the 2013 cohort was more adept at synthesising knowledge into their creative practice as demonstrated by their documentation of how specific information was applied into physical or system based design decisions. The processes of learning to research and researching to learn, witnessed a symbiotic relationship in research training – more depth in research as facilitated by the RSDF, which provided higher student satisfaction and self-motivation in the research process, and in turn fed better design outcomes and a thirst for more knowledge.

Conclusion

The above evidence illustrates the value of Library/Faculty partnerships in embedding research skill development into the curriculum for the purposes of learning to research, as well as researching to learn. Research results indicated strong links between student confidence and research ability. This cohort was extremely self-motivated, understanding the value and benefits of learning to research, providing feedback such as: "*I know where to find relevant and reliable resources online*" (Student B, 2013); "*I have a better understanding of the searching options*" (Student C, 2013); " *I have learned to be systematic and accurate with my research*" (Student D, 2013); "*I have learned to conduct the research task, leading to a more appropriate design outcome*" (Student E, 2013); " *I can now find higher level information*" (Student F, 2013); and "*I can find information in a faster and more coherent way*" (Student G, 2013).

This case study demonstrates the effectiveness of utilising a Project-Based Learning method, complemented with embedded research skill development, which enabled students to learn through research. Embarking on project-based research establishes the student as the learner, maintains motivation levels, and allows the student to contribute to knowledge in the field through the process of research. This model could be applied to other disciplines, particularly those linking to professions. The survey results indicated that the development of research skills – *learning to research* – was directly linked to employability skills, with students boasting high confidence levels in undertaking future research projects. The Project-Based Learning environment provides students with the opportunity to *research to learn*, and ultimately design a well-informed product, service or experience. Students *learned to research* through explicit research skill development in the curriculum, providing them with a transferrable skillset for additional assessment tasks, and future workplace projects. *Learning to research* within a Project-Based Learning environment coupled with a formalised and embedded research skill development programme accommodates the attainment of graduate employability skills and life-long learning.

Acknowledgements

This project is approved by the Monash University Human Research Ethics Committee, project reference number CF14/956 – 2014000400. The authors acknowledge the permission of students Maggie Phoeng and Michael Oechsle for the use of their work as examples in this chapter.

About the Authors

Linda Kalejs is Research and Learning Coordinator, and Team Leader for the Faculty of Art, Design and Architecture in the Library, Monash University, Australia. She can be contacted at this email: linda.kalejs@monash.edu

Robbie Napper is Senior Lecturer, PhD Program Director, Course Coordinator for Industrial Design, Faculty of Art, Design & Architecture, Monash University, Australia. He can be contacted at this email: robbie.napper@monash.edu

Bibliography

Baker, G. & D. Henson (2010). Promoting Employability Skills Development in a Research-Intensive University. *Education and Training*, Vol. 52, No. 1, pp. 62-75.

Bell, S. (2010). Project-Based Learning for the 21st Century: Skills for the Future. *The Clearing House: A Journal of Educational Strategies, Issues and Ideas*, Vol. 83, No. 2, pp. 39-43.

Blumenfeld, P.; E. Soloway; R. Marx; J. Krajcik; M. Guzdial & A. Palincsar (1991). Motivating Project-Based Learning: Sustaining the Doing, Supporting the Learning. *Educational Psychologist*, Vol. 26, No. 3-4, pp. 369-398.

Boyer, E. L. (1990). *Scholarship Revisited*. Princeton, NJ: Carnegie Foundation for the Advancement of Teaching.

Candy, L (2011). Research and Creative Practice. In L. Candy and E. Edmonds (Eds.) *Interacting: Art, Research and the Creative Practitioner*. Oxfordshire: Libri Publishing Ltd, pp. 33-59.

Careers Research & Advisory Centre (CRAC) Limited. (2014). Vitae Researcher Development Framework, Online Resource:
https://www.vitae.ac.uk/researchers-professional-development/about-the-vitae-researcher-development-framework [Accessed on 3 January 2015].

Cleland, D. I. & L. R. Ireland (2006). *Project management: Strategic design and implementation*. New York: McGraw-Hill.

Frank, M.; I. Lavy & D. Elata (2003). Implementing the Project-Based Learning Approach in an Academic Engineering Course. *International Journal of Technology and Design Education*, Vol.13, No. 3, pp. 273-288.

Green, L. & E. Bonollo (2002). The Development of a Suite of Design Methods Appropriate for Teaching Product Design. *Global Journal of Engineering Education*, Vol. 6, No. 1, pp. 45-51.

Holler Phillips, C. M (2011). Student Consultants' Perceptions and Valuations of Research Skills. *Reference Services Review*, Vol. 39, No. 3, pp. 514-530.

McKenzie, J.A (2000). *Beyond technology: Questioning, research and the information literate school*. Washington: FNO Press.

Monash University Art Design and Architecture (2013). *Unit Guide Semester 2*. Internal resource for students and faculty, Monash University.

Monash University Art Design and Architecture (2013). *Travel Light IDE3116 Project Brief*. Caulfield: Monash University

Monash University Employment and Career Development (2012). Employability Skills Research. Online Resource: http://www.monash.edu.au/careers/assets/docs/employability-skills/research.pdf [Accessed on 3 January 2015].

Monash University Employment and Career Development (2013). Employability Skills Research. Online Resource: http://www.monash.edu.au/careers/students-grads/employability-skills.html [Accessed on 3 January 2015].

Moursund, D. (1999). *Project-based learning using information technology.* Eugene, OR: International Society for Technology in Education.

Moylan, W. (2008). Learning by Project: Developing Essential 21st Century Skills using Student Team Projects. *International Journal of Learning*, Vol. 15, No. 9, pp. 287-292.

Nelson, H. G. & E. Stolterman (2003). *The design way: Intentional change in an unpredictable world: Foundations and fundamentals of design competence.* Englewood Cliffs, N.J.: Educational Technology Publications.

Rios, I.; A. Cazorla; J. Diaz-Puente & J. Yague (2010). Project-based learning in engineering higher education: Two decades of teaching competences in real environments. *Procedia Social and Behavioral Sciences*, Vol. 2, No. 2, pp. 1368-1378.

Thomas, J. (2000). *A Review of Research on Project-Based Learning.* San Rafael, California: The Autodesk Foundation.

Vygotsky, L. (1986). *Thought and Language.* Cambridge: MIT Press.

Webster, C.M. & J. Kenney (2011). Embedding Research Activities to Enhance Student Learning. *International Journal of Educational Management*, Vol. 25, No. 4, pp. 361-377.

Willison, J. & K. O'Regan (2012) *Research Skill Development for Curriculum Design and Assessment.* Online Resource: http://www.adelaide.edu.au/rsd/framework/ [Accessed on 3 January 2015].

Chapter Five

Learning to Research with Pre-Undergraduate Students: Curriculum as Support in the First-Year Experience

Phyllida Coombes

Introduction

This chapter contributes to the anthology by describing and analysing a pre-undergraduate enabling programme at a regional Australian university designed to prepare novice learners for undergraduate studies. My purpose is to provide readers with an insight into the nature of non-traditional students, the philosophy that underpins the programme and some of the skills students learn in achieving their goals, particularly those related to research. Traditional undergraduate students, who have completed their secondary schooling to matriculation level, have learned the skills of researching to a reasonable degree, but for non-traditional pre-undergraduate students, the process of academic research and writing is largely unfamiliar. This chapter explicates how a research-based programme, with a conceptual framework that promotes and values transitional and transformative learning, can support and encourage inexperienced learners. The theme of this chapter centres on the role played by the curriculum in enabling these learners to develop competency and confidence in the complex but rewarding field of research.

Students who enrol in a pre-undergraduate enabling course vary considerably in age, socio-economic status, gender and ethnicity, yet their reasons for choosing to involve themselves in the unfamiliar and possibly daunting milieu of academia appear remarkably similar. Their goals concern the desire to better themselves socially, economically and personally. The first step usually requires these individuals to change their perception of themselves as failed or damaged learners in their previous experience of formal learning in order to achieve a degree of confidence in their ability to succeed with undergraduate studies. An important element in this learning journey is for students to acquire the ability to become confident and competent researchers.

This chapter concerns students enrolled in a pre-entry programme (see Warner & Enomoto, this volume, for another example of a research-based pre-entry programme) at Central Queensland University, designed to equip them with the skills, abilities and confidence to progress to undergraduate study. Skills for Tertiary Education Preparatory Studies (STEPS) aims *"to provide a quality, tailored curriculum, within a supportive learning environment that fosters in adult learners the academic and personal skills for progression to undergraduate study."* (Central Queensland University, 2013:3). Regardless of their sometimes-negative previous encounters with formal education, students bring to this new stage in their lives a wealth of life experience and maturity despite not being entirely aware of the value of these advantages. The programme encourages them to begin with what they already know and understand, their own beliefs and attitudes, and to work outwards in widening circles of concern as they develop their proficiency as researchers.

Learning in the STEPS programme is a shared activity or community of practice (Lave & Wenger, 1991) between students, teachers, the academy and the wider world. The STEPS curriculum comprises one compulsory core unit, Preparatory Skills for the University, and a choice from eleven electives. In this chapter it is my intention to focus on the core unit that advocates the following learning outcomes (Central Queensland University, 2014:3):

1. development of effective study habits and learning strategies;
2. a capacity for critical self-reflection;
3. setting realistic goals towards individual study and career paths;
4. finding and evaluating relevant, scholarly research;

5. awareness of university procedures;
6. appropriate communication skills for tertiary study.

Through growing capability with Preparatory Skills, the aim is for students to learn to become self-directed, active and confident learners. Certain theories and concepts have been selected to provide focus and to assist students to develop practical skills and personal attitudes through critical self-reflection. The programme encompasses Mezirow's (2000) transformation theory as well as transition pedagogy promoted by a number of educationalists such as Kift *et al.* (2012). It also includes familiarity with Palmer's (2010) philosophy of learning as a healing process, and Campbell's (2008) and Butler's (1993) use of mythic structure as a conceptual framework. This chapter demonstrates how these notions have proved remarkably successful in encouraging the participants (over 8,000 since the inception of the programme in 1986) to become familiar with and competent in the process of research and to engage in lifelong learning. Reading this chapter you will:

1. gain insight into a curriculum designed to support and engage non-traditional students as they prepare to undertake an undergraduate degree course;
2. understand how personality and learning style indicators, mythic structure and transition pedagogy are important elements of a curriculum that aims to provide non-traditional students with the opportunity to know themselves and thence to extend their knowledge and understanding of their life-world;
3. familiarise yourself with transition pedagogy which enables students to accept and experience significant changes in their attitude towards and familiarity with learning skills to prepare them for undergraduate studies.

Conceptual Framework and Literature Review

During the 21st century issues of access and equity continue to replace elitism as the keystone of university education. A considerable body of research today considers the aspirations, experiences and outcomes of non-traditional tertiary students. Coates and Krause (2006) state that, in Australia, government policy continues to focus on widening participation in tertiary education for equity groups such as people of low economic status, a category shared by some of the students enrolled in the STEPS, programme. Marks (2009) is one among many who hold the view that the system of deferred payment through the Higher Education Contribution Scheme (HECS) has proved its worth in combating economic disadvantage. Evidence of developing access to tertiary education can be found in the statistics relating to increased numbers of mature-aged, international and equity students currently enrolled. It is the goal of enabling programmes, such as STEPS, to provide the necessary support for students to achieve academic success.

This chapter employs a conceptual framework that considers non-traditional students in ways that are positive and encouraging as evidence that they are able to develop the ability to learn about themselves and gain confidence, knowledge and understanding as they embark on their academic journey. Giroux (2005) through the theory of border crossing demonstrates how adult learners can achieve the ability to contest notions of marginalisation, a viewpoint they often assume when comparing themselves with seemingly privileged others. As they develop greater awareness of their potential strengths in the academic field, they may cross hypothetical borders from the margin to the centre, and sometimes they make the decision to return to the margin, which they come to perceive as possessing its own value and validity. For example, as students gain confidence in the area of research through consideration and practice, they frequently include valid experiences or opinions from their own background to support a particular viewpoint. Border crossing can be a worthwhile aspect of lifelong learning.

Continuity, change and regeneration comprise significant components of learning. STEPS students learn to respect the value of their particular life-world while accepting the need for change during their learning journeys and embracing subsequent regeneration. It is hardly surprising, therefore, that the theory of transformative learning, advanced by educational scholars such as Mezirow (2000) and Cranton (2006) provides a major component of the conceptual foundation of the STEPS programme. Genuine transformation can only eventuate from within as fledgling academic students, assisted, challenged and encouraged by fellow students and teachers, strive to complete a programme that will provide them with access to undergraduate study. The aim of the course comprises far more than the dissemination of skills and knowledge; through research and critical reflexivity (see Danaher, this volume; Hayes, this volume; Khong, this volume) students achieve awareness of themselves, their opinions, attitudes and dispositions. True transformation occurs when according to Lepani (1995), they accept the need to challenge and change their belief systems and behavioural patterns to meet new needs and opportunities and overcome disabilities and disadvantages.

The STEPS programme confronts students with a number of challenges, many of which have been addressed in current educational literature. Cullity (2006) advocates holistic curricula to confront challenges for novice learners in educational, social and economic areas in their quest for personal growth. In this regard the Core Skills Course aims to allow students to gain a broad overview of their role and identity as learners. The more specific electives also tend towards the dissemination and acquisition of skills related to future undergraduate study. Palmer (2010), whose ideas play an important role in the programme's philosophy, regards true education as providing ways of knowing that heal rather than damage. His phrase "*honest self-scrutiny*" (2010:2) meshes with Mezirow's (2000) notion of critical self-reflection. To this end unity and connectiveness (both social constructs) as opposed to competition would seem to best serve the tenets of transformative learning. Billet (2008) in his analysis of connections between lifelong learning and change, espouses the necessity for change in response to differing circumstances or significant events. Similarly, Danaher (2006:56) explores the idea of inalienable interconnectivity, "*the enduring connections between learner, community and environment*". As students become more familiar with these concepts in relation to their own situation, the possibility of emancipation from previous negative attitudes towards formal learning can be achieved.

Recent literature, while acknowledging the marked improvement in access to tertiary education, also reinforces the point that retention and success in completing a course of study form a necessary part of the process. Bragg and Durham (2012) for example contend that access and success are inextricably linked, and research in this field indicates the necessity for support programmes, particularly during a student's first year. Similarly Bailey and Morest (2006) claim that equity, for non-traditional students in particular, depends on access, readiness and success. While the first year for traditional university students comprises the introduction to the undergraduate course they have selected, it can be argued that for students in preparatory programmes such as STEPS the pre-undergraduate period provides their first experience of the opportunities and challenges of university life. STEPS is closely associated with degree courses at a preparatory level where students begin a journey leading to future undergraduate studies. Crossan *et al.* (2003) also indicate differences between traditional and non-traditional students when they argue that adult learners with limited or broken histories of previous education participation have difficulty in perceiving themselves as learners, and often regard institutions of learning with trepidation, antipathy or sometimes outright hostility. Their reason for subjecting themselves to the aim of completing pre-undergraduate and undergraduate studies may start out simply as a means to an end, but once they come to accept the concept of lifelong learning as a positive and fulfilling practice, their attitude towards learning usually becomes more positive.

Thus a pre-undergraduate programme plays an important role as part of the First Year Experience (FYE) at a tertiary institution. While the students have yet to commence undergraduate studies, they have the opportunity to become totally immersed in preparation for a degree course in the future as they learn about themselves, their strengths and weaknesses, goals and dispositions, as well as the requisite skills. The term transition pedagogy, according to Kift *et al.* (2012:1) explores the facilitation of a sense of *"engagement, support and belonging"* (see Danaher, this volume; Warner & Enomoto, this volume). They maintain that ensuring student retention is the business of everybody within the academy, including lecturers, tutors, administrative and support staff and fellow students. Similarly McInnis (2003) holds very strongly to the view that curriculum is the glue needed to hold knowledge and student experience together. Students who believe themselves to be supported and respected will tend to retain their commitment to the academy

According to transition pedagogy, curriculum is far more than a course of study, but as stated by Kift and Field (2009:2) comprises the totality of student experience and engagement as *"a guiding philosophy for intentional first year curriculum design"* (see Hayes, this volume; Khong, this volume; Warner & Enomoto, this volume). The curriculum needs to encompass not only what, where and when a student might be expected to learn, but also how and why certain goals are perceived as necessary and achievable. Other writers such as Tinto (2006, 2007) and Fasso (2013) also advocate transition pedagogy as a suitable philosophy and strategy to avoid attrition among first-year cohorts within higher education. While many students have indicated feelings of alienation when first experiencing the academic environment, with suitable guidance they soon come to expect and require the opportunity and support to learn, and most importantly to belong. A pre-entry programme such as STEPS needs to enable social and academic transition towards self-directed learning.

Notions of transition and transformation sometimes seem to imply a significant change on the part of the student from their essential self. This is not the case, and such an aim would be impossible to achieve. The Core Skills curriculum of the STEPS programme encourages the students through research to experience a wider understanding of the world beyond their own familiar environment. Students can undergo changes in opinion, attitude and disposition through critical reflection on the issues they encounter. As Kift *et al.* (2012) have stated, it is desirable for novice learners to gain the opportunity to access equitably the transformative effects of higher education towards a sense of belonging.

Many programmes have utilised curricula following the principles of transition pedagogy or transformative learning for a number of years. The question that needs to be asked is how the conceptual framework of the STEPS programme can best serve the needs of a seemingly disparate group of individuals, many of whom enrol with limited formal education and negative opinions about their own abilities as learners. The answer to a wide extent lies in the major theme of this book – learning to research and researching to learn. In the next section I provide some evidence-based suggestions for meeting the challenges facing pre-undergraduate learners and providing the support needed for them to achieve their goals.

Curriculum-Based Support for Students

As previously stated, according to Kift and Field (2009) a curriculum in its truest sense provides valuable support to students by demonstrating that their own particular life experience constitutes a valuable asset in their engagement with the programme. Pre-undergraduate students in the STEPS programme gradually learn to know themselves and to gain confidence in their ability to learn through research to form and perform connections between their inner and external worlds. Through the process of reading and absorbing information, discussion and debate, thinking and writing, students and teachers can reach an understanding of the challenges, frustration, exhilaration and transformed under-standing which all play their part in the process of research.

Thus learning can best be understood as making meaning of the world through interaction with natural and built environments and with people and their words through stories, instruction, opinions, ideas and theories. Learning is concerned with sharing experiences and feelings with others. For inexperienced students, the idea that they have something of value to share in the unfamiliar sphere of the University seems at first impos-sible if not ludicrous. For this reason they need to accept the possibility of changing their perceptions of self and to grow in confidence to be able to accept the challenges confronting them.

A useful starting point towards self-discovery for inexperienced students preparing for undergraduate studies concerns learning styles. The aim is to encourage individuals to explore the ways of learning that best suit their own personality, abilities and circumstances. The Keirsey Temperament Sorter (1998), the Myers-Briggs Type Indicator (1962) and the Soloman-Felder Index of Learning Styles (1991) have all proved effective as students respond to questions based on opinions rather than facts, thus achieving a deeper awareness of themselves and their preferred learning styles. The purpose is for them to recognise the possibility, indeed the likelihood, of significant change in their perceptions of self during their learning journey.

As border-crossers (Giroux, 2005) STEPS students learn to negotiate an unfamiliar world and become familiar with their preferred ways of learning and research. It is however difficult, if not impossible, for true learning to occur in isolation. The Preparatory Skills course curriculum is also designed to familiarise students with the notion that they are part of a web of connectedness that includes their community, country, world and universe, including all the living beings that inhabit that life world. Because such ideas can be difficult to grasp, particularly for non-tradi-tional students, the concept of mythic structure has proved invaluable in conveying the message in simpler and more familiar terms. Pre-undergrad-uate, graduate and post-graduate studies can be considered as a learning journey, and to this end the hero's journey myth provides a convincing allegory. Several examples of the hero's journey have grown familiar over time through the sagas and legends of diverse culture, including Homer's *Iliad* and *Odyssey*, the Anglo-Saxon *Beowulf* and John Bunyon's *Pilgrim's Progress*. In the STEPS programme Campbell's (2008) study of world hero myths, *The Hero with a Thousand Faces* has provided a favourite research source. Christopher Vogler (1996) adapted Campbell's *Hero's Journey* into twelve stages that fit comfortably into the particular learning journey of the STEPS programme. Students represent the hero in undertaking a quest after some hesitation and with the help of the mentor – in this case the teacher – learning to face the challenges of the journey to arrive safely and triumphantly at the end. Simpson and Coombes (2001) maintain that these analogous stages provide an apt research-based platform for the students to reflect on their learning journey.

Mythic structure through story telling provides the basis for the more complex skills of academic research and writing. From the outset the curriculum encourages the students to write constantly on a daily basis. These journals are private and personal, and there is no compulsion for the authors to share their written thoughts and feelings, positive and negative reactions, unless they wish to do so. As they learn about themselves and their situation in the academy, and as they gain confidence in their writing abilities, it is not unusual for them to become more eager to convey their feelings to fellow students and teachers. They are, in fact, becoming involved in the research process as both researchers and respondents, as they gain deeper knowledge and understanding about themselves and about their life-world through ever-widening circles of concern.

Singer (2012) explores the relationship between self-preservation and ethics. Thus learners can recognise both the need to care for and advance their self-interest as well as the existence of altruism, the desire to understand, relate to and protect others, starting with one's own family and community, and progressing towards other communities. For example, concern about the environment or about helpless people suffering as a result of civil war can be used as a basis for research to discover, write about, analyse and seek remedies for a particular situation. Empathy and altruism are key elements in the practice of connectivity.

Palmer's (2010) central theme in *To Know as we are Known* advocates ways of knowing and learning that heal rather than harm. This notion gains clearer perspective in the case of certain non-traditional students whose experiences of formal learning, perhaps many years previously, might have been unbearable and perhaps damaging to some degree. Once STEPS students are able to value themselves and to gain the capacity to embrace opportunities to work towards specific goals, they can look outwards towards the hidden wholeness of their life-world, to paraphrase the words of Trappist monk, Thomas Merton (cited in Palmer, 2010). The word education means drawing out, difficult to achieve in isolation. Students begin to recognise the pain of disconnection, particularly when they experience the inevitable setbacks, disappointments and difficulties that are part of the learning journey. The STEPS curriculum, therefore, is firmly linked to the importance and necessity of connectivity. Teacher support, while essential, is only part of the web of connection which also includes fellow students, family, friends and the wider network of the university, at the heart of co-operative learning. The more students learn, the more they come to depend on the widening circle of their world-view through their own experience, enhanced by the written and spoken word. As Parker (2010) contends, connections do not imply sameness but a rich tapestry of diversity, ambiguity and paradox.

In summary the Core Skills component of the STEPS programme uses a solid conceptual framework to support a philosophy of learning for inexperienced learners. Giroux's (2005) concept of border crossing assists students to combat feelings of marginalisation while Mezirow's (2000) transformative learning theory leads to the notion of critical self-reflection. Through transition pedagogy the curriculum is designed to provide students with the best possible support as they prepare to engage in undergraduate studies.

Learning to Research

Inexperienced mature-aged students need to acquire understanding of themselves and their role in the academy. It is equally important for them to learn the skills that will enable them to complete an undergraduate degree course, including the capability to research. The STEPS curriculum encourages students to be curious about themselves, their own culture and society, and the world beyond their immediate experience.

Considerable time and effort are often expended in academia in discussion about the relative merits of quantitative and/or qualitative research methods. Palmer (2010) among others argues that adherence to either objectivity or subjectivity is a myth; both should play a part in academic writing. The researcher discovers certain data relating to a specific topic and, through speculating on given facts and related theories, he/she can begin to form ideas, preferences and arguments that are partly subjective in nature. Students may have some difficulty in coming to terms with the notion of theory and theoretical literature, but once they learn to relate this to its original meaning (from the Greek word *theoros* meaning spectator) they can find clearer meaning for themselves. A theory cannot be purely objective since it involves a particular viewpoint on the part of the theorist. Intellectual rigour demands honest dissent where appropriate through careful examination and analysis of the data and the willingness to change perception in reaching conclusions. Thus through research, theories can remain relevant to changing ideas and circumstances.

Ethics too play an important role in the research process. As students begin to know more about their community and beyond, they learn to recognise the claims of others and to develop awareness and empathy through connectedness. Ethical responsibility in the research process requires self-reflexive consideration. Throughout their university studies, at all levels, students are confronted with a vast array of data: the facts, opinions, ideas and theories of academic writers or lecturers through structured or semi-structured interviews, discussion, tutorials, lectures or the vast resources of online or printed material. The ethical presentation of data is necessary to avoid risk to participants, usually anonymised, in responding to interviews and discussion with researchers. Another important consideration is the accurate acknowledgement of the spoken or written ideas of speakers and writers according to a specific system of referencing. The STEPS curriculum is designed so that students newly involved in academic writing are enabled to grow familiar with how, when and why to reference the ideas of others. Complete integrity is the keystone of rigorous research practice.

Researching to learn: Transition Pedagogy to Transformative Learning

An enabling programme such as STEPS provides the ideal opportunity for teachers and learners to observe transformative learning in action. Here, although a diverse group of individuals have come together from a wide range of backgrounds, limited past educational experience and a desire to acquire the skills to complete an undergraduate course are two important uniting characteristics of these students. Clearly, if they are to achieve their goals, significant educational transformation is desirable during their sojourn at the academy. For this reason, in this chapter I contend that a curriculum that best comprises the totality of student experience and engagement (Kift & Field, 2009) will rely on the conceptual frameworks of transition pedagogy and transformative learning.

Non-traditional students commonly have difficulty in coming to terms with the meaning and use of theory as a necessary scaffold in academic research and writing. The curriculum of the STEPS programme allows them to familiarise themselves with such concepts gradually and, as far as possible, in a non-threatening manner through the agency of transition pedagogy (Kift & Field, 2009) as a guiding philosophy. From the outset, they can come to accept the notion of change while they gradually accept and gain confidence in the essential nature of themselves and their potential capabilities. The best learning is accompanied by a sense of belonging as an integral part of the university.

While students will grow familiar with a wide range of theories and theorists during their undergraduate studies, I choose to focus here on transformative learning (Mezirow, 2000) as particularly relevant with regard to the conceptual framework of the STEPS programme. Rather than confronting students with a detailed and possibly confusing analysis of this theory at the outset of the course, through the more immediate processes of familiarity with learning styles, mythic structure and journaling, the students become personally involved in transformative learning. Thus when teachers need to explain how this concept can be employed as a theoretical basis for academic writing, students tend to recognise it as a familiar notion rather than a complex and daunting theoretical concept. Dirkx's (1997:79) description of transformative learning as *"a heroic struggle to wrest consciousness and knowledge from the forces of unconsciousness and ignorance, ...[to] guide the human spirit through the labyrinth of self, society, language and culture"* is particularly apposite.

Mezirow (2000) is recognised as one of the first educational scholars to conceive the theory of transformative learning. Subsequently writers such as Cranton (2006) have further developed this theory in the light of current thinking. She interprets transformative learning as the method by which learners confront, validate and redevelop their experiences and what they mean in terms of value to themselves and others. Valid learning needs to be a transformative process as students gain deeper awareness of themselves – their own personalities, abilities and values – moving towards knowledge and understanding of the culture and society of themselves and others. The process of transformative learning, according to Mezirow (2000) in Danaher *et al.* (2013), is progressive rather than linear. Each individual possesses a particular frame of reference comprising innate values and belief systems that guide, shape and dictate everyday attitude, dispositions and behaviour. Thus inevitably we adhere to particular assumptions on a range of matters. According to the tenets of transformative learning we need to be aware of these assumptions and should be prepared to test their validity and possibly revise them on the basis of acquiring more information and understanding through critical self-reflection. Thus Mezirow's definition of transformative learning is learning through critical self-reflection leading to the reformulation of our worldview to enhance understanding of our own experience. The assumptions that underlie our beliefs and values should become more inclusive and discriminating the more we learn. Critical self-reflection, questioning the validity of an assumption, can result in a new and transformed way of interpreting the world.

While the notion of transformative learning is reasonably straightforward, the process of critical self-reflection is a different matter. Thus the STEPS curriculum provides ample opportunities for students to engage with critical self-reflection from the beginning of the course, even though they might not recognise at first that this is what they are doing. For example, one assumption that many students need to confront is their view of themselves as unable or even unworthy to cope with the rigours of academic learning. The third stage of Campbell's (2008) *Hero's Journey*, Refusal of the Call, relates to this negative assumption. Once students, through critical self-reflection, learn to reject this negativity, they can regain their commitment to the programme. The optimal and most immediate ways of knowing evolve, not so much from being told things by teachers or reading about them in books, though this process has some value, rather – according to Dirkx (1997) through a personal and imaginative sense of one's own unique experience it is possible to know in the truest sense. Similarly Labouvie-Viet (1994) values the dimension of knowing through symbolism, myth and narrative. The use of mythic structure in the STEPS programme is supported by relevant literature and has proved effective in practice.

The recurring theme of this chapter is that the STEPS curriculum seeks to reinforce the notion of human experience and engagement as a two-way learning and research process between student and teacher. Critical self-reflection can best be understood not as a series of steps necessary to achieve some particular outcome, but as a dialogue between participants. Reflection can take place in solitude, with another or in a group through thinking, speaking or writing. A useful exercise might be for a student to select a particular deeply-held assumption, to read what has been written on this topic, to share this assumption with another student and to discuss it with a small group of class-mates. Finally the student needs to reflect, honestly and critically on the once entrenched belief and assess it in the light of new information, ideas and values gleaned from other sources. The likelihood is that assumptions will undergo change to some degree. This is the nature of transformative learning.

Cranton (1995) analyses Mezirow's theory of transformative learning through three distinct ways in which individuals make meaning of their world. Firstly the psychological perspectives determine their personal view, for example preferences, self-esteem and inhibitions. Secondly socio-linguistic meaning perspectives include social and cultural matters including language. Thirdly epistemic perspectives are based on knowledge and how they make use of it. Some STEPS students, for example, have a psychological perspective of themselves – at the beginning of the course – as failed learners. They have experienced the social and cultural norms of their own worldview and soon begin to understand those of the academy. As they acquire greater knowledge they gradually learn to overcome the negative aspects of their self-perception and develop confidence and self-esteem. The process requires critical self-reflection and is inherent to transformative learning.

Conclusion

The curriculum for the Skills for Tertiary Education Preparatory Studies (STEPS) programme has been carefully designed to support and engage non-traditional students as they prepare to undertake an undergraduate degree course. Of particular importance is the necessity to learn the skills and deeper meaning of effective research on the part of both students and teachers.

This chapter has sought to develop understanding of the particular nature of non-traditional students whose experience of formal learning has, in many cases, been interrupted at a relatively early age. Through procedures such as personality and learning style indicators, mythic structure and transition pedagogy, the curriculum aims to provide them with the opportunity to know themselves and thence to extend their knowledge and understanding of their life-world, growing familiar with factual knowledge and theoretical understanding as their academic perceptions widen and as they gain competency in learning to research and researching to learn.

The value of transition pedagogy (Kift *et al.*, 2012) to the STEPS curriculum is apparent when students acknowledge the willingness to accept and experience significant changes in their attitude towards and familiarity with learning skills to prepare them for undergraduate study. The curriculum itself has undergone significant change to accommodate the requirement for on-line external studies thus giving more students the opportunity to complete the programme.

The curriculum described and analysed in this chapter has proved its worth in supporting non-traditional students with limited prior formal educational experience through a programme preparing them for under-graduate study. Learning to research and researching to learn in a first year pre-undergraduate programme can provide a rich and fulfilling transformative learning experience.

> *We only preserve what we love;*
> *We only love what we understand;*
> *We only understand what we study.*
>
>   Tibetan Saying.

About the Author

Phyllida Coombes is an Independent Scholar from Bundaberg Queensland, Australia. She can be contacted at this email: cpcoombes@spin. net.au

Bibliography

Bailey, T. & V. S. Morest (Eds.) (2006). *Defending the Community College Equity Agenda*. Baltimore: The John Hopkins University Press.

Billet, S. (2008). Learning throughout Working Life: A Relational Interdependence between Social and Individual Agency. *British Journal of Education Studies*, Vol. 55, No. 1, pp. 39-58.

Bragg, D. & B. Durham (2012). Perspectives on Access and Equity in the Era of (Community) College Completion. *Community College Review*, Vol. 40, No. 2, pp. 106-125.

Butler, J. (1993). From Action to Thought: The Fulfilment of Human Potential. In J. Edwards (Ed.) *Thinking: International Interdisciplinary Perspectives*, Melbourne: Hawker Brownlow Education, pp. 16-22.

Campbell, J. (2008). *The Hero with a Thousand Faces*. London: Fontana Press.

Central Queensland University (2013). CZ01 *Skills for Tertiary Education Preparatory Studies: Guide for Students*. Rockhampton, CQU Press.

Central Queensland University (2014). SKIL 40025 *Preparatory Skills for University: Course Profile*. Rockhampton, CQU Press.

Coates, H. & K. L. Krause (2005). Investigating Ten Years of Equity Policy in Australian Higher Education. *Journal of Higher Education Policy and Management*, Vol. 27. No.1, pp. 35-47.

Cranton, P. (2006). *Understanding and Promoting Transformative Learning: A Guide for Educators of Adults*. San Francisco: Jossey-Bass.

Crossan, B.; J. Field; J. Gallacher & B. Merrill (2003). Understanding Participation in Learning for Non-traditional Adult Learners: Learning Careers and the Construction of Adult Learners. *British Journal of Sociology of Education*, Vol. 24, No. 1, pp. 55-67.

Cullity, M. (2006). Challenges in Understanding and Assisting Mature-age Students who Participate in Alternative Entry Programmes. *Australian Journal of Adult Education*, Vol. 46, No. 2, pp. 175-201.

Danaher, G. (2006). Inalienable Interconnective Lifelong Learning: Pathways, Partnerships and Pedagogies. In D. Orr; F. Nouwens; C. Macpherson; R.

E. Harreveld & P. Danaher (Eds.) *Fourth International Lifelong Learning Conference*. Rockhampton, Qld: CQU Press, pp. 56-60.

Danaher, M.; J. Cook; G. Danaher; P. Coombes & P. A. Danaher (2013). *Researching Education with Marginalized Communities*. Basingstoke, UK: Palgrave Macmillan.

Dirkx, J. M. (1997). Nurturing Soul in Adult Education. *New Directions for Adult and Continuing Education*, Vol. 74, pp. 79-88.

Doyle, S. (2006). *STEPS Celebrating 20 Years 1986-2006*. Rockhampton, Qld: Central Queensland University Press.

Fasso, W. (2013). First Year Distance Transition Pedagogy: Synchronous Online Classrooms. *The International Journal of the First Year in Higher Education*, Vol. 4, No. 1, pp. 33-45.

Giroux, H. A. (2005). *Border Crossings: Cultural Workers and the Politics of Education*. New York: Routledge.

Kift, S. M. & R. M. Field (2009). Intentional First-year Curriculum Design as a Means of Facilitating Student Engagement: Some Examples. In *Proceedings of the 12th Pacific Rim First Year in Higher Education Conference*. Queensland University of Technology, Townsville.

Kift, S. M.; K. J. Nelson & J. A. Clarke (2012). Transition Pedagogy: A Third Generation Approach to FYE: A Case Study of Policy and Practice for the Higher Education Sector. *The International Journal of the First Year in Higher Education*, Vol. 1, No. 1, pp. 1-20.

Labouvie-Vief, G. *Psyche and Eros*. Cambridge: Cambridge University Press.

Lave, J. & E. Wenger (1991). *Situated Learning: Legitimate Peripheral Participation*. Cambridge: Cambridge University Press.

Lepani, B. (1995). *Education in the Information Society*. Sydney: Australian Centre for Innovation and International Competitiveness, Sydney University.

Marks, G. N. (2009). The Social Effects of the Australian Higher Education Contribution Scheme. *Higher Education*, Vol. 57, No. 1, pp. 71-84.

McInnis, C. (2003). New Realities of the Student Experience: How should Universities Respond? Paper presented at *The 25th Annual Conference of the European Association for Institutional Research*. Limerick, Ireland.

Mezirow, J. (2000). Learning to Think Like an Adult: Core Concepts of Transformation Theory. In J. Mezirow & Associates (Eds.) *Learning as Transformation: Critical perspectives on a theory in progress*. San Francisco: Jossey-Bass, pp. 3-34.

Palmer, P. J. (2010). *To Know as we are Known: Education as a Spiritual Journey*. San Francisco: Harper Collins.

Simpson, J. & P. Coombes (2001). Adult Learning as a Hero's

Journey: Researching Mythic Structure as a Model for Transformational Change. *Queensland Journal of Educational Research*, Vol. 17, No. 2 pp. 164-177.

Singer, P. (2012). *The Expanding Circle: Ethics, Evolution and Moral Progress.* New York: Princeton University Press.

Tinto, V. (2006-2007). Research and Practice of Student Retention: What next? *Journal of College Student Retention*, Vol. 8, No. 1, pp. 1-19.

Vogler, C. (1996). *The Writer's Journey: Mythic Structure for Storytellers and Screenwriters.* London: Boxtree.

Chapter Six

Learning to Research in the Professions: Possibilities of Discovery Learning

Michelle Picard and Cally Guerin

Introductory background

This chapter contributes to the anthology by exploring how discovery-based research was introduced into the undergraduate curriculum across a whole university and how this was interpreted by professions-focused disciplines. This pedagogy, Small Group Discovery Experience (SGDE), draws on the basic concepts of an ideal research-focused university where individuals, free from state intervention, learn about and research the big questions of society under the leadership of senior scholars (Humboldt, 1850). Although drawing primarily on the work of Wilhelm Humboldt in nineteenth-century Europe, this initiative also has some synchronies with Boyer's (1990:17) *"scholarship of discovery"* since the focus of the students and researchers is on the discovery of new knowledge. SGDE in essence enacts the principles of "researching to learn"; however, interviews and focus groups with the academics involved in the implementation of SDGE revealed that they believed "learning to research" was a more appropriate focus for teaching an undergraduate cohort, particularly first-year students, in the Faculty of the Professions. Our respondents revealed that their experience in professions-based disciplines (e.g., Accounting, Law, and Education) indicated it is vital to teach students disciplinary knowledge construction in conjunction with discipline-specific research skills. Only then is it possible for students to actually engage in independent discovery.

By reading this chapter you will:

1. explore how Humboldt's and Boyer's philosophies of research play out within the contemporary university;

2. learn about models for research skills development within the constraints of an undergraduate, professions-based curriculum; and

3. understand that the way knowledge is constructed in professions-based disciplines necessitates more application than discovery-based research skill development.

Humboldt and the marketised university

Despite facing challenges from its very inception, the Humboldt model of the university, where academics and students work together as scholars focusing on *"not yet completely solved problems"* (Elton, 2008:226) and knowledge creation (*wissenschaft*) (Humboldt, 1850) has remained an important part of the global higher education discourse (Ash, 2006; Hohendahl, 2011). This is reflected in the increasing number of international and local associations and conferences promoting undergraduate student research, such as the Council on Undergraduate Research and its National Conferences on Undergraduate Research in the USA; the UK Office of Undergraduate Excellence and the British Conference on Undergraduate Research; and the Australasian Conference of Undergraduate Research.

In contrast with this focus on learning for its own sake and emphasis on knowledge creation, some have argued that the main task of universities is to prepare students for the job market (see, for example, Giret, 2011; Lehmann, 2009) and that this involves helping students to acquire knowledge along with *"developing their skills for using this knowledge in concrete situations"* (Nygaard *et al.*, 2008:33). Professions-based disciplines in particular seem inclined to take this second more utilitarian approach (Zamorski, 2002). Professions-based academic respondents in Zamorski's (2002) study believed that students must first gain a broad knowledge of disciplinary content and theory before undertaking the kind of independent research that requires in-depth exploration of disciplinary knowledge; without this foundation, the research activities might well be unsatisfactory.

In this chapter we explore the interplay between learning and teaching for professional purposes and more traditional views of research-based learning and teaching approaches within a professions-focused faculty at a research-intensive university in Australia. We show that, even within this tradition, academics experience tensions between preparing the students for their professional vocation and leading them towards knowledge creation. The study took place during the first year of an initiative in the Humboldtian tradition that aimed to *"return [the emphasis] to undergraduate research so that every student in every program has an opportunity to experience the thrill of discovery"* (The University of Adelaide, 2012:8). The specific form of the pedagogy was described as consisting of *"an individual research project in their final year, with preparatory skills and experience built through smaller exercises in the earlier years of their course"* (The University of Adelaide, 2013:5). This initiative was dubbed "Small Group Discovery Experience" (SGDE) in the University of Adelaide Strategic Plan: *The Beacon of Enlightenment* (The University of Adelaide, 2012:8). Here we present the experiences of academics within seven professions-based disciplines during the first year of implementation of this university-wide pedagogical change. As the initiative was implemented by a small group of academics in a limited number of Schools in the Faculty of Professions, in order to retain anonymity, any comments reflecting personal views of the SGDE intervention are not attributed to academics from a specific discipline.

What is Small Group Discovery and what are the experiences?

The Small Group Discovery Experience was introduced as a pedagogical policy responding to the twin issues of the massification of higher education in Australia and resulting large classes and impersonal experiences of university life, and the increasing demand for flexible and online delivery of classes. In large part, this pedagogical intervention was aimed at distinguishing the University from others where students might feel alienated from their lecturers and disengaged from their learning experiences because of current university pedagogies. SGDE was described in the official policy documents in the following terms:

> *"The Small Group Discovery Experience (SGDE) will engage students in the intellectual challenge of the scholarship of discovery, giving them the opportunity to develop skills of research and to engage actively with the content of the discipline.*
>
> *By adopting and generalising the SGDE, the University aims to uphold the value of the scholarship of discovery, as defined by Boyer i.e. 'the commitment to knowledge for its own sake', and 'the following, in a disciplined fashion, [of] an investigation wherever it may lead'. The University affirms the SGDE as an intrinsic defining feature of its pedagogy, in every year of all of its programs."* (The University of Adelaide, 2013:1).

As an experiment in developing a university-wide pedagogy, the concept of SGDE was at once appealing to academics working in a research-intensive university since it emphasised what is viewed as core business in this context, but also somewhat mystifying. How could such ambitious changes be implemented, and what would an SGDE actually look like?

General (and admittedly abstract) principles and guidelines were circulated to university staff in a one-page document. The "principles" of SGDE were described as follows:

"Principles of the Small Group Discovery Experience:

* *students are actively engaged with the content and an experienced academic;*
* *the Small Group Discovery Experience will enrich the on-campus experience;*
* *the scholarship of discovery is central to the learning activities of the University;*
* *the first year SGDE sets the foundation for a continuum of the scholarship of discovery;*
* *it will be a core component in a credit-bearing course of every undergraduate program."* (University of Adelaide, 2013:1).

These principles raised a number of questions. What was the meaning of "discovery experience"? What was the innovation or change in this pedagogical intervention from existing local and international models? There was uncertainty about whether it was merely a continuation of a commonly understood relationship of learning to research involving *"teaching informed by [the lecturer] or others' recent research"* in the discipline area, followed by an undergraduate capstone course (that is, a programme in which the student synthesises and applies content learnt in earlier levels to complex authentic problems, as discussed by Hauhart & Grahe, 2015). Or perhaps students were expected to develop complex research skills. Maybe actual research *"with or by the students"* was required (Zamorski, 2002:415).

In the initial focus group of key academics in the Faculty of the Professions in July 2013, the respondents were also confused about how SGDE and its accompanying notion of the "scholarship of discovery" was different from other initiatives they had previously participated in. As one academic noted, *"But [our accrediting body] has been focussing on experiential learning for years, what makes this different?"*

Indeed, as early as 1989, the term *"applied experiential learning"* had been used to refer to learning from a real-world situation that was combined with the application of concepts, ideas and theories to interactive settings (AACSB, 1989:3). This resulted in Business Schools being called upon to devise a curriculum that was *"interactive (other than between teacher and pupil) and is characterized by variability and uncertainty"* (AACSB, 1989:3). Participants felt that students would already *"discover"* and *"engage actively with the content of the discipline"* in such learning environments (The University of Adelaide, 2013:1).

Other academics who had been involved with university-wide learning and teaching initiatives wanted to know how this intervention differed from the problem-based learning as commonly used in Medical and Engineering disciplines. Woods (1994) describes problem-based learning as helping students to learn and develop skills and disciplinary confidence through formulating and addressing problems they have never seen before in consultation with academic experts. Surely this would enable students to *"discover"* and *"engage actively with the content of the discipline"* (University of Adelaide, 2013:1)? Many considered that this met the criteria of students engaging actively with *"an experienced academic"* (The University of Adelaide, 2013:1).

The content of a workshop run by the senior learning and teaching academic at the University charged with driving the implementation of SGDE soon disabused our respondents of these notions. Academics were admonished to view SGDE as exclusively related to Boyer's concept of the *"scholarship of discovery"*, thus focusing on students conducting research and discovering "new" knowledge (Boyer, 1990:17). In a follow-up workshop in September, the respondents expressed their trepidations regarding this clarification of SGDE. Several noted that even their own research activities involved more of Boyer's *"scholarship of integration"*, since they tended to either *"synthesize, provide conceptual frameworks and elaborate a sociological understanding of the world"* or write *"integrative literature reviews and meta analyses of empirical findings"* (Atkinson, 2001:1220). One respondent went as far as to claim that *all* research in their field involved Boyer's *"scholarship of application"* rather than the *"scholarship of discovery"* (Boyer, 1990:17); researchers in that particular field took part in *"a dynamic process through which theory and practice interact"* (Atkinson, 2001:1220). However, along with Atkinson (2001), this respondent felt that "the scholarship of application" also included discovery, since *"in the process of applying theory to a social problem we not only help ameliorate the problem but refine the theory with empirical insights"* (Atkinson, 2001:1220).

At the same time as the academics were debating and trying to come to grips with very concept of SGDE, they were desperately rushing to prepare for its introduction in Semester 1 of 2014 (starting early March in Australia). The plan was to ensure that all first-year students commencing their studies at the University would participate in an SGDE in 2014. Introduction of second-year and third-year SGDEs were planned for 2015 and 2016, respectively. While many lecturers were excited by the prospect of putting a clear focus on developing research skills through a Humboldtian process of discovery, the timeframe was tight and limited resources made available to design and develop activities to meet the requirements.

Models of SGDE

The Context: Faculty of the Professions

Implementing the SGDE initiative was particularly challenging in the Faculty of the Professions, which at the time of the research consisted of the following undergraduate teaching Schools: The Adelaide Business School, The School of Economics, The Adelaide Law School, The School of Education, and The School of Architecture and the Built Environment. The Faculty of the Professions is the largest Faculty at the University of

Adelaide. In 2012, out of a student body of 20,088, just under a third of the students (6,170) studied within the Professions, with the remaining 13,918 shared between the four other faculties. The cohort is also characterised by a large percentage of international students (just over 42% in 2012) and large undergraduate classes of 300 to 500 in some courses.

In the Faculty of the Professions, many of the courses must meet the accreditation standards of industry bodies such as the Teacher Registration Board, the College of Architects, the Board of Chartered Accountants and the Law Society. Courses that fail to cover the content demanded by these industry bodies will not be endorsed by them, resulting in degrees that do not allow graduates to be employed in the capacity they believe themselves to be qualified for. It was very important to find ways of introducing the new pedagogy of SGDE that would not disrupt these crucial requirements of existing degree structures. Another issue was the definition of *"experienced academic"*. At the time of implementation approximately half of the teaching in the Faculty of the Professions was done by sessional staff on casual or short-term contracts of a year or less. There were also very few Professors or even Associate Professors in most of the Schools. The Faculty thus decided to define *"experienced academic"* in this context as *"a full-time academic with an ongoing position who is research active"*. As the process of developing possible activities advanced, it became clear that SGDEs would need to be treated as an extra activity to be included in the curriculum, rather than a whole-curriculum transformational mode of learning.

Models of SGDE

As might be expected, the basic principles and guidelines were interpreted very differently in the various disciplinary contexts. However, the first step was to identify the core courses in first-year undergraduate programmes that would cover all students. Key senior academics were identified in each School and Centre and were made responsible for the development and/or delivery of the SGDE. By the first semester of 2014, seven different versions of SGDE were devised.

1. Education

An activity was designed to teach students about how educational issues are reported in the media. Students are split into groups of four and instructed to monitor a given news group's reporting of educational issues. They bring their findings to compulsory one-hour weekly tutorials (eight in total), where the senior academic facilitates discussion of the articles, encouraging the development of critical thinking skills in assessing the stories. Articles are posted to an online news board for future reference. Thus, "discovery" is enacted as a process of auditing the media for education policy decisions. Students learn to apply policy analysis skills to media events. This is a precursor to an assessment task in which the student teachers are required to find and read policy documents in schools during their first Professional Experience Placement; their earlier experience aids their ability to identify such documents and appreciate their implications in real-life school situations.

2. Architecture

A design studio task was created which required students to explore the relationships between the specific details of a technical issue and the big-picture questions these issues might feed into. The idea is to use the city around the campus as a design laboratory. Groups of five students meet with an academic mentor three times during the second half of the semester for 30-40 minutes each time. "Discovery" here takes the form of learning about disciplinary principles such as typography and methods, concepts in design, and design solutions through students working in small groups on real-life design projects. The aim, according to the "experienced academics" involved, was to provide disciplinarily relevant research experience. Lecture content would be available online to inform students' project work and to free up time in the class schedule for the mentor meetings.

3. Economics

Groups of four students in a Mathematics Economics class work together learning about the modelling of contemporary economic issues using the mathematical tools introduced in weekly classes. Tutorials are used to critique Economic issues in newspaper articles provided by the lecturer; students learn how to extract key information, notice political bias, and analyse the validity of arguments and statistical interpretations put forward in the articles. In this class, that is focused on mathematics, students discover the social meaning behind the words that are used alongside numerical information. Time for this focus on newspaper articles is created by putting weekly lectures on theoretical principles online and then face-to-face classes in lecture theatres are devoted to working through applications of that theory.

4. Law

Law students work in groups of three or four to perform research into contemporary public law problems, including recognition of Aboriginal and Torres Strait Islander peoples in the constitution using key cases recommended by their lecturers. These research topics are an extension of the areas that are covered in their course. Instead of having their usual classes in a three-week period towards the end of the semester, sessions are held in the library with senior academics who supervise the group research projects. Attendance is required at these sessions. Some scaffolding is provided to facilitate group work in advance. This SGDE mimics the "research" lawyers perform to prepare for cases or reports.

5. Accounting and Finance

Groups of five students develop the ability to understand "accounting language" and how it is applied in practice so they can identify relevant information for decision makers. Each group is provided with a newspaper article regarding a current accounting issue. The lecturer poses a question about this topic that requires research. Group discussions about how the task can be approached are conducted on a wiki; then groups present their report on how they would construct an answer to the question. Importantly, students are encouraged to go beyond the textbook to find solutions. One aspect of this is teaching students how to unpack the type of questions presented by clients in real-life situations. The focus is not so much on attempting to provide answers to the questions as on teaching the students to "discover" the principles underpinning the approach to those questions. Some lectures are provided in the form of a flipped classroom (online lectures focused on content which the students access in advance as preparation for the classes) to create space in the programme for this extra activity.

6. Marketing

Students work in groups of five on a simulation game. The course aims to provide opportunities for the practical implementation of the main concepts covered and the development of problem-solving skills through the use of a simulation. Groups design a product and then compete against one another or against a computer through several rounds of the simulation game. They are able to seek advice from the kinds of experts that one would have access to in a real-life company (e.g., the marketing research coordinator, the CEO, etc.). Two mentoring sessions are provided by academic staff, and six weeks of online lectures free up time for the simulation—one session for a trial run, then five rounds of the game.

7. Management

Groups of five students work together on a research project designed to train students in the skills of teamwork. Multidisciplinary projects explore issues relating to contemporary and future management perspectives. Common perceptions about management are explored. "Discovery" is emphasised by focusing on the possible future of management, rather than the usual historical view of where today's practices have come from—that is, students are encouraged to speculate in a reasoned and well-informed manner about what we don't know. Research skills this can develop include using data to support an argument for their vision of the future, and the ability to develop an argument about what students believe management will be and why they think it won't be something else. A PowerPoint presentation explains how the group arrived at their final outcome. Time for mentoring sessions for each group is freed up by delivering ten tutorials instead of twelve.

Key SGDE Elements in the Faculty of the Professions

A number of elements appeared to be uniform across the seven SGDEs in the Faculty of the Professions. Some of these followed the standard University model of SGDE such as:

+ the size of group;
+ active, face-to-face engagement with an experienced academic; and
+ enriched on-campus experience with active participation.

However, other elements appeared to be more specific to the Faculty of the Professions:

+ SGDEs became an "add on" presented within tutorial groups (or outside of class times) in two instances; and
+ "discovery" here relates to professionally relevant tasks and includes "synthesis" and "application" of knowledge

"Small" was generally interpreted as three to six students, while "group" nearly always became group work or team work, often with grades attached to the activity. The required "interaction with an experienced academic" has usually meant that academics meet in person with the students, either during scheduled tutorial time or in extra face-to-face mentoring sessions; "experienced" has been interpreted as a full-time, research-active lecturer, rather than casual, hourly paid teaching staff. "Discovery" in these models has become a description of open-ended tasks in which students are set problems or exercises that require them to work together to find answers for themselves (as opposed to a transmission style of lecturing). In this sense, then, students actively participate in finding relevant information as they research the topic of the task. Thus, in the Faculty of the Professions, the "discovery" element for students was not necessarily discovery of new knowledge.

Small Group Discovery Experience: Research or just disciplinary learning?

Although the Humboldtian model espoused in the University's strategic plan appears to emphasise what Boyer (1990:17) dubbed *"the scholarship of discovery"*, the development of new knowledge (or at least the skills to eventually do so) is not the primary focus of the Professions SGDE models. Instead, in the Education, Economics, Accounting and Finance, and Law first-year SGDEs, there is an emphasis on integrating knowledge (theory) and its manifestation in real-world problems (as seen in the media, schools or legal problems), followed by application of that knowledge to real-world contexts. In the Marketing, Management and Architecture examples, there is direct application of disciplinary skills to real-world projects. Thus, the Professions SGDEs seem to resemble Boyer's scholarships of *"integration"* and *"application"* more than discovery. However, as one of the respondents articulated: *"This is the kind of 'research' we do in [Respondents' Discipline]: looking at real life and changing practice. There needs to be a pragmatic element. I need to answer students' questions: how is this relevant to me as a (future) [accountant/architect/teacher]?".*

What were the challenges for staff charged with the responsibility of implementing this new pedagogy?

In March to July 2014, the SGDE intervention was implemented with the first-year cohort. At focus groups throughout the first semester and in interviews in late 2014, a number of challenges in implementing the SGDE pedagogy were identified by lecturers. Although they enthusiastically embraced SGDE because it allowed more active participation on the part of both staff and students, made their courses more entertaining and fun, and encouraged students to engage in more complex ways with the knowledge of their future professions, they also encountered a number of logistical and pedagogical frustrations along the way.

Large Classes

Pragmatically, implementing a pedagogy that required active, virtually one-on-one engagement and conceptual mentoring as suggested by the Humboldtian ideal was extremely difficult in the Faculty of the Professions where large classes were the norm. One respondent noted that the Faculty of Professions academics had *"laughed [their] heads off"* when academics from other Faculties had expressed their concerns during a university-wide workshop about *"doing [SGDE] with 30 students"*, since *"[they] had 44 groups [of 30 or more] to look at..."* Clearly, great pressure was placed on those who had sole responsibility for teaching the two experiences to all tutorial classes. One respondent described the process as *"exhausting"* and another noted that: *"I will need the rest of the semester to recover from this"*. Other respondents shared the workload with colleagues, since it was *"too much to do on my own because we have a hundred students"*. In one of the models, all research-active academics participated in the SGDE and had groups of students coming to see them after hours; however, this was done on a *"voluntary basis"* with no *"workload recognition"* and the respondents expressed concern that the model was unsustainable.

Credit and Commitment

Due to the logistical issues raised above, in most cases the SGDE really became an "add on" activity, which was reflected in the percentage of grade allocated to the SGDE activity. Although one respondent stated, *"I made it worth 10 percent of their final grade...I had to make it worth their while"*, most of the SGDEs had a very low percentage allocated. One respondent noted that this affected student commitment: *"We put like 5%...which is not much...We did not want to put the whole burden on that... we understand if they don't like it...we just didn't know what to expect. It was the first time we were running it...so like let us just put 5%... but sometimes the students are willing to give up 5% because they are just lazy to come... maybe it was not enough"*. In contrast, two of the respondents felt that the SGDE was a core part of the course and merely a formal articulation of what the disciplinary team had *"already been doing"*. Since the SGDE took the students through the learning processes required for the entire course, no separate mark allocation was required.

Group/Teamwork

A central challenge for most of the models is the complications created by the requirements of team work. The complaints that students make about working and being assessed in groups are well documented in the learning and teaching literature (e.g., Cumming *et al.*, 2014; Elliott, 2014). The respondents, echoing common findings in the literature, realised that *"some [students] all they did was tend to piggyback on someone else"*. Most of the respondents addressed this issue by devoting time to setting up the guidelines of team work in terms of roles and responsibilities. Others created marking systems that rewarded those who put time and effort into the tasks (with the recognition that some students can be inclined to take over and not allow space for others to participate in the ways they might want to). Another respondent staggered the access to material to ensure that work was only done after students had had class interactions, since *"you want them to talk to each other and to think about it and to disagree with each other so that they kind of have a little debate going on… so that is what is going on…if we give them earlier some people would work like crazy on it and others would be playing and it would be just a disaster…"*

Despite the challenges of managing the team dynamics, many felt that this was a valuable learning experience for students (even if the students themselves sometimes struggled with being good team contributors): *"I strongly believe in the importance of working together in teams, I can definitely see the benefit of getting them engaged with research, with research tasks… so I think in general it's a good idea"*.

The respondents also indicated that the active use of group/team work would put lecturers in a better position to answer the question that students will inevitably ask: how is this relevant to my future profession? For example, one respondent explained that the capacity to work with unknown colleagues on a professional basis is central to the jobs that his students are likely to undertake:*"[The] nature of our profession is that a lot of work is done in teams, but the teams may not necessarily be in the same office, may not necessarily be in the same building, may not necessarily be in the same country. So people may work in teams with people they have never ever met and never likely to meet"*.

Progression and Repetition

Another concern raised was that the implementation of SGDEs across programmes and over subsequent years may begin to seem rather repetitive to students. Other respondents viewed this repetition as *"a strength"*, since it could potentially *"encourage all course coordinators to map the activities they plan across the whole program, which will in turn allow for better planning of research skill development across the years"*. On the whole, though, the sheer variety of models of SGDE documented in this chapter indicates that there are multiple ways in which this pedagogy can be implemented. In sharing their thinking and experiences, academics involved in designing SGDE will undoubtedly find inspiration from those around them.

Resourcing

Decisions about SGDE models were also influenced by the available teaching spaces. Sometimes attempts to engage groups in discussions were hampered by students being trapped in traditional raked lecture theatres with fixed seating. Other interventions that employed synchronous Internet activity were abandoned because lecturers did not know in advance if the computer labs would have sufficient (working) computers for their requirements. Although many students might have mobile devices, making it a requirement to bring their own laptop or tablet was regarded as inequitable.

Many lecturers were frustrated by the inadequacies of the online technologies available to them through the formal university systems. Some of the technical requirements of their planned interventions turned out to be very time-consuming and cumbersome as reflected in the following quotations from different respondents:

> "We had lots of issues with technology...It was a nightmare!"

> "Not all of them [the students] could use the technology... so it took a lot of time just teaching them that aspect."

> "The problem was I gave them too many electronic tools and it was difficult to measure some of them... with the blog it was easy to measure participation...but like with the discussion board..."

Others chose early on not to grapple with what they regarded as inadequate facilities: "It would have been a bit more 'fun' to have things [online], having the question popping up, having the article and pushing them out to the other. You need to first fill in the first one and then you type the number, and find out if you were right or wrong, before you move onto the second one, and then it gives you a little transcript". Although this respondent regarded interactive tasks as technically possible, the complexities of preparing such an activity for a large group was seen as taking an unreasonable amount of time. Further, it was anticipated that the extra time required to set up computers in the teaching room for such a task and then train students in how to use the new "app" would have cut deeply into the students' face-to-face session time. Nevertheless, resorting to a paper copy of materials, with *"no colour, no pictures"* and no online interaction *"to entertain them a little"* was regarded as part of the reason one SGDE *"fell a bit flat"* with this particular group of first-year students.

Discovery versus Synthesis and Application

At the development and implementation stages of the SGDEs, the key issue for the respondents remained the tension between implementing Boyer's *"scholarship of discovery"* (Boyer, 1990:17) and their disciplines' preferred scholarships of *"integration"* and *"application"*. While the *"scholarship of discovery"* might work well in some disciplines such as Architecture and the *"Studio Model of design and critique"*, this was less comfortably adapted to other areas where a premium is placed on integration and application, as Healey (2005) reminds us. This resulted in clearly defined disciplinary tasks, rather than the *"not yet completely solved problems"* (Elton, 2008:226) espoused by Humboldt. This is illustrated, for example, in the following description for the motivation of one SGDE: *"The task arose out of my perception that the students did not understand how to answer a question..... I use the example 'Do you know the time?' and most of the students answer the actual time, whereas the actual answer is 'yes' or 'no'. This is really important in [my field], that you precisely answer the question"*.

Like Zamorski's respondents (2002), several of the respondents in this study were concerned that "discovery" was not possible before gaining a thorough understanding of disciplinary content and theoretical grounding. Because that groundwork had not been established, respondents were concerned that the students were not ready for independent discovery, or that tasks had to be limited to small-scale discoveries and application of knowledge. As one respondent noted: *"No it was very different because this is just a [subject] course...and we have to give them the basic tools... I know sometimes we could have done it better and this could help us do that...On the other hand, because this is a [Subject] 1 basic course it was hard to find topics that were easy enough that we could ask them to do something… they were really low level".*

Conclusion

The notion of the Small Group Discovery Experience encapsulates many of the ideals associated with a pedagogy based on both "researching to learn" and "learning to research". The University of Adelaide policy and advice provided to academics implementing the SGDE intervention suggests its implementation will enable undergraduate students to learn about research and the processes of research, as well as undertake knowledge creation (*"wissenschaft"* (Humboldt, 1850)) themselves. In the context of educating undergraduate professions-based students, however, this is not always an easy fit. Rather, accrediting bodies may demand specific content to be covered in the ways they deem appropriate (Healey, 2005). Indeed, sometimes the concerns of academic research are not regarded as relevant to the conduct of the profession (Harrington & Booth, 2003).

Nevertheless, our academic respondents suggest that students can benefit from opportunities to use discovery-based activities to learn disciplinary knowledge in the professions and other applied disciplines, and that this kind of intervention can assist academics in conveying disciplinary content. While the pedagogy of SGDE resembles enquiry-based or problem-based learning, it has its own foundations in the Humboldtian ideals of the student and academic researching new knowledge together. In practice, the ideal may not entirely be possible, especially when resourcing limitations related to class sizes, technology and staffing intervene. However, despite the significant challenges, the seven SGDEs referred to in this chapter all managed to design disciplinarily scaffolded activities, which enabled their students to undertake "discovery" and start to participate in research or research-like activities with various degrees of autonomy. The first iteration of this exciting new direction in university pedagogy has met a number of challenges, but is also already proving to embody the kinds of engagement that many twenty-first-century university students respond to in very positive ways. It is now vital for the University of Adelaide—and any other institutions following similar bold initiatives in the face of marketisation and massification—to put the resourcing and systems in place that will support academics in this endeavour.

About the authors

Dr Michelle Picard is a senior lecturer in the School of Education and Director, Researcher Education and Development Unit at the University of Adelaide. She can be contacted at this email: michelle.picard@adelaide.edu.au

Dr Cally Guerin is a lecturer in the Researcher Education and Development Unit at the University of Adelaide. She can be contacted at this email: cally.guerin@adelaide.edu.au

Bibliography

American Assembly of Collegiate Schools of Business (AACSB) (1989). Report of the AACSB Task Force on Outcome Measurement Project, St Louis, MO.

Ash, M. G. (2006). Bachelor of What, Master of Whom? The Humboldt Myth and Historical Transformations of Higher Education in German-Speaking Europe and the US. *European Journal of Education*, Vol. 41, No. 2, pp. 245-267.

Atkinson, M. P. (2001). The Scholarship of Teaching and Learning: Reconceptualizing Scholarship and Transforming the Academy. *Social Forces*, Vol. 79, No. 4, pp. 1217-1229.

Boyer, E. L. (1990). *Scholarship Revisited*. Princeton, NJ: Carnegie Foundation for the Advancement of Teaching.

Cumming, J.; C. Woodcock; S. J. Cooley; M. J. G. Holland & V. E. Burns (2014). Development and Validation of the Groupwork Skills Questionnaire (GSQ) for Higher Education. *Assessment & Evaluation in Higher Education*, pp. 1-14.

Elliott, C. J. & M. Reynolds (2014). Participative Pedagogies, Group Work and the International Classroom: An Account of Students' and Tutors' Experiences. *Studies in Higher Education*, Vol. 39, No. 2, pp. 307-320.

Elton, L. (2008). Collegiality and Complexity: Humboldt's Relevance to British Universities Today. *Higher Education Quarterly*, Vol. 62, No. 3, pp. 224-236.

Giret, J.-F. (2011). Does Vocational Training Help Transition to Work? The 'New French Vocational Bachelor Degree'. *European Journal of Education*, 46, No. 2, pp. 244-256.

Griffiths, R. (2004). Knowledge Production and the Research-Teaching Nexus: The Case of the Built Environment Disciplines. *Studies in Higher Education*, Vol. 29, No. 6, pp. 709-726.

Harrington, J. & C. Booth (2003). Rigour versus Relevance, Research versus Teaching? Evidence from Business and Management Studies. Paper presented to *Society for Research into Higher Education Annual Conference: Research, Scholarship and Teaching: Changing Relationships?* 16.-18. December, 2003, Royal Holloway, University of London.

Hauhart, R. C. & J. E. Grahe (2015). *Designing and Teaching Undergraduate Capstone Courses*. John Wiley & Sons.

Healey, M. (2005). Linking Research and Teaching: Exploring Disciplinary Spaces and the Role of Inquiry-Based Learning. In R. Barnett (Ed.), *Reshaping the University: New Relationships between Research, Scholarship and Teaching*. McGraw Hill/Open University Press, pp. 67-78.

Hohendahl, P. U. (2011). Humboldt Revisited: Liberal Education, University Reform, and the Opposition to the Neoliberal University. *New German Critique*, Vol. 38, No. 2, pp. 159-196.

Humboldt, W. von (1850). *Thoughts and Opinions of a Statesman*. London: W. Pickering.

Lehmann, W. (2009). University as Vocational Education: Working Class Students' Expectations for University. *British Journal of Sociology of Education*, Vol. 30, No. 2 , pp. 137-149.

Nygaard, C.; T. Højlt & M. Hermansen (2008). Learning-based Curriculum Development. *Higher Education*, Vol. 55, No. 1, pp. 33-50.

The University of Adelaide. (2012). *Beacon of Enlightenment: Strategic Plan* 2013-2023.

The University of Adelaide. (2013). *Small Group Discovery Experience: Principles and Guidelines*, 27 March 2013.

Woods, D. R. (1994). *Problem-Based Learning: How to Gain the Most from PBL*, Waterdown, Ontario.

Zamorski, B. (2002). Research-led Teaching and Learning in Higher Education: A Case. *Teaching in Higher Education*, Vol. 7, No 55, pp. 411-427.

Chapter Seven

Encouraging the intellectual craft of *living* research: tattoos, theory and time

Sarah Hayes

Introduction

This chapter contributes to the anthology on *learning to research – researching to learn* because it emphases a need to design curricula that enables *living* research, and on-going researcher development, rather than one that restricts student and staff activities within a marketised approach towards *time*. In recent decades higher education (HE) has come to be valued for its contribution to the global economy. Referred to as the neo-liberal university, a strong prioritisation has been placed on meeting the needs of industry by providing a better workforce. This perspective emphasises the role of a degree in HE to secure future material affluence, rather than to study as an on-going investment in the self (Molesworth *et al.*, 2009). Students are treated primarily as consumers in this model, where through their tuition fees they purchase a product, rather than benefit from the transformative potential university education offers for the whole of life. Given that HE is now measured by the numbers of students it attracts, and later places into well-paid jobs, there is an intense pressure on *time*, which has led to a method where the learning experiences of students are broken down into discrete modules. Whilst this provides consistency, students can come to view research processes in a fragmented way within the modular system. Topics are presented chronologically, week-by-week and students simply complete a set of tasks to 'have a degree', rather than to 'be learners' (Molesworth *et al.*, 2009) who are *living* their research, in relation to their own past, present and future. The idea of *living research* in this context is my own adaptation of an approach suggested by C. Wright Mills (1959) in The Sociological Imagination. Mills advises that successful scholars do not split their work from the rest of their lives, but treat scholarship as a choice of how to *live*, as well as a choice of career.

The marketised slant in HE thus creates a tension; firstly, for *students* who are *learning to research* – Mills would encourage them to be creative, not instrumental, in their use of time, yet they are journeying through a system that is structured for a swift progression towards a high paid job, rather than crafted for reflexive inquiry that transforms their understanding throughout life. Many universities are placing a strong focus on discrete skills for student employability, but I suggest that embedding the transformative skills emphasised by Mills empowers students and builds their confidence to help them make connections that aid their employability.

Secondly, the marketised approach creates a problem for *staff* designing the curriculum if students do not easily make links across time over their years of study and whole programmes. By *researching to learn*, staff can discover new methods to apply in their design of the curriculum, to help students make important and creative connections across their programmes of study. In this chapter I address these points in two ways. I invite readers to engage in conversations about how we approach time, both practically and theoretically, firstly in relation to developing student research skills as they are *learning to research* and secondly, in building collective knowledge about curriculum design amongst staff by *researching to learn*. As staff, *researching to learn* we can seek new understandings of *time*, beyond merely the chronological, that might then be applied in design of the curriculum. For example, Currie (2007) provides us with three broader conceptions of time: *time–space compression, recontextualisation* and *archive fever*. I use these ideas to open new ways of thinking about learning and curriculum development. I discuss how I designed tasks to help students who are *learning to research* in a final year Sociology module I created: *Tattoos, TV and Trends, Understanding Popular Culture*. This course demonstrates my own attempt to introduce different conceptions of time to student thinking and thus bridge the modular approach to curriculum and Mills' idea of research as a *living* process. Whilst clear curriculum design principles, such as *constructive alignment* (Biggs, 2003) are endorsed, encouraging students to think more imaginatively about time in their tasks helps them relate their learning reflexively to past and future events. More discussion is invited on the merit of reviewing both practice and theory concerning time, when planning a curriculum. How the research process is taught should not be viewed in isolation from constraints that modern capitalist culture places on academic practices. Given the marketisation of HE that has taken place in recent decades, students are encouraged to think of universities as effectively providing 'the student experience' *for* them, but this hides from them the demanding on-going personal endeavour of academic study at university level.

In reading this chapter, you will gain the following insights:

1. a better understanding of how, through the concept of *research-led teaching* (Griffiths, 2004, Healey and Jenkins, 2005), the intellectual craft of *living* research might be designed into modules, considering both ideas from C Wright Mills on the benefits of treating scholarly research as a choice of how to *live*, and theory about time from Currie (2007), as inspiration to innovate in designing the curriculum;

2. an appreciation of ways to develop *research-oriented teaching* to encourage students to question rigid approaches towards theory and time. This extends into *research-based teaching*, where autonomous student inquiry-based activities are negotiated for their final assessment (Griffiths, 2004, Healey and Jenkins, 2005); and

3. an invitation to share ideas on how, within an aligned curriculum, we might optimise the conditions of quality learning for students in relation to time. Is it possible to plan within programme teams for both the practical timing of modules and also allow flexible spaces for reflexive, theoretical approaches towards time?

I would like to credit Lee Barron, whose book: *Social Theory in Popular Culture* I used as a key text for this module. The ideas presented by Barron (2013) help students to resist simply treating research as a chronological process. Instead they are encouraged to look to what could happen, to inform what has, and review both classic and contemporary theory in their own cultural experience of the present.

Challenges for academics in a knowledge-based economy

One significant problem faced by academic staff in a *knowledge-based economy* (Jessop, 2008), where our modern culture strongly values flexible skills to support global competition, is that students can come to view their learning in a fragmented way. They may be presented with a lot of information but not always make the necessary connections we would wish them to make across their modules of study. Equally, our final-year students (who at Aston University are often returning from a busy work placement year) may take little time to reflect back to modules they studied in their first or second year. The modular system in HE has provided consistency, in terms of credit ratings for courses and progression, but it has also led to distinct modules (courses), with taught sessions confined within weekly folders concealed within virtual learning environments (VLEs). As students complete each assessment, they perceive these modules to be 'done'. Yet past topics also contain vital elements of their curriculum, such as research training, theoretical connections and skills that if applied by students in their final year, can contribute to strong dissertation work. A colleague of mine, in her recent publication on student experiences in the learning and teaching of sensitive issues, explains that: *"much of the work on educational journeys has looked at transitions between places, such as the transition to university, or following degree studies into work"* (Lowe, 2014:2). Less attention has been focused on the transitions between years at university (Willcoxson et al., 2011). Students encounter problems moving from guided learning within modules to the independence of undertaking research for a dissertation. They respond emotionally to aspects such as uncertainty and time management (Todd et al., 2004).

In designing programmes (and modules (courses) within programmes), using clear language, which states what students will do in the form of measurable learning outcomes is a first stage to making students feel more secure. Aligning the assessment to clearly show how outcomes are met by students is important too (Biggs, 2003). Once this structure is in place though it provides a framework onto which, if encouraged, students can map their own individual life experience and learning aspirations. Their achievement of small successes is central to maximising skills in researching to learn (see Warner & Enomoto, this volume). Students from diverse backgrounds need reassurance to self-reflect critically on their identity within the research process and to see their own personal input as valid (see Coombes, this volume). Given students are surrounded by simple, flexible and vague narratives in HE policies and marketing texts within a knowledge-based economy, honesty can be hard for students to uncover. For example, in the UK Government White Paper: Higher Education: students at the heart of the system (BIS, 2011), it is inferred that students take their custom to the marketplace and universities efficiently provide the service they require, which misleads students. It hides from students the demanding personal endeavour of academic study at university level, shrouding this is in a simple consumer-based rhetoric around "the student experience". The individual nature of transformative study and critical self-reflection becomes marginalised and replaced by a form of self that calculates the quickest route to completion. Many universities have responded to this agenda by accepting the notion of students as customers of the higher education "offer" (Hayes & Bartholomew, 2014). However this tends to reduce university learning into simply a "means to an end". The deeper learning required to develop innovative student researchers, through active application of theory to the world, is replaced by an instrumental "time is money" approach. I therefore encourage readers to imagine *time* in broader terms than simply linked to economic gain, given that in HE we have now set the clock to tick to the pace of *"emergency as rule"* (Thrift, 2000).

Time and transformation

Social acceleration is a significant problem in modern society (Rosa, 2013) and academic acceleration is a problem for staff and students in HE (Gill, 2009). Gregg (2009) refers to "function creep", the requirement to do more with less in HE. Alongside an intensification of work in academia there is also extensification (Jarvis & Pratt, 2006) across time and space. There is not only more work to fit into less time, there is less physical space too. Open plan spaces are noisy and do not allow tasks to be completed until later at home, or via mobile devices on the move. An "academia without walls" (Gill, 2009) leaves us all in danger of being so "busy" that no time is scheduled for staff or students to examine, reconsider and recontextualise themselves within these changes. If our *"whole society is placed at the disposal of profit"* (Negri, 1989:79) then what, realistically, are the options in HE for resisting an impoverished version of Mills vision of *living* research? We need to confront how we currently value time in academia before we can begin to imagine alternatives (Hayes, 2015). Whilst research is powerful, we also have powerful tools at our disposal in the context of teaching, for re-writing the curriculum. Perhaps if we critically explore how we apply the concept of time in our design of taught programmes we might re-focus on the design of real spaces for transformative experiences. This in turn could open new routes for research for ourselves and our students. In Figure 1 below, a broader picture is illustrated.

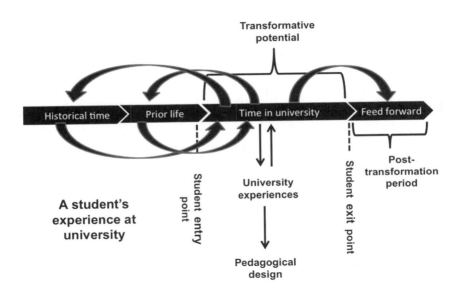

Figure 1: A student's experience at university along a timeline that links historical time, a student's prior life and their post-transformation period after university.

This is a reminder that university study, from student entry point to student exit point, offers transformative potential (Mezirow, 2000) if the activities designed for students are not merely instrumental. Mezirow (2000) suggested that purely instrumental learning reinforces ideology, fosters conformity and impedes development of people's responsibility and agency. If this is the case then we deny students vital employability skills and fail to empower them for the workplace. Yet if curriculum is designed with historical time, prior life and future employment in mind then student university experiences can also feed back into exciting new pedagogical designs. Reviewing how we communicate the notion of time, both theoretically and practically, in curriculum design could provide a resistance to contradictions within a knowledge-based economy. For example, tensions students may perceive between the idea of undertaking research to generate knowledge as a collective resource for social benefit, or a more calculating approach which views a dissertation as just one of a series of tasks to be ticked off a list. Innovative ideas about time can provoke more reflexive thought for students once they understand a chronological approach is just *one* way to view their learning. Staff too (given time) could within their programme teams revisit the ways they map time to student learning to liberate their thinking. The chronological sequencing of study may be necessary in some subjects. It may simply be convenient, but it can also conceal refreshing alternative ideas. Larger classes, wrought by pressure to recruit more students, has resulted in students often experiencing a simple transmission of vast amounts of content, but with fewer opportunities to apply and better understand how to live the practice of their craft (Mills, 1959).

The role of imagination in learning to research

When teaching Sociology undergraduates, a key text that first year students are often asked to engage with is: *The Sociological Imagination* by C. Wright Mills (1959). In this accessible piece of writing, Mills explains his own intellectual craftsmanship for the benefit of student under-standing. He makes the important point that successful scholars do not split their work from the rest of their lives and so scholarship is a choice of how to *live*, as well as a choice of career. Here I would emphasise that this is indeed an active *choice* – a conscious decision – to live research in a personally meaningful way, rather than simply a 24/7 response to be "always on" due to function creep. Mills instructs students to learn to use their life experience in intellectual work, and continually to examine and interpret it (Mills, 1959). With reference to Figure 1 it becomes possible to visualise what Mills is referring to in relation to a student's experience at university. Figure 1 reminds us that in a broader approach to university study, from a student entry point we can help students to look ahead and back, taking into account both historical time and prior experience, as well as anticipating their careers to come.

Mills reminds students that their past plays into and affects their present and as such it defines their capacity for future experience (Mills, 1959). This shifts the focus from education as a "product" that the student-consumer "buys", to a personal involvement. Mills explains to students that education is in every intellectual product upon which the student may work (Mills, 1959). Here I suggest we not only encourage students to understand the transformative potential of their university experiences personally, through the projects they work on, but that we also place strong value on their input into the pedagogical design of our future courses to come.

It is my personal belief that Mill's advice from 1959 is as relevant now as it was then for student researchers, from the moment they enter university education (across all disciplines – not just Sociology) to the point where they move into future employment and feed-forward this experience into their post-transformative lives. Furthermore, in modern global society there are new demands on how we handle time. As discussed in the next section, new technologies have altered how we experience and react to time. We need to open new discussions on practical and theoretical links to how we approach time in both *learning to research* and *researching to learn*.

New ways to think about time and the curriculum

In this section I briefly examine a theoretical framework where time is discussed via 3 concepts from Currie (2007): *time–space compression*, *recontextualisation* and *archive fever*. The first concept of *time–space compression* concerns the ways that pace and time are now represented differently through new technologies such as fast telecommunications and the speed of jet travel. Humans can now experience a simultaneity of being able to move across physical spaces, yet communicate in different time zones. The result is a form of "contaminated present", through the collapse of temporal distance (Currie, 2007). The second concept of *recontextualisation* is a model where the present is understood as *"the bearer of historical traces"* (Currie, 2007). We now experience very rapid forms of accelerated recontextualisation due to technologies that close the gap between original styles, for example, and newer versions of styles that are recontextualised. The present both anticipates its own past and is experienced, like everything else in the contemporary world, as the object of a future memory. For example, in a restaurant we may be served a meal, we might photograph it and text it across the world to friends who view the image or video in another time zone, before we have even finished eating. *"The process which consigns the present to memory is conducted at infinite speed, since the present commodity is always already in the past"* (Currie, 2007:11). This links to the last concept discussed by Currie of *archive fever*, where the present is lived as if it were the object of a future memory. Derrida described this as a "future orientation", a mode of anticipation which structures the present through the promise of a future that is always yet to come (Derrida, 1996). In our highly developed capitalist society, rather than an event being recorded *because it happens*, the event happens *because it is recorded*. I record a "selfie" (a snapshot of myself) in anticipation of its future action, as something that will make a good story.

Compression of time and space has implications for how we experience the present (including our capacity for critical and reflexive learning), because we can now encompass places once thought to be at a considerable spatial, and therefore temporal, distance (Currie, 2007). What these examples do is help to free our thoughts from the constraint that we must design research skills in only a linear, processional way. For some subjects, topics must to be taught in a particular order because, for example, patient health may depend on it. This does not mean these courses need to be taught in a cultural vacuum. Instead we can raise student awareness that how we treat time is a social and political construct that in a knowledge-based economy has implications for both *learning to research* and *researching to learn*, before, during and after university education.

Approaches towards the teaching-research relationship

Curriculum design is a powerful tool for lecturers to use to develop student engagement. A careful and explicit alignment of what students will do, linked with how their attainment will be measured, if planned at the design stage of learning, provides clarity for both students and staff. In Figure 2 an academic's experience of course (module) delivery is shown in the wider context of his or her life, along a timeline that includes historical time, prior life and the period within a university when a course they are teaching is delivered and reviewed as part of quality processes. The course may have been running before the academic arrives and begins teaching, but the programme the course belongs to is subject to a six year review process (within the model of academic quality enhancement of UK HE), which provides an opportunity for a programme team to review how the different elements of the programme align with each other. Within this process, stakeholders such as students, employers and professional bodies should be consulted and the programme philosophy revisited. Here it would be worth discussing the role of time within the programme philosophy. How is time practically applied by the programme team and indeed theoretically understood to have bearing on both course delivery and student understanding.

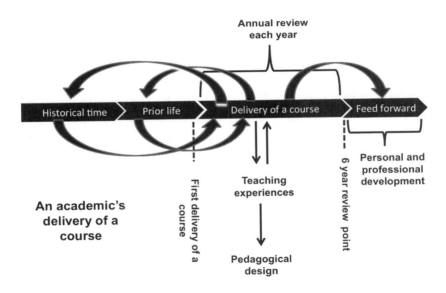

Figure 2: An academic's experience of course delivery is shown along a timeline that links historical time, prior life and the period within a university when the course is reviewed as part of quality processes.

A rigorous design approach need not restrict an educator's imagination in bringing ideas from their own disciplinary research into their teaching, and in turn, drawing from their experience of teaching, new reflections that inform future research. This is understood as *research-led teaching* (Griffiths, 2004; Healey & Jenkins, 2005). This is a process that for me, as I adopted it in the design of my popular culture module: *Tattoos, TV and Trends* "*extends beyond the notion of formal curriculum into the wider process of co-learning, engagement and social learning*" (Chapman & Ishaq, 2013:235). Referring once more to Figure 2, the experience of the academic includes both teaching and personal and professional development. Academics belong to many communities for their teaching and research activities, and these are not mutually exclusive. Full scholarly engagement can lead to a cross-pollination that not only develops the individual academic but extends the professionalism of a community (see Bartholomew, this volume).

In exploring the teaching-research relationship however, there are other positions to consider which, whilst open to interpretation, can be helpful in thinking through specific teaching aims and student learning outcomes. For example, *research-oriented teaching* is concerned with developing a research ethos in students. As this extends into student inquiry-based activities it might be described as *research-based teaching*, whilst *research-informed teaching* describes a teaching process derived from specific research into learning and teaching processes (Griffiths, 2004; Healey & Jenkins, 2005). Personally, I perceive some problems arise in detaching learning and teaching processes from the contexts in which these are applied. I prefer instead to imagine ways to encourage students to develop a research ethos that critically questions a dominant status quo in wider society. By this I refer to how corporate models have flooded higher education to limit and distribute knowledge in specific ways linked to global competition and profit. To help students who are *learning to research* to develop strong critical research skills and make important temporal connections to understand how past, present, and future might connect with their studies, I constructed some particular learning outcomes and linked assessments. In the next section I describe for others how the theory of C. Wright Mills informed my final year undergraduate Sociology module: *Tattoos, TV and Trends: Understanding Popular Culture*, which I designed and taught during 2013, at

Aston University. With such a title, the module attracted over 60 curious students, who were not fully aware of how they would be required to use their imaginations to develop and challenge their ideas about research across time.

Designing learning to research into Tattoos, TV and Trends

Tattoos, TV and Trends was one of several optional modules in the Sociology programme designed to provide final year students with choice and autonomy of decision in their last year of study. To encourage students to practise research skills and build understanding that would serve them well, both on this module and in preparation for their impending dissertation projects, I planned two key learning outcomes:

Students will:

a) gain a greater awareness of how *classical theories* covered during their degree studies are evident in our culture and brought to life through *daily experience*; and

b) practise skills of defining a topic, drafting an abstract, presenting, writing up and applying the work of a key classical social theorist to a trend in popular culture.

In terms of skills and knowledge, these learning outcomes were designed to operate at two levels that are relevant to the interrelated theme of this anthology. Via learning outcome a) students are *researching to learn*, as they explore literature to connect this with their daily experience of popular culture. In learning outcome b) students are *learning to research* as they practise (at the very start of their final year) an important set of skills that are needed again as they begin to develop their dissertation topics.

Learning outcome a) might fall into the category of *research-oriented teaching*, which is concerned with developing a research ethos in students. Outcome a) is there to help students gain a deep understanding of how classical Sociological theorists (such as Marx, Durkheim, Weber, Adorno, Simmel, Parsons, C Wright Mills and others) might be applied to everyday activities in our modern global culture industry. This includes linking ideas from a classical theorist with issues related to a chosen form of popular culture, for example: listening to hip-hop music, reading "chick-lit", buying fashion items, visiting the cinema, watching Reality TV, or YouTube, getting a tattoo or body piercing. Though important for Sociology at their time of writing, given the time lapse between the research of these early critical theorists (who may have written their key works between the early 1800s and the early 1900s, or have their roots in the culture of that period), it would be easy for students to assume these "long-dead thinkers" lack any relevance to the here and now (Barron, 2013). Since the death of these classical writers our modern technologies have developed to extend the standardised "mass culture" described by Adorno and Horkheimer (1944) as able to suppress and control individual consciousness. We have since been able to experience convergent media, where groups watch and interact with reality TV, access footage through the Internet, send comments through mobile phones and devices to have real-time effects on the fate of live participants. How would early critical theorists be able to comment on the many extensions to human experience that digital technologies have permitted? Furthermore, the majority of these "classics" were white, heterosexual men, so how can their ideas be applicable to our modern multicultural media "texts", which include feminist issues such as sexual oppression, gender and the body, as well as more traditional topics like class conflict, the economy and social status? Nevertheless, these theories/theorists dealt with many centrally important social issues and so still have much to say on everyday cultural life.

In the second learning outcome b) students gain early practise of an important set of skills that are needed to develop their dissertation topics. These student inquiry-based activities might be described as *research-based teaching*. Towards the end of the Autumn term students are expected to defend their choice of dissertation topic in a viva where they explain to staff and other students their chosen methodological approach and related literature. Students returning from placement to undertake the final year of their degree studies can therefore feel anxious about what pressure lies ahead. Quickly becoming proficient in time management, to define a topic and draft and present an approach can make a big difference in building student confidence. In planning assessments linked to these learning outcomes I wanted students to own their final-year research at an early point and gain skills they would be able to translate across their other modules.

Linking the negotiated assessment with the learning outcomes

In designing the assessment tasks I wanted to give students the freedom to negotiate their individual topic and choice of classical theorist with me. As they would soon be doing this for a much larger piece of work (their dissertation project), this was a chance for them to practise selecting a subject of personal interest and planning how they would research it. I took a *research-informed teaching* approach by adopting a negotiated assessment to both encourage student autonomy and interest and foster original pieces of work. This builds students' metacognitive strategies, as they become more aware of their learning process, their judgements and limitations, and a need to modify their thinking as they explain these stages to others (thinking ahead to their dissertation vivas). Jacobson summarises metacognition as *"knowing the process by which one learns"* (Jacobson, 1998:3). In the end of module feedback comments on what was liked about this module one student comment expresses this particularly well:

> *"the topic and the way it is conducted enables me to put together theoretical concepts of previous years, systemises knowledge in the relevant and interesting content"*

The assessment involved 2 Tasks:
+ Task 1: a 500-word abstract (15%)
+ Task 2: a 2,500-word essay (85%)

Task 1: 500-word abstract (15%) Submission deadline: Week 4
Task 1 was a proposal really; I asked students to write this as if they were preparing an abstract for a research paper they might present at a conference. Their instructions were:
To prepare your abstract you will first need to do the following:
+ select your media topic from popular culture;
+ consider what issue(s) you plan to research in relation to this case/topic?
    E.g. class, conflict, sexual oppression, gender, power,

consumerism, ethnicity, the body, social relations, economic systems, stability, social status…;

+ decide on the classic social theorist you are going to align with your topic;

+ research your theorist carefully to note what their main works have covered:
  a. consult the reading list and library catalogue
  b. does your classic theorist link well with your chosen topic?
  c. look at what is required for the essay
  d. book into my office hours to confirm with me your theorist/ topic

+ try drafting your abstract to get a feel for the information you can include;

+ it takes time to write an abstract well. As you read further, refine it to provide an overview of what your essay will do and any limitations;

+ include a reference list of the sources you consulted in the correct format,

+ submit by the deadline in Week 4;

  feedback will be given through: written feedback on your abstract, and on your essay, when it is returned, plus on-going feedback during classes and office hours.

In the Week 1 seminar, students were given examples of abstracts to discuss and to consider what information should be included. They were informed they would submit in Week 4 and therefore advised to begin researching directly after the Week 1 lecture and seminar, to allow time to decide on a topic, classic theorist, and to discuss it with me before writing and submitting the abstract. The face-to-face meeting with me was non-negotiable and all students came for a short consultation individually, or in pairs. This was a considerable time commitment on my part, but one I believe shaped the later submission of many original essays of a high quality. Comments from students on what they liked included:

"Assessment! Really clear, and it was useful to have an abstract before an essay"

> *"I like the idea of having 2 assessments. The first assessment helps the bigger essay"*

> *"Useful assessment to build grounding for later essay"*

The length of the abstract was questioned by some students in the feedback as well as the early deadline for submission of this first piece of work:

> *"Maybe shorter abstract? Felt more like an extended intro"*

> *"Allowing more time to submit abstract"*

The abstract I believe could be shortened to around 300 words. However, the early deadline was intentional on my part and an aspect I would be reluctant to change.

Task 2: 2500-word essay (85%) Submission deadline: Week 12

The final essay was a well-argued and well-referenced formal research paper, based on the abstract. It was expected that students would critically discuss classic social theory within popular culture. This meant taking the thought of a classic theorist and applying it reflexively to a chosen popular culture media example. Their instructions were:

Your topic choice

* ✦ it is your choice as to what topic within popular culture you choose;
* ✦ it is also your choice as to whose arguments you use to critique, your topic.

What your essay should include

1. introduce your classic theorist;
2. introduce the media example from popular culture you have chosen, through which you will illustrate the key relevant ideas of your theorist;
3. discuss the main issue(s) you have researched that led you to link this media example with your choice of classic social theorist (Some examples might be:-class, conflict, sexual oppression,

gender, power, consumerism, ethnicity, the body, social relations, economic systems, stability, social status......but this will vary with your choice of classic theorist);

4. critically appraise the theory/theorist to discuss their contributions;

5. dicuss limitations of their work on the issues you defined, citing contemporary social theorists that support this critique and drawing your final conclusions;

6. include a full list of references in the correct Harvard format.

Feed-forward not back

In designing *Tattoos, TV and Trends*, I applied one of my own research interests around perceptions of time in modern culture and linked this with the approach taken by Barron in *Social Theory in Popular Culture* (2013). For more discussion on reconsidering how we treat time in higher education see Hayes (2015). A further element of *research-informed teaching* I introduced were *feed-forward* techniques. I wanted to encourage students to see lecturer comments on their work as active and dynamic, rather than something finite at the end of a piece of writing. There is a tendency in education to treat previous assessment and experience in a simple chronological sense, i.e. what happened to me in childhood has shaped my current state and my past. Feedback reinforces a focus on what has occurred and not on the infinite possibilities that might happen in the future.

Feed-forward is instead *anticipatory*, which has a number of advantages (Hounsell, 2007). Firstly, by providing comments to students on their first assessment (the 500 word abstract) in time for them to read these before they write their later essay, it enables them to respond. It also allows a lecturer the opportunity also to avoid the disappointment of marking many scripts where errors could have been avoided. Feed-forward is taken less personally and emotionally by students, as it offers more control than simply collecting feedback at the end of a module. Students have told me they frequently do not collect feedback as they do not want to read negative comments, particularly when they perceive the course to be over.

Practising researching to learn

Recalling learning outcome a), in order to respond to the requirement of applying classical theories to phenomena that are evident in current popular culture, students were requested to reflect on how these are brought to life through *daily experience*. They were instructed to adopt a similar approach towards their research as that mapped out in *The Sociological Imagination* by C. Wright Mills (1959). Mills offers really practical advice to those *learning to research* on how they might go about *research, in order to learn*. He stresses the importance of conversations *"in which experienced thinkers exchange information about their actual ways of working"* (Mills, 1959). This becomes even more important when, for the final dissertation, students are often collecting primary data. All too frequently they rush to gather this information without adequately planning how to analyse their data within a framework where they can defend their epistemological stance and related methodology with supporting literature. What they require are clear examples of how others have done this and at an early stage to practically understand and apply different methods. In the curriculum we tend to teach students in first year the epistemological implications of knowledge. We explain the different paradigms through which inquiry might be approached and we examine related attitudes towards the key categories of experience, reasoning and research. Then we seem to rarely refer again to this important topic that literally affects *all* that we do.

Enriching research through our daily lives, past, present and future

Describing in detail his own "craft" Mills suggests students should not disassociate their work from their lives, but rather let each enrich the other (Mills, 1959). In working towards perfection of their craft, students can realise their own potentialities and opportunities, constructing their own qualities of good workmanship. It is this acknowledgement of self and personal understanding of what we believe knowledge to be that undergraduates can often overlook in their research. For example, the decision to indelibly mark the skin with ink is both individual, but also cultural. The meaning associated with acquiring a tattoo has deep and diverse interpretations that also vary across time. Mills suggests that the past plays into and affects our present and defines our capacity for future experience (Mills, 1959). This is an idea I develop later, in relation to the three concepts described by Currie (2007). So much of what we require from students is focused in the "here and now", but we need to help them connect this with the "past and future" – and in a very personal, non-linear way, if they are to become accomplished in the intellectual craft of living research. Students' comments on what they liked about the temporal and experiential aspects of *Tattoos, TV and Trends* included:

- "*links between history and modern day*"
- "*incorporates and builds on previous academic knowledge gained in 1st and 2nd year*"
- "*new applications of classic theory, eg Weber – film etc. Also scope to design our research question/topic. And abstract – good idea*"
- "*the topics have been interesting and have been backed up with contemporary examples to aid the understanding of the ideas. It is interactive and it's great to hear other examples from the class – something that Sarah encourages very well*"

This last comment emphasises the importance of the "conversations" Mills describes, where thinkers interact to exchange information about their perceptions and ways of working. As the last student comment points out, I did encourage this! However, as voiced by another student below, getting a mixed balance of class participation and lecturer explanation is necessary:

- "*concepts need to be explained more thoroughly, less class participation in lecture*"

Yet, as often is the case when considering student feedback, there are conflicting comments and some readers will smile to see that a different student added:

- "*lecture is quite slow paced. I think we could look at more contemporary examples than the ones we look at in class and engage in further discussion*"

Despite some differing opinions on the amount of class participation that should be involved, having students voice their understanding about, for example, how they might research the semiotics of tattoos, in relation to theory from Ferdinand de Saussure (1916), was enlightening. Many students were unaware of just how long a history might be traced back in the art of tattooing.

Mills discusses the collection of ideas and notes on different topics that a researcher works with as an on-going filing system. As students re-arrange such records, Mills (1959) advises them that they will often find themselves loosening their imagination. This link between the practical storing and organising of ideas and the theoretical and conceptual production of knowledge remains relevant despite many new digital ways for researchers to work. Students presented their ideas on their abstracts to me on paper notepads, mobile phones, ipads and laptops. Students can now explore topics across many devices and in countless different media formats, but they are in a sense overloaded by exposure to content. To unleash imaginative thought they may require new tasks to try to make sense of what they are observing. Experimenting with connections across time between new trends in popular culture and original works by classical theorists offers one way to disrupt complacency and trigger imaginative thought. Each student can apply their daily experience of popular culture to consider what it tells them about the past, the present and indeed the future, in terms of their research. Student comments endorsed the inclusion of video and audio clips in class of, for example: hip hop music, reality TV shows, soap operas and movies. When asked what they liked comments included:

- *"the variety of topics – new concepts and put across in an effective way"*
- *"the content"*
- *"the different topics"*
- *"the content was very interesting"*
- *"the topics are varied and theories applied to make them academic"*
- *"references to modern examples that we can easily relate to"*
- *"thank you so much for a great module. It really has been fascinating and I have really enjoyed your teaching style and the resources you have used"*

What the students "crafted" in terms of their essays was equally fascinating. I enjoyed marking some diverse combinations of classical theorists and examples in popular culture. These included a critique of the popularity of crime thrillers, a study of *One Direction* and a critique of how religion is presented through the media, each of these topics examined through the lens of Durkheim. Other essays explored dating websites, Disney princesses, premier league footballers and the approach of *Nike* to employment in developing nations, these were scrutinised through Marxist theory. The thought and ideas of Weber were applied by other students to the topic of degradation of women in hip-hop music, and theory from Simmel was used to discuss pop music, fashion and theories about the body.

Theories of "time" and curriculum design in higher education

So, having described (in terms of practice) how I sought to enhance undergraduate applications of classical Sociological theory to examples in popular culture, across time on *Tattoos, TV and Trends*, I will now explore some more general thoughts about time and curriculum design. Whilst the notion of how students (and indeed staff) perceive time may not be the first principle lecturers consider in the design of their programmes and modules, it is an important one, given our widespread modular system and the links we are expecting students to make for themselves in a knowledge-based economy. How a curriculum is organised practically and which stakeholders are consulted in its design underpins many of the issues, or successes, that students ultimately experience. In an age where "the student experience" has been brought under the spotlight it is worth examining what leads to superficial, rather than deeper learning engagements. By way of defining curriculum design I mean the activities involved in organising and sequencing elements of instruction, such as objectives, classes, tasks, assessments, into a flow of learning to facilitate student performance. It is, I believe, worth considering how time is understood and applied, both theoretically, as well as practically, by teams designing curricula.

A practical use of time in designing curricula

When allocating time to courses across a programme of study, in our modular system in universities, it is necessary to consider the amount of "credit" that will be allowed for each module, as students build their study towards a whole degree. This credit value determines how long a module will run for and how much time will be spent by students studying it. The lengths of classes, activities and assessments are also allocated specific time periods. In efforts to improve what is now commonly referred to as "the student experience", the number of hours for tutorials outside of class may also be specified. In planning the whole programme, it is helpful to refer to the theory of *constructive alignment* (Biggs, 2003), which is an approach to curriculum design aimed at optimising the conditions of quality learning, by focusing on what the student does, rather than what the teacher does, and helping students to understand how their learning outcomes on a module align to their module assessment. These are important practical considerations to build clear frameworks students can relate to. However, in creating such clearly defined time slots, does this also give students the impression they need do no more? How might we also within programme teams encourage students to imaginatively *live* research as an on-going scholarly project, and not a time-limited exercise?

A theoretical understanding of time in planning a curriculum

Dicussing some more theoretical considerations of how time is perceived by both staff and students across a programme of study could also be a part of a curriculum design dialogue. I say this because there have been global changes in modern society in recent decades that might be incorporated into new theories about curriculum design, as well as new practices. If as humans (with the aid of modern technologies) we are constantly in a form of simultaneity, where we move back and forth across time and spaces, then what we discover in the present might also change what was once conceptualised rather differently in the past. Equally, we might draw in new insights from historical theories to better explain what we experience now. In planning new taught programmes, or in redesigning older ones, there are opportunities to look ahead and also to reflect on how learning has been organised in the past. If our students now have new practices then we may review how face-to-face or online time is managed. Are there ways to invite students to also think more reflexively about what time, in past and future theory, might mean to them within the subject they are studying? In a knowledge-based economy, perceptions of time and how a curriculum is taught and assessed can run the risk of remaining within an economically-focused linear approach. Yet modern technological developments (in for example medicine, transport and online communications) have led to expectations of people living longer, moving ever more quickly and now able to communicate differently across time and space. There are reasons to take stock of these developments in relation to how we imaginatively and reflexively explore the treatment of time in planning curricula and developing student research skills.

Conclusion

In this chapter I explained firstly the problem of a "marketised" approach in neo-liberal universities, where students are discussed as consumers purchasing a product, rather than benefitting from the transformative potential university education offers for the whole of life. Mills (1959) shifts the focus from education as a product students buy to explaining to students the importance of their own personal endeavour in *learning to research*. As staff, by *researching to learn*, we can draw on theory from Currie to innovate in designing a curriculum that that is not simply chronological and fragmented. In Figure 2, the experience of the academic who is teaching is reflexively drawn from links to historical and prior life, as well as personal and professional development anticipated. I explained my own *research-led* approach in designing the idea of *living* research into my module. This helps students understand scholarly research as a choice of how to *live* and incorporate their own identity into the research-writing process (see Benzie, this volume). In a knowledge-based economy, we tend to confine learning experiences within weekly folders, ordered neatly across terms and years, inviting disconnected thought. I sought to disrupt this problem and to design both *research-oriented teaching* to encourage students to question rigid approaches towards theory and time and *research-based teaching*, where my students were able to undertake inquiry-based activities and negotiate their final assessment. Lastly, I extended an invitation to others to share their ideas on time and how, within an aligned curriculum, we might optimise the conditions of quality learning for students. The educational journeys of students *learning to research* are enriched by both practical advice on how to manage time and also opportunities to map their own individual life experiences to what is being learned across time, as shown in Figure 1. Techniques that encourage students to imagine ways their current experience informs on the past, as well as the future, can liberate thought.

In a final anecdote, I was recently tattooed myself for the first time. The decision was informed by theory from the topic I taught, but this was also a conscious individual act that has altered some of my own ideas about the theories I have read. Were I to teach my module now, I might discuss how this experience has changed my own reading of de Saussure (1916) on semiotics. If the self is understood as a *"reflexive project"* (Giddens, 1991:75-77) then how we approach our research across time is ever-changing. So this is simply a call for others, not to feel they need to have a tattoo, but to simply pick up this discussion and see where it may take us if we apply these ideas to curriculum design. It took me on a journey with students that examined what classical Sociological theory might say to develop our understanding of popular culture about tattoos, reality TV, hip hop music and other topics of their choice with students researching and explaining both the insights and limitations of theories from more than a century ago could provide. Technology has in a sense enabled us to "converse" simultaneously with both the past as a drama, and future acts that may undo what has gone before. We can use these ideas when *researching to learn*. With such knowledge, we might then wonder at why we would write programmes for those who are *learning to research*, as if ordered processes ever take place in linear, chronological patterns of time.

About the author

Dr. Sarah Hayes is a Lecturer in Technology-Enhanced and Flexible Learning in the Centre for Learning Innovation and Professional Practice at Aston University, Birmingham, England. She can be contacted at this email: s.hayes@aston.ac.uk

Bibliography

Adorno, T. W. & M. Horkheimer (1944). *Dialectic of Enlightenment*. New York: Seabury.

Barron, L. (2013). *Social Theory in Popular Culture*. London: Palgrave Macmillan.

Biggs, J. B. (2003). *Teaching for Quality Learning at University*. Buckingham: The Open University Press.

BIS (2011). Higher Education: Students at the Heart of the System. London: TSO, June 2011 Cm 8122.

Chapman, D. & A. Ishaq (2013). Beyond the Curriculum: Deepening Reflective Practice and Widening Student Engagement. In C. Nygaard; S. Brand; P. Bartholomew & L. Millard (Eds) *Student Engagement, Identity, Motivation and Community*. Oxfordshire: Libri Publishing Ltd., pp. 235-250.

Currie, M. (2007). *About Time: Narrative, Fiction and the Philosophy of Time*. Edinburgh: Edinburgh University Press.

Derrida, J. (1996). *Archive Fever: A Freudian Impression*. Chicago: University of Chicago Press.

De Saussure, F. (1916). *Nature of the Linguistic Sign*. Course in General Linguistics.

Giddens, A. (1991). *Modernity and Self-Identity: Self and Society in the Late Modern Age*. Cambridge: Polity Press.

Griffiths, R. (2004). Knowledge Production and the Research-Teaching Nexus: The Case of the Built Environment Disciplines, *Studies in Higher Education* Vol 29, No 6, pp. 709-726.

Gill, R. (2009). Breaking the Silence: The Hidden Injuries of Neo-liberal Academia. Secrecy and Silence in the Research Process. *Feminist Reflections*, pp. 228-244.

Gregg, M. (2009). Function Creep: Communication Technologies and Anticipatory Labour in the Information Workplace. *New Media and Society*.

Hayes, S. & P. Bartholomew (2014). Where's the Humanity? Challenging the Policy Discourse of Technology Enhanced Learning. In *Technology Enhanced Learning in Higher Education*. London: Libri Publishing, forthcoming.

Hayes, S. (2015). A Sphere of Resonance for Networked Learning in the 'non-places' of our Universities. *Networked Realms and Hoped-For Futures Special Issue of E-learning and Digital Media*. Oxford: Symposium Journals Ltd.

Healey, M. & A. Jenkins, (2005). *Institutional Strategies to Link Teaching and Research*. York: Higher Education Academy.

Hounsell, D. (2007). Towards More Sustainable Feedback to Students. In D. Boud & N. Falchikov (Eds.) Rethinking Assessment in Higher Education. Learning for the Longer Term. London: Routledge, pp. 101-113.

Jacobson, R. (1998). Teachers Improving Learning using Metacognition with Self Monitoring Learning Strategies. *Education*, Vol.118, No 4, pp. 579-589.

Jarvis, H & A Pratt (2006). Bringing it all Back Home: the Extensification and 'overflowing' of Work, the Case of San Francisco's New Media Households. *Geoforum*, Vol. 37, pp. 331-339.

Jessop, B. (2008). The Knowledge Based Economy. Article Prepared for Naked Punch. Online Resource: http://eprints.lancs.ac.uk/1007/1/ Microsoft_Word_-_I-2008_Naked_Punch.pdf [Accessed 3 January 2015].

Mills, C. W. (1959). *The Sociological Imagination*. London, Oxford and New York: Oxford University Press.

Mezirow, J. (2000). *Learning as Transformation: Critical Perspectives on a Theory in Progress. The Jossey-Bass Higher and Adult Education Series*. San Francisco: Jossey-Bass Publishers.

Molesworth, M; E. Nixon & R. Scullion. (2009). Having, Being and Higher Education: the Marketisation of the University and the Transformation of the Student into Consumer, *Teaching in Higher Education*, Vol. 14, No 3, pp. 277-287.

Negri, T. (1989). *The Politics of Subversion: a manifesto for the 21st Century*. Cambridge, Polity Press.

Rosa, H. (2013). *Social Acceleration: a new theory of modernity*. New York: Columbia University Press.

Thrift, N. (2000) Performing cultures in the new economy. *Annals of the asssociation of American Geographers*, Vol. 90, pp. 674-692

Todd, M.; P. Bannister & S. Clegg (2004). Independent Inquiry and the Undergraduate Dissertation: Perceptions and Experiences of Final-Year Social Science Students. *Assessment & Evaluation in Higher Education* Vol. 29, No 3, pp.335–355.

Willcoxson, L.; J. Cotter & S. Joy (2011). Beyond the First-year Experience: The Impact on Attrition of Student Experiences throughout Undergraduate Degree Studies in Six Diverse Universities. *Studies in Higher Education* Vol. 36, No 3, pp. 331–352.

Chapter Eight

Developing Deeper Learning in Adult Learners: A Research-oriented Curriculum in Leadership for School-Family and Community Engagement

Lana Y.L. Khong

Introduction

This chapter contributes to the anthology by offering some further insights into the effectiveness of using a research-based curriculum design to facilitate deeper learning among adult learners in the field of educational management and leadership in Singapore. Benefits to learners of an active learning approach accrued in integrating theoretical knowledge, instructor input and peer discourse that together supported a practical research-based experience outside the classroom. Participants collaboratively designed and conducted a single case study interview, then presented and assessed the range of evidence offered by each research team. A research-based instructional approach in higher education, carefully designed and executed, can effectively support subjective meaning-making and thus, deeper learning. Marton and Säljö (1976) made a distinction between those who took an *understanding* approach to learning, as opposed to those who took a *reproduction* approach to learning. This chapter advocates the former approach as the author is convinced that learners who can be led beyond a surface level of learning (for instance, gained through memorisation of information) to engage in an active search for meaning can then be empowered to discover and imagine alternative possibilities for their own work and practice. They would be enabled to expand, and perhaps even transform, prior assumptions and initial frames of reference that may have limited their earlier understandings of the field. Reading the chapter, you will:

1. understand that learning to research coupled with researching to learn can assist the development of deeper, more reflective, structures of learning that may better support learners in twenty-first century higher education;

2. be offered an example of a curriculum design for more actively and deeply engaging adults in learning together with a professional community with peers; and

3. see that an active research-oriented approach that directly interrogates real-world challenges can develop or strengthen higher-order learning competencies such as reflective and autonomous thinking for problem-solving in a knowledge society.

This chapter discusses the learning design of a 13-week Masters of Arts in Educational Management module (course) offered by the author. At the time of initial writing of this chapter, the course was still in the design phase and by the end of the writing process, it had completed the full cycle of implementation. As a result, this chapter now includes additional insights derived from the benefit of hindsight as well as directly from student feedback and reflection at the end of the course. The research-based approach in this chapter includes both themes of this anthology, but focuses more on the second half, that is, *researching to learn*. Transformative learning of skills, dispositions and understandings is said to comprise the essence of adult learning (Mezirow, 1991); thus, this chapter also describes the learning of skills, specifically research skills, in order to allow learners direct access to the field of interest. Participants were equipped with basic investigative tools adequate for them to conduct a single case study to interrogate one school leader about his or her beliefs and practices in school-family and school-community engagement. Bartholomew (this volume) discusses the finer distinctions of case study research in much detail, and I agree with his argument that the process of case study research includes the development of thinking beginning from rich narrative accounts of *lived experience* (ie., perceived realities) moving towards higher (or deeper) levels of understanding as sense-making occurs. In addition, the case study research undertaken here is a collective effort, based on single cases produced by thirty participants who were divided into ten separate research teams. This had the potential of leading to shared meaning-making and therefore, more accurate understandings of the field on the part of the novice researchers. The curriculum design discussed in the chapter is also framed by the related ideas of constructive alignment, community-based discourse and the importance of critical reflection, which will be discussed in turn.

Rethinking Teaching in Higher Education

As a teacher in higher education, I am committed to creating student-centred learning spaces based on a conception of self-directed meaning-making. This requires me to make a deliberate shift from a passive model of learning where an instructor would merely provide and transmit information on prescribed content to a more active learning model where my students are given real opportunities to take on the responsibility of negotiating values and meaning for themselves, and thus learn at a deeper level. I personally believe that such an approach would better suit mature learners who are fueling the current expansion of the higher education sector globally. Not only do such learners often bring a rich stock of practitioner knowledge and prior experience to the classroom but also, as I have observed, possess a stronger commitment and drive to master learning material than younger students.

The research literature into learning and teaching in higher education provides relevant information about how these students approach studying, their conceptions of learning, and their perceptions of the academic context. Marton (1976) had earlier concluded that students who adopted a deep approach are more actively engaged in learning for themselves, while those who adopted a passive surface approach tended to see learning as something that *just happens* to them. In reviewing this large body of work, Richardson (2005:674) proposed that an important aspect of students' perception of effective instruction by teachers in higher education is an *"emphasis on independence"* and also that students taught using a problem-based learning approach were more likely to adopt a deep approach to learning. As mentioned earlier, this is qualitatively different from an instrumental surface approach that may be based on routine memorising and reproducing course materials in order to pass the exams. Learning environments are also linked to important issues such as the process of learning, transferability of learning, and competent performance which are in turn influenced by degrees of student-centredness, knowledge-centredness, assessment-centredness and community-centredness in the classroom.

According to research on learning (Bransford *et al.*, 2001), learners use prior knowledge to increase understanding and construct new knowledge. This is activated when learners are required to think and apply what they know in order to solve problems. Assessment based on formative feedback over the course of time also provides learners with opportunities to revise and improve their thinking and understanding, especially when this is done in a community of learners that value interaction, feedback and learning. In rethinking teaching in higher education then, while designing and developing appropriate courses to teach, an important question that university teachers need to address is: *how best to balance expert (or subject) and practitioner knowledge in a curriculum that can add value to the longer-term learning needs of adult learners.*

The Value of Researching to Learn

Scholars like Schön (1987) and Boyer (1990) have long advocated a scholarship of teaching that shifts from a traditional transmission model of university teaching to one that includes, respectively, a "reflective practicum" as well as one that engages and fosters active student learning. Specifically, a reflective practicum must be *"learned by doing"* (Schön, 1987:311), an idea quite similar to that later suggested by Tinkler *et al.* (1996) of *experiential praxis*. This means that a key challenge for an instructional leader in higher education lies in effectively facilitating a transformative learning environment that leverages on active learning processes to move learners beyond merely assimilating or accumulating declarative knowledge. *Researching to learn* thus performs an important function in raising the quality of student learning, as this is inextricably entwined in the very nature of *doing research.*

Doing research is an effective practice through which learners are given the opportunity to find empirical evidence for (or against) pre-existing beliefs and assumptions, as well as to interrogate the theoretical concepts they learn in the classroom through direct instruction and through reading the research literature. This implies that the experience and practice of research can actually lead to higher-quality and higher-order learning outcomes for students who are thus engaged (Kuh, 2001; Kuh *et al.*, 2007). In this way, students' learning is doubly informed – theoretically and evidentially – resulting in a more robust understanding and a stronger personal ownership of what they learn, with the potential of eventually transforming their own perspectives and workplace practices. Mezirow (1990, 1997) further insists that the quality of adult learning be judged by how well the instructor selects appropriate practices to help learners transform their existing frames of reference through critical reflection on their assumptions, *"validating contested beliefs... taking action on one's reflective insight, and critically assessing it"* (1990:11). In contrast, he also declares that transformation in learning is unlikely to occur as long as the material fits comfortably in learners' existing frames of reference.

In addition, Wenger (1998) has highlighted the importance of community-based engagement in the learning process where there are opportunities for individual and mutual engagement around a shared enterprise (such as a research-based project), founded on a respect for the particularity of experience and insight. This necessarily requires an integration of teaching and research, – where learning, meaning and learner identity can occur. An approach that encourages active learner engagement with the material, namely, reading and reflexively critiquing the literature, having conversations with other learners and school leaders in actual field research situations was thus also deemed to be essential in my curriculum and pedagogy. This approach fostered a stronger likelihood of higher quality learning outcomes, especially for adult learners who already have a large stock of prior knowledge, work and life experiences that often act as filters to what they can effectively learn. The research cited earlier further supports the notion that student motivation is related to opportunities for autonomy and appropriate choice because these allow learners to feel that they have ownership over their own learning. This in turn creates a natural desire to want to learn and a persistence to pursue the learning tasks given to them (Bransford *et al.*, 2001; Deci and Ryan, 2002; McCombs, n.d.).

Table 1 below summarises some clear differences in process and outcomes between the teacher-centred, transmissive, disseminative model of teaching and student-focused, research-oriented, community-based teaching. As indicated, conceptual change in students' perspectives is more likely in the latter approach, as is more durable learning. In many higher education disciplines today, including educational management, learners require vital competencies to help them effectively acquire authentic knowledge and manage people in a wide range of increasingly complex workplaces. These include acquiring, interpreting, analysing and using information, identifying and managing resources to solve problems, working with others, communicating ideas, and understanding a diversity of social and cultural relationships for making socially responsible decisions. As such, it is still necessary, yet certainly not sufficient, to teach in ways that input or transmit theoretical, abstract, or, as Nygaard and Andersen (2004) have termed it, "*decontextual*" knowledge to learners. Rather, learners need to also have the experience of actually constructing and producing meaningful, context-based knowledge for themselves. This meaning-making process necessitates engaging them in critical reflection of their own frames of reference, higher-order thinking (including the validation of what is considered to be of value), collaborative modes of learning, analysis and synthesis of information in real-world contexts, and communication skills in giving voice to what they have learned in discourse with others. This daunting range of skills that learners in higher education today need to master can usefully be developed in a well-structured research-oriented academic curriculum.

Stages of Learning	Surface Learning	Deeper Learning
Content is…	Declarative, theoretical	Constructive, meaningful
	Expert knowledge – "what is known?"	Expert + practitioner knowledge – "how to come to know?"
	Decontextualised, isolated facts	Contextualised, evidence-based
	For "reproduction" and rote application	For "'understanding" and application to real-world problems
Pedagogy is…	Teacher-focused, little choice	Student-focused, choices given
	Unilateral, transmissive "lecture"	Reflexive, interactive, discursive
	Individual-based learning	Individual + community-based learning
Outcomes are…	Conceptual change unlikely	Conceptual change likely
	Short-term learning	Longer-term Learning

Table 1a: Curriculum design for surface vs deeper learning in higher education – content, pedagogy, outcomes.

Learning about Leadership and School Engagement

In designing a course to encourage deeper learning among my class of mature Masters-level students, I considered the many benefits of getting them to acquire and apply basic research skills that would empower them to engage in hands-on investigation of a single case of one school leader in Singapore. This had the overall objective of helping the students become more active learners, reflective and autonomous thinkers and practitioners within a professional field of interest. With clear course objectives and instructional modes coherently and constructively aligned, participants would be facilitated to explore how school leaders engage their communities (including parents of their students) in order to strengthen the academic learning and holistic well-being of children and youth. In explaining his notion of constructive alignment, Biggs (2003) pointed out that the *constructive* aspect refers to what learners do in constructing meaning for themselves, while the *alignment* aspect refers to what instructors do in setting up environments to support the appropriate learning activities for achieving desired learning outcomes, especially with reference to teaching methods and assessment tasks. In part, my course synopsis stated that *"the course will require participants to exercise basic research skills in discovering for themselves the centrality of leadership in prioritising and managing school-stakeholder collaboration..."*. The research-oriented approach was designed to facilitate students in collectively learning how leaders grapple with real-life challenges of stakeholder engagement and partnership work. Selecting the specific sample and site, learning to craft meaningful research questions, and actively conducting data-collection and data analysis would thus enable adult learners to learn at a deeper level.

In his work with classroom teachers, Entwistle (2000:1) emphasised the need to *"transform the knowledge base relevant to learning into effective and efficient teaching...practices"*. Furthermore, Trowler (2010:48) pointed out that *"data informs and refines theory, theory shapes the interpretation of data; concepts are crystallised out of that interaction and themselves are applied to the situation on the ground"*. This circularity of understanding and application, similar to Laurillard's (2002) "conversational framework", could then pave the way for deeper learning to further help students to reconsider (or even challenge) their current understandings and prior assumptions acquired earlier. As all of my students were either educators or management-level staff in related professions, this learning would potentially enhance their future applications of an expanded stock of experiential knowledge.

Three Stages of Conceptual and Contextual Learning

In this research-oriented view to curriculum design, I naturally had some concerns about standards, ethical considerations, and coverage of the curriculum which also had to be designed and managed. In its final version (*Figure 1* below), the 13-week (39 hours) Masters-level course/module progressed in three more or less distinct, yet overlapping and iterative, stages of understanding, both enabling and enabled by a *researching to learn* approach.

There was an initial *conceptualising* of school-family-community engagement as the first key element of the module. Course objectives were clearly stated and the conceptual frame and schedule drawn out. This foundational segment of the course guided students to relevant readings as well as initial self-reflection to provide them an early conceptual entry point into the field of school leadership and stakeholder engagement. This included the introduction of conceptual frameworks of leadership for family and community engagement as the initial stimulus for active class discussion, and the unpacking of prior assumptions. At the end of this stage, assessment of student learning was carried out in class in order to gauge how effectively students had learned the material. Feedback tools used included asking learners to collectively create concept maps that made visible the underlying thinking that learners had about connections among key concepts; another one was posing a hypothetical problem that required brainstorming and application of the concepts in order to solve it. Instructor input and adaptations of the learning environment were then made in areas where student learning was still 'muddy'.

The second stage of the course was the *contextualisation* of school-family-community engagement through an expanded critical literature review of community partnership efforts in local and international educational and cultural contexts. Interestingly, McDermott (1999:15) defined context as *"an order of behaviour of which one is part"*, emphasising the social and relational (that is, cultural) processes of learning that complement the structural elements of learning. In this light, pair and group discussions on the topic, including first-person experiences and examples, made the reading and review of literature a relevant learning activity. Students also had in-class opportunities to listen to excerpts of an actual interview I had conducted with a school leader, as well as role-play and reflect on steps to establish rapport so as to encourage more candid conversations. This modelling helped not only to familiarise the students with an actual research conversation, but also had the added benefit of them perceiving me not just as the 'expert' but also as a co-learner/practitioner.

When the conceptual grounding was more or less firmly laid, students were deemed ready for the third stage, namely, to be introduced to learning and then, putting into practice basic research skills related to case study research. Stake (1995:xi) defined case study as *"the study of the particularity and complexity of a single case, coming to understand its activity within important circumstances"*. Specifically, students were facilitated to design and conduct semi-structured interviews that explored and allowed inter-pretation of unique examples of *"real people in real situations"* (Cohen *et al.*, 2007:253). Yin (2009:18) defined a case study as *"an empirical inquiry that investigates a contemporary phenomenon within its real-life context"*. Hitch-cock and Hughes (1995) clearly delineated a case study as including the following characteristics:

1. the focus is on individual actors within a drawn geographical, organisational and temporal boundary (for example, a school or community) and their perceptions of, and thoughts and feelings about events;

2. specific events that are relevant to the case are highlighted and blended with a detailed description of events with analysis based on systematically collected subjective and objective data;

3. the richness of the case is portrayed in the research report by allowing the events and situations to "speak for themselves".

Learners were given the autonomy to select the research sites and sample participants purposively in order to gain rich information about the central phenomenon of stakeholder engagement in schools with fami-lies and the wider community. Informants were drawn from all four school zones in Singapore, covering a variety of levels and types of school (namely, primary, secondary, mainstream government, independent, single-gender, co-educational). In most cases, participants' own social and educational networks were successful sources for finding a school leader who was willing to be interviewed for the limited purposes of the class. For students who had no contacts within the education arena, I activated my own network of school leaders as an available source of interviewees. Ten research teams comprising between two to five students were formed and encouraged to collaboratively create, review and critique sets of inter-view questions addressing three key research questions as part of their preparation for actual fieldwork. Guidelines for research ethics and other research procedures were given here, including the need to be reflective in identifying self-beliefs and assumptions about school leadership roles. Interview questions were finalised after groups took turns to practise role-playing the interview with one another and giving peer feedback on the questions in terms of clarity and appropriateness. In addition, a guest speaker, an experienced school leader with deep practical knowledge in the area of stakeholder partnerships, was invited into the classroom around this time to reinforce the practitioner element of managing the processes and challenges of family and community engagement practices. This not only sparked off much discourse and self-reflection on the part of learners in further unpacking their conceptions of engagement and partnership in the local schooling context but also provided an authentic context for them to ask some of their prepared interview questions. In this meaningful conversation, they were encouraged to reflect not only on their understandings from readings of the international research literature but also on their own beliefs, lived experiences as past students or current teachers (and present parents for some), as well as habitual patterns of assumptions and expectations. These subjective perspectives, which adult learners bring along in abundance to class, provide the natural filters by which people interpret what they learn through selectively organising and delimiting what they perceive and are thus *enabled* to learn. The uncovering of these underlying assumptions and embedded values through an iterative dialogue based on critical reading and interactions with peers and expert practitioners further engaged learners in scrutinising their own habits of mind and the existing mental models influencing their meaning-making of schools' policies and school engagement practices.

Having students work in small teams, instead of individually, certainly generated many benefits of collaborative learning while also providing a vital element of mutual support within a new, possibly risky, learning experience. The learning process at this stage helped them gain an awareness of the ethics of planning and implementing research, addressing considerations such as gaining access to the research settings and positioning themselves to respondents as researchers, collaborating on the research protocols, and understanding a researcher's responsibility to the research community such as maintaining confidentiality.

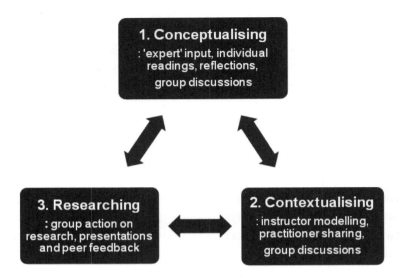

Figure 1: Stages of Understanding with Researching to Learn.

In terms of course assessment, it is clear that assessment requirements have much influence on student learning in higher education. In a well-aligned research-based curriculum designed for deeper learning, the instructor is also faced with significant challenges in rethinking the role of assessment, such as how to balance formative/process and summative/product requirements, or put simply, assessment *for* and *of* learning respectively. Table 1b below shows the broad differences and directions of assessment that drive surface and deep learning. I attempted to use the course assessment as a formative tool for deeper learning and engaged participants actively in peer assessment as well as using feedback to strengthen their own knowledge and skills. Indeed, a global review of assessment research by the OECD (2005) showed that substantial gains were effected through the use of formative assessment procedures, which furthermore, is one of the most effective strategies for developing skills for *learning to learn*. As such, assessment components in my course were integrated into the learning process, where students were able to cumulatively build upon previous work done instead of having to work on separately-assessed disparate pieces of work. This was deemed a better fit with the constructivist, contextualised and qualitative paradigm of learning that I espoused (Segers *et al.*, 2003).

Overall, each component was aligned and embedded, helping students to *do more with less* and be rewarded by a gradual holistic growth in personal understandings over the duration of the module. A research-based course design that strategically employs meaningful assessment components of self-reflection, class participation, collaborative work, and oral presentation, can help foster cognitive capital and practical knowledge to help learners leverage on their learning and transform their appreciation and understanding of complex environments beyond the university classroom. Both formative and summative modes of assessment are therefore integral to the deep learning cycle. This implies an acceptance that learners will attain different levels of understanding and qualitatively different learning outcomes. Biggs and Collis' (1982) SOLO (Structure of the Observed Learning Outcome) taxonomy ranging from 'prestructural' to 'extended abstract' levels offered me useful guidelines for course assessment in terms of five levels of understanding, as did Wiggins and McTighe's (2005) six *facets of understanding* encompassing various levels and degrees of explanation, interpretation, application, perspective, empathy, and self-knowledge.

Assessment is...	Surface learning:	Deeper learning:
	Based on superficial coverage of unconnected facts.	Based on depth and synthesis of ideas.
	Decontextualised, isolated and atomistic.	Contextualised, use of skills in context.
	Focused on "one right answer".	Focused on "many right answers".
	Solely teacher's responsibility.	Shared responsibility of students.

Table 1b: Curriculum design for surface vs deeper learning in higher education – assessment.

Thus, assessment comprised the following three main components: individual class work, group case study (including an individual reflection essay), and a group case study presentation. These included active class participation, group discussions, individual reflective writing on the process and product of the case study research, as well as an intensive process of case presentations of leadership practices conducted (and evaluated) by everyone in the respective research teams to arrive at new meaning-making of the overall evidence. Assessment being thus embedded into the process of teaching and learning enabled the learners to refine, elaborate on, and differentiate new ways of thinking from their own prior assumptions and understandings, as was voiced by several students in the final reflections, which will be shared in the final section of this chapter. Peer evaluation of the case studies looked mainly at content such as *identification of main issues and challenges, analysis of issues and challenges, analysis of leadership effectiveness, and overall findings about stakeholder engagement*. Final instructor evaluation of student learning was based on the four broad criteria of *relevance, authenticity, meaning-making and meaningfulness*, and *applicability of ideas*. These were elicited through guiding questions requiring students to reflect deeply on, and construct meaning from, their personal experience of the overall research process and product.

In summary, this relatively short module for mature students (who were also novice researchers) utilised qualitative research of single-case studies of the descriptive *snapshot* type (Merriam, 1988) to generate deeper learning of a specific aspect of educational leadership and management. The intention was not to generalise the findings but rather, to develop deeper understandings on the part of the learners. Each case study produced deeper understanding of a particular school leader's beliefs about engagement and partnership work and how those beliefs shaped school leader's actions. At the initial design stage, I envisaged that each of these snapshots would usefully contribute a unique illustration to the emergent collective account of how school leaders in Singapore responded to the policy call to engage stakeholders for bolstering the learning and developmental needs of students. Each case study was expected to contribute an interesting piece to the (w)holistic yet more complex puzzle of the issues faced by leaders, providing micro-scale, on-the-ground evidence of the effects of macro government policy on specific individuals and schools. In the process of researching this issue, learners would experience opportunities to develop higher-order thinking skills such as reflection, comparison and evaluation. Indeed, reflection was a strong underlying theme and thread of the course and the next section briefly examines its contribution to both my students' and my own learning.

Reflection for Meaning-Making in Learning

Boud *et al.* (1985:3) broadly defined reflection as *"a generic term for those intellectual and affective activities in which individuals engage to explore their experiences in order to lead to new understandings and appreciation"*. Mezirow (1990) asserts however, that reflection requires not just assessing the *whats* and *hows* of such experiences but also involves a critical assessment of the *whys*, that is, one's assumptions and presuppositions, and the justifications of what one believes. This he terms *critical* reflection. The impact that research can have on the transformation of one's knowledge base thus depends on the process and findings provoking critical reflection on practice and generating new ideas for useful changes made to improve the current situation, perhaps similar to what Entwistle (1994) terms *pedagogical fertility*. Research, by definition, involves problem-solving of all kinds and critical reflection addresses the presuppositions and patterned habits of thinking on which we pose these problems. These may threaten or disorientate the meanings learners have hitherto drawn from their experiences, but if there is openness to new meanings based on the gathering of evidence in the situations investigated, there can be a shift in personal learning, or even a transformation of earlier cognitive and affective perspectives, to reorient learners' understandings of the problem.

The personal research encounter with school leaders thus engaged my learners in ways of understanding "reality" and in turn, may have redirected them in the ways they subsequently take action in their world. In reflectively assessing their own perspectives of the research process and learning conversations, students were given many opportunities to step back to consider, individually and collectively, the reasons for, and consequences of, leadership decision-making and action. In this way, there was some realisation of how prior beliefs and assumptions (or perhaps, merely limited experiences) may have constrained understandings of leadership work. The research experience motivated learners to understand better the meaning of this work, helping them to be more open to a broader range of perspectives (notably those of leaders, but also other stakeholders such as parents and community members), as well as to apply these insights to different work contexts. To better integrate their experiences and refine their thinking around effective (educational) interventions, ongoing peer discourse and discussions within a professional community of learners were invaluable. The classroom and the discourses therein provided a safe space for newfound collective insights to emerge.

As Student A reflected, *"before I took this course, I was a skeptic based on my own work experiences... I couldn't see how partnerships with parents would ever work out. After the course, I've gained fresh insights into partnerships... now I recognise that all schools are at a different stage, there needs to be a suitable starting point for my school, and growth will take time. After hearing from Mdm S's sharing in class and after the interview with Mr. B, my conviction has been renewed".*

Student B also realised that *"in this learning journey, I have learned a lot about leadership and partnership. My initial shallow understanding has deepened as I learned about leadership styles and acquired new knowledge about authentic engagement. My perspectives have also widened through my reading of articles locally and internationally. The initial phase of the module not only deepened my knowledge but also equipped me with skills to approach and conduct my interview as I went through a trial with my peers. The interview with the principal was one of the main highlights of the whole module because it helped me to relate and have the opportunity to practice what I learned."*

As the course instructor, the student-centred approach I took required me (to some extent) to gradually release some control of the traditionally powerful role of the expert *sage on the stage* and take on more of the facilitator-provocateur *guide on the side*, or even, a *meddler in the middle* role, as McWilliams (2009) advocates. This is somewhat similar to the "control wedge model" discussed in Warner and Enomoto's chapter (this volume). Student learning was scaffolded and progressively enhanced as they moved through their initial perception of me as firstly, an "expert" and then, as a co-learner who was also currently actively engaged in research into this area. This was facilitated through the use of teaching material drawn from my own published work as well as excerpts from my own research as examples. The learners were progressively led to collectively explore essential issues I was able to highlight first-hand from my own research work, and enabled the growing together into a professional community of learners to support and expand their shared understandings of the sometimes-entangled partnership problems faced by school leaders. In the process, students who were leaders in their own right in education and even other fields (such as nursing and the military) were able to draw relevant lessons they said they would apply to their own workplace. Many pointed to the value of *"hearing it directly"* from, and understanding the subjective perceptions of, leaders themselves. The development of a shared enthusiasm in investigating and thinking about related issues enriched student-instructor interactions in the classroom setting, as well as peer interactions, another aspect that is positively related to student learning gains for those in higher education and, in turn, found to be an essential component of strong adult learning environments.

Conclusion

Researching to learn can powerfully contribute essential aspects to the development of authentic student "knowing" of a complex world. This chapter therefore hopes to have contributed some insights into how curriculum design for deeper learning can foster better *knowing and understanding* among adult learners at higher levels of education. In embracing the opportunity for active hands-on research activities, students stand to gain on several learning fronts: developing more in-depth (as opposed to naive) explanations and interpretations of their world, developing more thorough critical perspectives of current knowledge and school practises, growing in empathy for others, communicating ideas, and co-constructing knowledge they can apply to the management of real-world problems. A research-oriented approach thus seeks to fruitfully and constructively align student research as an essential component in academic coursework so as to intentionally encourage the development of essential twenty-first century competencies for critical and creative thinking, professional problem-solving, and collaborative learning. Through a coherent set of conceptual and inquiry procedures that comprise effective pedagogical content knowledge, learners in such a course can be provided with multiple supported opportunities to take responsibility for their own learning, clarify and have opportunities to voice their personal perspectives, experience learning not just from the formal instructor, but also from peers who can be seen as collaborators instead of competitors, and to deepen their learning by practising putting new knowledge to work.

About the Author

Lana Khong is a Lecturer in the Policy and Leadership Studies Academic Group at the National Institute of Education, Nanyang Technological University, Singapore. She can be contacted at this email: lana.khong@nie.edu.sg

Bibliography

Biggs, J. B. (2003). *Teaching for Quality Learning at University – What the Student Does.* SRHE / Open University Press, Buckingham.

Biggs, J. B. & K. Collis. (1982). *Evaluating the Quality of Learning: the SOLO Taxonomy.* New York: Academic Press.

Boud, D.; R. Keogh & D. Walker (1985). *Reflection: Turning Experience into Learning.* London: Routledge & Kegan Paul.

Boyer, E. (1990). *Scholarship Reconsidered: Priorities of the Professoriate.* New Jersey: The Carnegie Foundation for the Advancement of Teaching.

Bransford, J. D.; A. L. Brown & R. R. Cocking (2001). *How People Learn: Brain, Mind, Experience, and School.* Committee on Developments in the Science of Learning, Commission on Behavioral and Social Sciences and Education, National Research Council. The National Academies Press.

Cohen, L.; L. Manion & K. Morrison (2007). *Research Methods in Education.* London and New York: Routledge.

Deci, E. L. & R. M. Ryan (2002). Overview of self-determination theory: An organismic dialectical perspective. In E. L. Deci & R. M. Ryan (Eds.), *Handbook of Self-determination Research.* Rochester, NY: University of Rochester Press. pp. 3-33.

Entwistle, N. (1994). Generative concepts and pedagogical fertility: Communicating research findings on student learning. Presidential address to the European Association for Research on Learning and Instruction. *EARLI News,* June, pp. 9-15.

Entwistle, N. (2000). *Promoting deep learning through teaching and assessment: conceptual frameworks and educational contexts.* Paper presented at TLRP Conference, Leicester, November.

Hitchcock, G. & D. Hughes (1995). *Research and the Teacher.* London: Routledge.

Kuh, G. D. (2001). Assessing What Really Matters to Student Learning: Inside the National Survey of Student Engagement. *Change,* Vol. 33, No. 3, pp. 10-17.

Kuh, G. D.; J. Kinzie; J. A. Buckley; B. K. Bridges & J. C. Hayek (2007). Piecing Together the Student Success Puzzle: Research, Propositions, and Recommendations. *ASHE Higher Education Report*, Vol. 32, No. 5. San Francisco: Jossey-Bass.

Laurillard, D. (2002). *Rethinking teaching for the knowledge society.* EDUCAUSE Review, Vol 37, No.1. pp. 6-25.

Marton, F. (1976). What does it take to learn? *Strategies for Research and Development in Higher Education.* Amsterdam: Swets & Zeitlinger, pp. 32-43. Marton F. and Säljö R. (1976) On qualitative differences in learning. *British Journal of Educational Psychology*, Vol. 46, pp. 4-11.

McCombs, B. (n.d). Developing Responsible and Autonomous Learners: A Key to Motivating Students. *American Psychological Association.* Online Resource: http://www.apa.org/education/k12/learners.aspx [Accessed on 3 January 2015].

McDermott, R. P. (1999). On becoming labelled – the story of Adam. In P. Murphy (Ed.) *Learners, Learning and Assessment.* Learning, Curriculum and Assessment Series. London: Paul Champan Publishing Ltd., pp. 1-21.

McWilliam, E. (2009). Teaching for Creativity: from sage to guide to meddler. *Asia Pacific Journal of Education.* Vol. 29, No. 3. September, pp 281-293.

Merriam, S. B. (1988). *Case Study Research in Education.* San Francisco, CA: Jossey-Bass.

Merriam, S. B. (2009). *Qualitative Research: A Guide to Design and Implementation.* San Francisco, CA: Jossey-Bass.

Mezirow, J. (1990). How Critical Reflection Triggers Transformative Learning. In J. Mezirow & Associates. *Fostering Critical Reflection in Adulthood.* San Francisco, CA.: Jossey-Bass, pp. 1-20.

Mezirow, J. (1991). *Transformative Dimensions of Adult Learning.* San Francisco, CA.: Jossey-Bass.

Mezirow, J. (1997). Transformative Learning: Theory to Practice. In *New Directions for Adult and Continuing Education*, No. 74, Summer. Jossey-Bass Publishers.

Nygaard, C. & I. Andersen (2004). Contextual Learning in Higher Education: Curriculum Development with Focus on Student Learning. In R. G. Milter; V. S. Perotti & M. S. R. Segers (Eds.) *Educational Innovation in Economics and Business IX. Breaking Boundaries for Global Learning.* Berlin: Springer. Part 5, Chapter 15.

OECD/CERI, (2005). *Formative Assessment – Improving Learning in Secondary Classrooms.* OECD Publishing

Richardson, J. T. E. (2005). Students' Approaches to Learning and Teachers' Approaches to Teaching in Higher Education. *Educational Psychology*, Vol. 25, No. 6. December, pp. 673-680.

Segers, M.; Dochy, F. & Cascallar, E. (Eds). (2003). *Optimising New Modes of Assessment: In Search of Qualities and Standards*. Dordrecht: Kluwer Academic Publishers.

Stake, R. E. (1995) *The Art of Case Study Research*. California: Sage

Tinkler, D.; B. Lepani & J. Mitchell (1996). *Education and technology convergence*. Commissioned Report No. 43. National Board of Employment Education and Training. Canberra, Australia: Employment and Skills Council. Australian Government Publishing Service.

Trowler, V. (2010). *Student Engagement Literature Review*. The Higher Education Academy.

Umbach, P. D. & M. R. Wawrzynshi (n.d.). *Faculty Do Matter: The Role of College Faculty in Student Learning and Engagement*. Online Resource: http://nsse.iub.edu/pdf/research_papers/faculty_do_matter.pdf [Accessed January 15, 2015].

Wenger, E. (1998). *Communities of Practice: Learning, Meaning, and Identity*. Cambridge: Cambridge University Press.

Wiggins, G., & J. McTighe (2005). *Understanding by Design*. Alexandria, USA: Association for Supervision and Curriculum Development.

Yin, R. K. (2009). *Case Study Research: Design and Methods*. 4th edition. Beverly Hills, CA: Sage.

Chapter Nine

Postgraduate Research Assistantships as Spaces for Researching, Learning, and Teaching

Michelle K. McGinn

Postgraduate Research Assistantships

This chapter contributes to the anthology by exploring postgraduate research assistantships as venues and means for researching to learn and simultaneously for researching to teach. In the current knowledge-intensive environment, academics at institutions around the world are expected to produce research and contribute to the development of subsequent generations of researchers. These expectations may be fulfilled in part through the appointment of Master's or Doctoral students as research assistants (also known as apprentices or interns) who contribute essential labour to produce research under the direction of research supervisors.

Paid and unpaid research assistantships are co-curricular opportunities for postgraduate (Master's or Doctoral) students to engage in research activities that may deepen or extend learning associated with their research-based degree programmes. Typically, postgraduate research assistants are newcomers to research and hence have much to learn about research in order to fulfil their research responsibilities. Postgraduate research assistants learn to research by researching. Simultaneously, research supervisors are positioned to teach research through open or informal means as they engage postgraduate research assistants in their research activities.

Readers of this chapter will:

1. gain an appreciation for synergistic relationships involving researching, learning, and teaching within postgraduate research assistantships;

2. become familiar with various possible forms, content, and outcomes of postgraduate research assistantships; and

3. be encouraged to draw inspiration and potential models for their practice from the cases identified herein.

Theoretical and Conceptual Foundations for this Chapter

Research learning in this chapter is conceptualised in terms of the actions, interactions, and self-perceptions of postgraduate research assistants and their research supervisors. The work is formulated with respect to educational theories that emphasise learning, knowing, doing, and being as inherently intertwined and social functions (Lave & Wenger, 1991; Wenger, 1998, 2000; Packer & Goicoechea, 2000). These theories and the related research show that when students perform the kinds of tasks and engage in the kinds of conversations that practitioners perform, those students can begin to develop identities as practitioners rather than students. In the context of research education, students may conceive of themselves and be treated as senior learners, colleagues-in-training, or junior colleagues (Nyquist & Wulff, 1996) or as students of research, consumers of research, assistant researchers, or researchers (McGinn, 2002), depending upon the depth and breadth of their experiences. Development as a researcher has been characterised in terms of enhanced confidence, greater recognition as a researcher, higher levels of research productivity, or more sophisticated approaches to research (Åkerlind, 2008).

Postgraduate students engaged as research assistants have opportunities to perform the activities of established researchers, including completing research tasks, communicating about research, and contributing to research knowledge. The experiences of postgraduate research assistants emphasise synergistic relationships involving researching, learning, and teaching (see Figure 1). These synergistic relationships are reinforced through consideration of a situated learning perspective that emphasises the impossibility of separating doing research, learning research, and being research workers. As postgraduate research assistants engage in research activities, they learn research and they become research workers. Doing research, talking research, and creating research documents (i.e., tasks, talk, and texts) are all evidence of research learning and research performance, and important bases for perceptions of one's self as a researcher.

Research is not a singular pursuit, but a community practice. Postgraduate research assistants engage alongside established researchers who lead the research projects (i.e., their research supervisors). Sometimes postgraduate research assistants work with other team members. Beyond their individual research projects and teams, postgraduate research assistants are engaged in research that is part of a larger community of scholars and scholarship. Even when an established researcher or a postgraduate research assistant is working independently, research is *very much a social practice, in the sense that the individual investigator acts within a framework determined by the potential consumers of the products of his or her research and by the traditions of acceptable practice prevailing in the field*" (Danziger, 1990:4). Established researchers and postgraduate research assistants contribute to scholarly communities and scholarly conversations through their actions and interactions, and in the ways they present themselves as researchers and the ways they respond to other researchers.

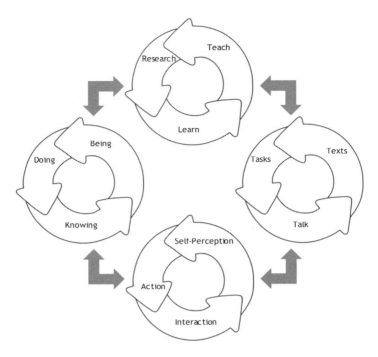

Figure 1: Synergistic relationships involving researching, learning, and teaching within postgraduate research assistantships.

To understand postgraduate research assistantships as spaces for researching, learning, and teaching, it is important to appreciate the individual and collective actions, interactions, and self-perceptions of postgraduate research assistants and their research supervisors. Research activities (including tasks, talk, and texts) provide opportunities to engage in research and to be researchers, which is all part of learning and knowing research. The synergistic relationships involving researching, learning, and teaching that are depicted in Figure 1 provide the backdrop for the following discussion of existing evidence about possible forms, content, and outcomes of postgraduate research assistantships.

Postgraduate Research Assistantships in Action

This chapter draws upon the existing body of empirical research about research learning in postgraduate research assistantships (McWey *et al.*,

2006; Jiao *et al.*, 2011; Grenville & Ciuffetelli Parker, 2013; Maher *et al.*, 2013; McGinn *et al.*, 2013; Moore *et al.*, 2013) and presents evidence from a range of postgraduate research assistantships to demonstrate tasks, conversations, content knowledge, research skills, and senses of identity for postgraduate students engaged as research assistants. Through my programme of research, I have observed and talked with many postgraduate research assistants, their research supervisors, and their team members to understand their practices and perceptions about researching, learning, and teaching. Throughout this chapter, I draw from this data corpus as well as published studies about postgraduate research assistantships.

Research work is highly varied. Different disciplines, projects, and scholars emphasise diverse skills and activities. A sociologist may be engaged in frontline fieldwork as a full participant in a particular community. A historian may be sequestered away in an archive, immersed in rarely-seen documents. A bench scientist may be experimenting with chemical or biological agents in a heavily controlled laboratory setting. A linguist may be travelling the world catching snippets of conversation in uncharted languages and dialects. These examples illustrate that the spaces and means for undertaking research are limitless as scholars engage in disciplinary and idiosyncratic ways with documents, people, and ideas.

Given the considerable diversity in research work, it is evident that the work of postgraduate research assistants must also be varied. For the hypothetical scholars mentioned above, the relevant kinds of assistance are necessarily quite distinct. As research materials and methods vary, so too must the activities of postgraduate research assistants and established researchers. In the context of any project, postgraduate research assistant activities may be small or large, peripheral or central, mundane or engaging, repetitive or singular, cognitively simplistic or demanding, individualistic or collaborative. As a result, the skills, knowledge, and learning potentials associated with the work of postgraduate research assistants varies substantially (Grundy, 2004). In what follows, I consider the ways, tasks, talk, and texts intertwine and influence learning for postgraduate research assistants, including the development of their research selves, and also how they relate to the teaching roles of research supervisors.

Research Tasks

Common research tasks for postgraduate research assistants vary according to discipline, project, and research phase (Grundy, 2004; Niemczyk, 2010; McGinn *et al.*, 2013). Research tasks during early phases of a project might include searching publication databases, reading theoretical or empirical articles, creating annotated bibliographies, or formulating applications or bids for research funding. Later publication and dissemination tasks might include writing sections of research reports, writing research or conference proposals, designing conference posters, presenting at conferences, researching publication outlets, securing copyright permissions for reproductions, communicating with journal editors, or editing papers. Communication tasks at any phase of a project might involve attending research team meetings, maintaining a project website, or nurturing a social media presence. Administrative tasks throughout the life of any project in any discipline might involve photocopying, organising, or filing research materials. Tasks at the heart of empirical research projects might include recording fieldnotes, maintaining research journals, entering data, coding and analysing data, or preparing data displays. In social science disciplines, specific tasks might include preparing applications for human ethics review, recruiting research participants, scheduling research sessions, distributing questionnaires, conducting interviews, or transcribing data. In science disciplines, specific tasks might include preparing applications related to human or animal ethics, drawing human tissue samples, mixing chemical compounds, sterilising laboratory environment, or calibrating equipment. Specific tasks in humanities disciplines might include locating archival documents, scanning original materials into digital formats, or conducting fine-grained analyses of texts or images. Postgraduate research assistants may be involved in any one or more of these tasks at any point in a research project.

Whether behind the scenes or in the foreground, these research tasks are essential to research endeavours. The activity of engaging appropriately in any one of these tasks is evidence that the postgraduate research assistant has learned how to do that task and hence the postgraduate research assistant has learned something of research. Doing a research task is evidence of learning and knowing that aspect of research. Khong (this volume) presents a similar argument for doing research in the context of a formalised module at the Master's level. As illustrated through the synergistic relationships in Figure 1, doing and knowing are inherently inseparable.

This does not mean, however, that all research tasks contribute equally to the process of researching to learn. The extent of the learning potential within a postgraduate research assistantship depends upon the nature of the task or tasks undertaken, and the ways those tasks are connected to the research project as a whole. For example, my colleagues and I have written about a postgraduate research assistantship in which the postgraduate research assistant was a full collaborator in designing, conducting, and presenting an interview-based research study with her research supervisor (McGinn et al., 2013). Over an eight-month period, the postgraduate research assistant was involved in almost every step in Hershey et al.'s (1996:305) "expert research script", which was compiled from the most frequently cited actions or steps identified as part of the social science research process (see Table 1). Consistent with Hershey et al. (1996), high-consensus events (mentioned by at least 60% of the original study participants who were academics with PhDs) are shown in all capitals in Table 1, moderate-consensus events (mentioned by 40–59% of PhD participants) are shown in upper and lowercase letters, and low-consensus events (mentioned by 20–39% of PhD participants) are shown in lowercase italics. As is evident from the table, the postgraduate research assistant was engaged in the key steps of research, which means she was doing research.

Step	Postgraduate Research Assistant's Involvement
Get Idea (anchor)	no, research supervisor introduced idea
READ LITERATURE	yes
Discuss idea with colleagues	yes
Conceptualise project	yes
Determine participant population	yes
Formulate Hypotheses	yes (limited due to qualitative research approach)
DESIGN EXPERIMENTAL METHODS	yes
Obtain materials or measures	yes
Construct materials or measures	yes
Obtain research assistants	yes
Pilot Test Procedures	yes
Refine procedures based upon pilot test	yes
Recruit Participants	yes
COLLECT DATA	yes
Code and organise data	yes
ANALYSE DATA	yes
Determine if hypotheses are supported	yes (limited due to qualitative research approach)
Make presentation	yes
Conduct final literature review	yes
WRITE DRAFT	yes
Get feedback on draft paper	yes
Submit for Publication	scheduled after data-collection period ended
Make post-review revisions	scheduled after data-collection period ended
Publish Paper (anchor)	scheduled after data-collection period ended

Table 1: A postgraduate research assistant's involvement in steps from the expert research script identified by Hershey et al. (1996).

Given the high level of involvement of the postgraduate research assistant throughout the whole research project, she was credited appropriately as a second author for their conference paper and on the manuscript they were preparing for submission to a journal. The postgraduate research assistant was clearly engaged in the research process; through this engagement, she was simultaneously doing research and learning through research (i.e., she was researching to learn). As we have explained previously (McGinn *et al.*, 2013), the postgraduate research assistant began with no research experience, expressing intimidation and nervousness, and anticipating that she would be able to assist with typing and filing. After part-time employment over 8 months (a total of 130 hours), she presented herself as a confident researcher, prepared to complete her Master's thesis and committed to pursuing doctoral studies and an academic career. She identified the postgraduate research assistantship as the source of her newly emerged research skills and confidence, and her revised career goals.

As Table 1 shows, this postgraduate research assistant was involved in a range of research tasks, representing a full research cycle. Other postgraduate research assistants might be restricted to a single behind-the-scenes step in a research project. Repeated exposure to a single complex task provides opportunities for learning and building expertise. However, repeated exposure to a mundane task can be discouraging. For example, "Laura Reid" (a pseudonym), a postgraduate research assistant quoted in Grundy (2004:85), bemoaned the limitations of one postgraduate research assistant contract that was almost exclusively focused on photocopying research articles for her research supervisor: "*Photocopying: Literally 78 hours of photocopying. Time-consuming, menial—redundant . . . . I hated it*". Photocopying research articles is not part of Hershey *et al.*'s (1996) expert research script; it is, however, a possible component of locating and obtaining relevant literature, which was identified by 16% of the PhD participants in that earlier study. The lack of attention to photocopying research articles in Hershey *et al.*'s (1996) expert research script reinforces Laura's perception that this postgraduate research assistant work was marginal and a poor use of her skills and education. Although Laura was "*doing*", her task was insufficiently related to the overall research goals for her to perceive the work as valuable and educational. For her, photocopying was disconnected from the research project and hence provided a limited educational experience.

In contrast to Laura, "Lin" (a pseudonym), a postgraduate research assistant in chemistry, found educational value in a procedural task (Maher *et al.*, 2013). Sterilising bottles in a laboratory may not provide substantial learning on its own; however, when Lin experienced the effect of sterilisation—or failure to sterilise—on the outcomes of her research project, her learning was much more profound: "*I spent the holiday learning how to do the purification of the virus because it is a very complicated protocol. It influences the virus, and you can get different yield. The first time I did that, it was totally wrong because some other user used a bottle as waste and I used it . . . . From this process of the purification, actually I learned a lot, not only depending on somebody to tell you how to do that*" (Maher *et al.*, 2013:12). By sterilising the bottles herself, Lin learned how to sterilise the equipment, learned the importance of sterilisation, and learned to be self-reliant as a researcher. She connected the procedural task of sterilising bottles to the outcomes of the research project and hence saw the task as a research task. The task provided context and opportunity to advance her learning. This example is a reminder that repetitive procedural tasks may be critically important to research and to research learning.

Tilley (2003a) presented Ken and Kathy as two further examples of postgraduate research assistants who recognised the educational value of their assigned research tasks. Ken was hired to transcribe audio recordings of research interviews in one project and subsequently agreed to participate in a parallel study about transcription work; Kathy was hired as a research assistant for the parallel project about transcription work. They each described the ways they connected their transcription tasks with the broader activities and goals of their respective research projects and the reasons they perceived their work as educational and considered it helpful in preparing for employment opportunities and degree requirements. Tilley (2003a:770) articulated the educational advantages of assigning transcription work to postgraduate research assistants rather than "*proficient typists outside the research context*". As Tilley (2003a:751) argued, transcription work need not be considered "*a mundane, time-consuming chore*"; it is instead a critical space for preparing research data, commencing data analysis, and formulating deep understandings of data. Given the importance of transcription in developing research understandings, Tilley (2003a, 2003b) also provided advice for researchers to minimise potential losses to the research when transcription tasks are delegated to others. Transcription is important research work that can provide spaces to learn whilst researching, including learning the specific procedural tasks of converting audio to text, as well as broader lessons about research methodology, data quality, and the content focus of a specific research project.

Postgraduate research assistants who are encouraged and supported to see their work as important work are best positioned to learn from the opportunities. Differences in perception between meaningful and meaningless tasks are reinforced through the surrounding conversations. Together the actions and interactions associated with a postgraduate research assistantship influence the learning opportunities for postgraduate research assistants.

Research Talk

Postgraduate research assistants engage not only in research tasks, but also in talk about research. Through scheduled research team meetings, phone calls, email messages, and chance encounters with research supervisors and other research team members, they have opportunities to discuss tasks to be accomplished, methods to be used, advantages and disadvantages of possible actions, the progress of the research, and many other topics. Ratković *et al.* (2014) emphasise the importance of communication in ensuring task understanding, keeping up to date on progress, and circumventing or resolving conflicts within postgraduate research assistantships.

Research talk is a major component of postgraduate research assistantships. For example, we recorded 24 research team meetings between a postgraduate research assistant and a research supervisor (McGinn *et al.*, 2013). These meetings represented 22% of the postgraduate research assistant's allotted time for the project. Many more hours were spent in conversational interviews with their research participants. The postgraduate research assistant and her research supervisor also shared speaking responsibilities for their conference presentation. Certainly, the postgraduate research assistant was engaged in a lot of research talk.

During their meetings, the postgraduate research assistant and the research supervisor talked predominantly about their research project. The majority of their meeting time focused directly on discussing their research project (representing 75% of the codes assigned to the transcriptions). All this time talking about research provided opportunities for the postgraduate research assistant to crystallise her thinking by articulating her ideas. At the same time, talking allowed her to demonstrate her ability to use research terminology appropriately, which is an important aspect of research knowledge. Appropriating the discursive practice of established researchers allows one to connect with other researchers and contributes to one's recognition as a researcher (Bunch, 1995).

Postgraduate research assistants may also discuss research through formal conference presentations and networking meetings with other scholars, as well as in interactions with research participants, gatekeepers, and sometimes funders. These conversations require postgraduate research assistants to know and demonstrate their research process, content, and reasoning.

Interactions between postgraduate research assistants and others in the academic or research enterprise may also include conversations that extend beyond an individual research project. For example, in our analysis of postgraduate research assistant meetings, we assigned 22% of the codes to conversational topics about academic issues unrelated to the research project, including discussions about other research findings and projects, aspects of postgraduate study, and general considerations about the work of academics (McGinn et al., 2013). The postgraduate research assistant described these broader conversational topics as informative and valuable, and perceived them as evidence that her research supervisor was interested in her personally and committed to supporting her development and not just concerned with completing the research project they were pursuing.

The postgraduate research assistant was particularly appreciative of the conversations that focused on personal topics beyond research or academe (2% of the codes assigned). Paré et al. (2009:185) described "chats about children or hobbies or current affairs as essential to creating working relationships" in supervisory dyads. In another of my studies, a postgraduate research assistant described a restaurant meal with her research supervisor as a significant moment in the evolution of their mentoring relationship from employer–employee or professor–student towards a personal connection and friendship (Saudelli et al., 2013). Personal connections respond to the emotional work associated with identity development (Benzie, this volume).

Conversing together about research is key in coming to understand research, and in communicating about that research to others. Opportunities to talk about a research project or field and about broader topics of interest with other established researchers provide entrée into a community of researchers. These conversations allow postgraduate research assistants to draw from and contribute to the wider community (Bartholomew, this volume). Talking research can be considered essential to doing research and to knowing research. Much research talk is also captured in textual form.

Research Texts

A significant portion of research involves textual documents of various kinds. Reading and creating these various texts is a key element of research and is central to engaging in a community of research. Postgraduate research assistants may be expected to create an extensive array of textual documents for a broad range of audiences, including their research supervisors, research collaborators, research participants, research review committees, publishers and editors, and many others. Creating these documents requires strong comprehension of research methods and reasoning, as well as appropriate uses of research terminology and writing genres suitable for different audiences. As Benzie (this volume) argues, writing is integral to researching.

Many of these textual documents, especially those intended for presentation beyond the immediate research team, are created through "*joint texting*" (Kamler & Thomson, 2006:53) in which postgraduate research assistants and their research supervisors co-construct the texts. There were many examples of joint texting for the postgraduate research assistant and research supervisor that we wrote about in McGinn *et al.* (2013). The postgraduate research assistant volunteered to write the first drafts of the application for ethics review and the conference proposal, even though both genres were new to her. The research supervisor provided samples to serve as models for these two writing tasks and she provided detailed feedback about the postgraduate research assistant's initial drafts. The conference paper was their third major writing task. The two divided up responsibilities for the initial draft of different sections of this paper and also wrote some pieces collectively during extended working meetings in the weeks leading up to their conference. For all three writing tasks, the joint texting involved multiple iterations of drafting and revising. Through these various cycles, the postgraduate research assistant enhanced her familiarity with the requirements of these different genres, which she was then able to apply in her own subsequent research projects.

The postgraduate research assistantship in McGinn *et al.* (2013) involved three major writing tasks (the ethics application, conference proposal, and conference paper), all of which were created through joint texting. In other postgraduate research assistantships in my data corpus, there was evidence that over time some postgraduate research assistants began to create finished research texts with more limited intervention from their research supervisors, but there was always some element of joint texting as is to be expected for any jointly authored document.

In addition to these finished research texts, many interim research texts are created in the natural course of a research project. Postgraduate research assistants are frequently involved in the preparation of field-notes, interview transcriptions, annotated bibliographies, and other such research materials for the use of research team members and seldom seen by broader audiences. As Tilley (2003a) argued, interview transcriptions are essential to research and can provide important learning opportunities for postgraduate research assistants. The same is true for fieldnotes and other interim research texts. However, postgraduate research assistants must see the connection between these interim research texts and the overall research project; if no such connections are made, there is a danger that the quality of the interim texts might not receive sufficient attention, which could undermine the overall research project. For example, Grundy (2004) documented the shortcomings of an interview transcription prepared by a research assistant and the resulting enhanced quality of the subsequent interview transcription after the significance of the transcription was explained to the research assistant. It is important to attend to the purpose and audience for interim texts, just as it is for finished texts.

Given the central role of writing in research (Benzie, this volume; Kamler & Thomson, 2006), opportunities for postgraduate research assistants to create progressively more focal research texts allow them to engage at deeper levels in the research and to see themselves as valuable contributors to the work. As their work moves from behind-the-scenes interim texts to the front stage finished research texts, postgraduate research assistants place themselves more firmly in the research and recognise their contributions to the work.

Research Selves

Postgraduate research assistants engage in research by doing, talking, and documenting research. Performance of these various activities shows their learning and knowledge of research. Performing specific research tasks, engaging in the discourse of research, and creating research texts are all components of the interrelated functions of doing research, knowing research, and being researchers. Through these various activities, there are opportunities for postgraduate research assistants to take ownership of research and begin to self-identify as researchers. In one of the research meetings I have recorded, the postgraduate research assistant described her changing sense of herself as a researcher in the following way:

> "I think when I first started on this project I kind of saw myself in that role like coming to do a job and then that's it. As we're getting close to, and we're doing the interviews, and we're going to start writing up the paper and everything. I really don't want to let it go. I'm really enjoying this. And I am starting to feel like a researcher. I'm not worried at all about the interviews and the ethnography; I know that I can do that".

In studies where I have asked postgraduate research assistants about whether they do or do not perceive themselves as researchers, their responses typically reference factors such as the specific activities involved, the level of control they feel in selecting activities and determining how those activities are accomplished, their interest in the activities, the kinds of skills demanded or built through the activities, and the feedback they receive from others (McGinn, 2002; McGinn & Lovering, 2004). Individuals become researchers by doing research, and their self-identities as researchers are influenced by the kinds of research undertaken and the conditions for that research.

Findings from my data corpus indicate that postgraduate research assistants who have opportunities to contribute over time and to experience first-hand their emerging research accomplishments are most likely to see themselves as emerging researchers. They describe their experiences as challenging and rewarding, and they characterise these experiences as formative to their thesis or dissertation work and to their future academic and career aspirations.

As we have theorised elsewhere, identity is a social construction that emerges from the confluence of accomplished tasks, self-presentational strategies, and the reception by others (McGinn & Pollon, 2004). Across studies, postgraduate research assistants report that working on meaningful research tasks in conjunction with others (e.g., research supervisors, other research team members) contributes to their well-being as postgraduate research assistants and to their identities as researchers. Engaging meaningfully in research tasks prompts increased confidence and higher self-esteem for postgraduate research assistants, and ultimately contributes to their senses of themselves as capable (future) researchers.

Research Supervisors

Postgraduate research assistants are partnered with research supervisors, and both parties have opportunities to develop as researchers through their work together. As the more experienced partners in these relationships, research supervisors are the ones who hold the greatest responsibility for education within the context of postgraduate research assistantships. This responsibility establishes a teaching–learning relationship between research supervisors and postgraduate research assistants. Research supervisors must provide adequate instruction and supervision to postgraduate research assistants in order to ensure the fidelity of their research.

For research supervisors who are employed in academic positions with teaching and research duties, there is an expectation that they contribute to the intellectual development of postgraduate students, including postgraduate students who are engaged as research assistants. Strike *et al.* (2002) indicated that these research supervisors are ethically obligated to ensure postgraduate research assistantships are educative, such that postgraduate research assistants are able to demonstrate their competence in research tasks and their preparedness to continue in research beyond their postgraduate degrees. It is therefore appropriate to assert that research supervisors are expected to teach postgraduate research assistants.

The ways that research supervisors enact teaching practice within postgraduate research assistantships have ramifications for the research projects and the postgraduate research assistants. Strike *et al.* (2002) present several cases that show the possible consequences when teaching and learning are insufficiently emphasised in postgraduate research assistantships: research tasks do not meet the expected standards, postgraduate research assistants do not improve their work over time, research supervisors are disappointed, postgraduate research assistants feel uncertain and underappreciated, heated emotional interactions ensue, research participants may withdraw from the study, or other negative outcomes may emerge.

Teaching within postgraduate research assistantships matters. The process of teaching may be highly or loosely structured, depending upon the circumstances and the people involved. For example, Grenville and Ciuffetelli Parker (2013) described a structured instructional process for a postgraduate research assistant engaged in a case study research project. Documenting fieldnotes from observational visits was important for their project. Prior to beginning data collection, the research supervisor provided detailed instructions to the postgraduate research assistant about the expected form and content of fieldnotes. She then reviewed the postgraduate research assistant's initial fieldnotes and provided constructive feedback for improving these fieldnotes. The research supervisor also explained where and how the fieldnotes fit into the overall research project, and recommended readings to enhance the postgraduate research assistant's understandings about the research approach they were using and the content focus of their research. In this way, the postgraduate research assistant became increasingly comfortable and confident in recording fieldnotes and in undertaking other research tasks.

A second example of instruction provided by a research supervisor involved a scaffolded learning approach to introduce the postgraduate research assistant to the interviewing process (McGinn *et al.*, 2013). For the first three interviews, the postgraduate research assistant observed as the research supervisor conducted interviews (role modeling). The postgraduate research assistant then conducted a series of interviews with student participants as the research supervisor observed (guided practice). Next, the postgraduate research assistant interviewed a professor as the research supervisor observed (more guided practice). Eventually, the postgraduate research assistant conducted interviews without the research supervisor (independent practice). The research supervisor was physically present and engaged alongside the postgraduate research assistant until the assistant asserted her comfort in acting independently. Advancing through the stages from role modeling to guided practice to independent practice was under the complete control of the postgraduate research assistant who dictated when the scaffolds were withdrawn. This scaffolded learning approach is reminiscent of the Control Wedge Model implemented in Warner and Enomoto (this volume) or the Research Skill Development Framework implemented in Kalejs and Napper (this volume). Across these models, students (postgraduate research assistants) gradually adopt greater control and autonomy as they move from structured direction provided by an instructor (or research supervisor) towards independent practice.

When research supervisors focus consciously on instructional interactions with postgraduate research assistants, the relationship may shift from teaching and learning towards mentoring. Nyquist and Wulff (1996) asserted that postgraduate research assistants who come to see themselves as researchers or junior colleagues tend to treat their research supervisors as mentors rather than managers or role models, which was evident in the two examples above (Grenville & Ciuffetelli Parker, 2013; McGinn et al., 2013). Consistent with the published literature (Jiao et al., 2011; Grenville & Ciuffetelli Parker, 2013; Moore et al., 2013; Saudelli et al., 2013; Godden et al., 2014), the language of mentoring has been prevalent in many of my interviews and informal conversations with postgraduate research assistants. It seems that the greatest learning potential emerges when there is space and opportunity for mentoring relationships to develop.

Whether the relationship is characterised as mentoring or teaching, a clear commitment to the postgraduate research assistant's learning has a critical influence on the progress of the research and the development of the postgraduate research assistant. The research supervisor is responsible for ensuring that the needs of the postgraduate research assistant are considered alongside the needs of the project. The ethical obligation to fulfil this responsibility (Strike et al., 2002; McGinn et al., 2013) is coupled with a pragmatic rationale: a postgraduate research assistant who is well prepared and supported has the most to contribute to the current research project and to future research endeavours.

Revisiting the Synergies of Postgraduate Research Assistantships

The research literature and the accumulated evidence from my research projects show that postgraduate research assistantships can be powerful spaces for researching, learning, and teaching. Postgraduate research assistants can acquire, practise, and enhance their research knowledge, skills, interests, and confidence as they complete the activities associated with their positions. These activities may involve doing any number of possible research tasks, including reading or creating varied research texts, as well as talking about research. This variety is embedded in the tasks–talk–texts cycle in Figure 1. Postgraduate research assistants can engage in research in multiple and varied ways. Meaningful actions and interactions that allow postgraduate research assistants to connect behind-the-scenes work with finished research products and understandings enhance the quality and value of these activities.

The varied actions and interactions associated with postgraduate research assistantships provide multiple opportunities for postgraduate research assistants to try new things and to begin to think of themselves as someone who can accomplish these things. Realising that they are doing research and being treated as researchers tends to expand their considerations that they indeed could be researchers. This self-realisation is introduced in the action–interaction–self-perception cycle of Figure 1. The typical reasoning might be conceived along the lines that since research is something done by researchers, and they are doing research, that they might just be researchers.

The third cycle in Figure 1 connects doing research and being researchers with knowing research. This chapter was framed in terms of foundational learning theories that articulate doing, knowing, and being as inherently inseparable (Lave & Wenger, 1991; Wenger, 1998, 2000; Packer & Goicoechea, 2000). The accumulated evidence presented herein supports this theoretical perspective as a way to conceptualise postgraduate research assistantships as learning spaces. Doing research simultaneously provides opportunities for postgraduate research assistants to learn research, to demonstrate their knowledge of research, and to be researchers.

A central contribution of this chapter is to extend this theoretical conceptualisation beyond doing, being, and knowing to also draw attention to synergies within learning–teaching relationships. The final cycle in Figure 1 emphasises the overall synergy of researching, learning, and teaching as cued in the title of this chapter. Doing, being, knowing, learning, *and teaching* are all intertwined. Postgraduate research assistantships are most productive when learning is prioritised as postgraduate research assistants research to learn. Prioritising learning involves a corresponding commitment to teaching. Through this work, I have come to see postgraduate research assistantships as important teaching or pedagogical spaces for the research supervisors who work with postgraduate research assistants. These research supervisors have obligations to support learning and development for the postgraduate students involved as research assistants. A commitment to teaching informs and influences the potential for learning.

The multiple synergies involving researching, learning, and teaching in postgraduate research assistantships serve as a reminder and a resource to consciously and proactively contemplate how best to engage as research supervisors and research assistants. Researching together provides rich opportunities for learning and for teaching. It is my hope that research assistants, research supervisors, and institutional administrators will draw inspiration and potential models for their practice from the cases and evidence identified herein.

About the Author

Michelle K. McGinn is Professor and Associate Dean of Research and International Initiatives in the Faculty of Education at Brock University, Canada. She may be contacted at this email: mmcginn@brocku.ca

Acknowledgements

This research was supported in part by the Social Sciences and Humanities Research Council of Canada (Standard Research Grant 410-2006-0308) and informed by contributions from Ewelina Niemczyk, Snežana Ratković, Mary Saudelli, and Julie Dixon.

Bibliography

Åkerlind, G. S. (2008). Growing and Developing as a University Researcher. *Higher Education*, Vol. 55, No. 2, pp. 241–254.

Bunch, S. M. (1995). *The Context of Community: The Initiation of Graduate Students into the Discourse of Mathematics Education Researchers.* Paper presented at the American Educational Research Association annual conference, San Francisco, CA.

Danziger, K. (1990). *Constructing the Subject: Historical Origins of Psychological Research.* Cambridge: Cambridge University Press.

Godden, L.; L. Tregunna & B. Kutsyuruba (2014). Collaborative Application of the Adaptive Mentorship© Model: The Professional and Personal Growth Within a Research Triad. *International Journal of Mentoring and Coaching in Education*, Vol. 3, No. 2, pp. 125–140.

Grenville, H. & D. Ciuffetelli Parker (2013). From Research Assistant to Researcher: Being Wakeful in a Mentorship Journey about Methodology, Poverty, and Deficit Thinking. *Journal of Research Practice*, Vol. 9, No. 2, Article M7.

Grundy, A. L. (2004). *Learning Experiences and Identity Development as a Research Assistant.* Master's thesis, Brock University, St. Catharines, Canada.

Hershey, D. A.; T. L. Wilson & J. Mitchell-Copeland (1996). Conceptions of the Psychological Research Process: Script Variation as a Function of Training and Experience. *Current Psychology*, Vol. 14, No. 4, pp. 293–312.

Jiao, X.; R. Kumar; J. Billot & R. Smith (2011). Developing Research Skills and Capability in Higher Education: Combining Collaborative Research with Mentoring. *Journal of Educational Leadership, Policy and Practice*, Vol. 26, No. 1, pp. 42–55.

Kamler, B. & P. Thomson (2006). *Helping Doctoral Students Write: Pedagogies for Supervision.* Milton Park: Routledge.

Lave, J. & E. Wenger (1991). *Situated Learning: Legitimate Peripheral Participation.* Cambridge: Cambridge University Press.

Maher, M. A.; J. A. Gilmore; D. F. Feldon & T. E. Davis (2013). Cognitive Apprenticeship and the Supervision of Science and Engineering Research Assistants. *Journal of Research Practice*, Vol. 9, No. 2, Article M5.

McGinn, M. K. (2002). *Researcher Identities: Research and Researcher Training in Graduate School.* Paper presented at the Society for Teaching and Learning in Higher Education annual conference, Hamilton, Canada.

McGinn, M. K. & M. Lovering (2009). *Researcher Education in the Social Sciences: Canadian Perspectives About Research Skill Development.* Paper presented at the European Association for Research on Learning and Instruction biennial conference, Amsterdam, the Netherlands.

McGinn, M. K.; E. K. Niemczyk & M. G. Saudelli (2013). Fulfilling an Ethical Obligation: An Educative Research Assistantship. *Alberta Journal of Educational Research,* Vol. 59, No. 1, pp. 72–91.

McGinn, M. K. & D. E. Pollon (2004, May). *Researcher Identity Construction.* Paper presented at the annual Qualitative Analysis Conference, Ottawa, Canada.

McWey, L. M.; T. L. Henderson & F. P. Piercy (2006). Cooperative Learning through Collaborative Faculty–Student Research Teams. *Family Relations,* Vol. 55, No. 2, pp. 252–262.

Moore, J.; J. A. Scarduzio; B. Plump & P. Geist-Martin (2013). The Light and Shadow of Feminist Research Mentorship: A Collaborative Autoethnography of Faculty–Student Research. *Journal of Research Practice,* Vol. 9, No. 2, Article M8.

Niemczyk, E. K. (2010). *Expanding the Research Horizon in Higher Education: Master's Students' Perceptions of Research Assistantships.* Master's thesis, Brock University, St. Catharines, Canada.

Nyquist, J. D. & D. H. Wulff (1996). *Working Effectively With Graduate Assistants.* Thousand Oaks: Sage.

Packer, M. J. & J. Goicoechea (2000). Sociocultural and Constructivist Theories of Learning: Ontology, Not Just Epistemology. *Educational Psychologist,* Vol. 35, No. 4, pp. 227–241.

Paré, A.; D. Starke-Meyerring & L. McAlpine (2009). The Dissertation as Multi-Genre: Many Readers, Many Readings. In C. Bazerman; A. Bonini and D. Figueiredo (Eds.). *Genre in a Changing World,* Fort Collins, CO: WAC Clearing House, pp. 179–193.

Ratković, S.; E. K. Niemczyk; L. Trudeau & M. K. McGinn (2014). *Faculty of Education Handbook for Research Assistants and Supervisors.* Faculty of Education, Brock University.

Saudelli, M. G.; E. K. Niemczyk & M. K. McGinn (2013). *Revealing Moments of Mentorship: Social Exchanges Between a Graduate Research Assistant and a Professor.* Unpublished manuscript.

Strike, K. A.; M. S. Anderson; R. Curren; T. van Geel; I. Pritchard & E. Robertson (2002). *Ethical Standards of the American Educational Research Association: Cases and Commentary.* Washington: American Educational Research Association.

Tilley, S. A. (2003a). "Challenging" Research Practices: Turning a Critical Lens on the Work of Transcription. *Qualitative Inquiry*, Vol. 9, No. 5, pp. 750–773.

Tilley, S. A. (2003b). Transcription Work: Learning Through Coparticipation in Research Practices. *International Journal of Qualitative Studies in Education*, Vol. 16, No. 6, pp. 835–851.

Wenger, E. (1998). *Communities of Practice: Learning, Meaning, and Identity*. Cambridge: Cambridge University Press.

Wenger, E. (2000). Communities of Practice and Social Learning Systems. *Organization*, Vol. 7, No. 2, pp. 225–246.

Chapter Ten

Reflecting on Feedback in a Peer-led Research Writing Group

Helen Benzie

Introduction

This chapter contributes to the anthology by analysing the collegial processes employed by a group of doctoral students who in the process of researching to learn have met regularly to provide feedback for each other on writing. A key aspect of doctoral studies is learning to write with the authority and confidence expected of an expert in the field. Where once it was expected that candidates would be proficient writers before starting their studies it is now accepted that they may, for many reasons, struggle with the writing process. Indeed research writing is a complex and challenging process involving students' identity, confidence and development as a person and a researcher (Kamler, 2008; Kamler & Thomson, 2006). The affective domain of writing development tends to have been neglected in favour of the cognitive, underestimating the role of confidence, motivation and self-belief in learning to research (Wellington 2010). One means of addressing this issue is through access to the peer support provided in writing groups. Scholarly writing groups are often set up by supervisors for their students (Lassig *et al.*, 2009) or developed by groups of academics who wish to increase their publication rate (Bosanquet *et al.*, 2014; Danaher, this volume). Groups run by candidates who support each other through providing feedback on writing are however less often reported on.

One way of developing skills in research writing is through having the opportunity to give and receive feedback on drafts. This chapter explores the experiences of a peer-led research-writing group, which has met fortnightly for almost nine years to provide this kind of support. A focus on giving and receiving feedback on writing highlights factors leading to the success of the group which has, like others described in the literature (Aitchison, 2009; Guerin *et al.*, 2012), achieved an important goal — timely completions. By placing group members' experiences as individuals against the wider context of Doctoral student supervision and research education, this chapter demonstrates that outcomes for the group were much more wide-ranging than simply completing the degree on time. Members not only developed their own researcher/professional identities, through researching to learn in the group they also developed dispositions and techniques for giving and receiving feedback, skills in contributing to group processes, and taking part in a supportive research writing community.

By reading this chapter you will:

1. gain insights into how informal peer-led writing groups can make an important contribution to research education by complementing the work of supervisors and research education specialists;

2. be informed about the importance of the affective side of writer/researcher development in feedback processes because of the becoming and identity work that are involved; and

3. learn how peer-led research writing groups can contribute to the development of early career researchers, helping to build professional communities and healthy institutional writing cultures.

Research education

The traditional hands-off approach to Doctoral studies assumes that candidates will be largely self-sufficient. Research skills, if required, are taught through the supervisor adopting a mentoring role and guiding the candidate through the process of completing their research. However, aside from differing conceptions of what mentoring involves, seeing it as the sole activity in supervision underestimates the role of power in the supervisory relationship (Manathunga, 2007). Furthermore, increased workloads for supervisors, increases in the numbers of candidates, their varying backgrounds, and competing demands on supervisors and candidates mean that the close supervisor-student relationship is less workable than it may have been in the past (Aitchison & Guerin 2014). Both supervisors and candidates can require more assistance than such an approach implies and a mixed model is suggested where the supervisor role is complemented by institutional supports (McCallin & Nayar, 2011; Manathunga, 2005). The field of research education or supervision pedagogy has also developed and matured (Boud & Lee, 2005). Supervision pedagogy assumes that candidates need to be taught skills such as researching, writing, applying for ethics clearance, reviewing the literature, analysing data and managing their project. Moves towards developing research education curricula aim to develop candidates' *"capability expansion"* (Walker, 2010:29) but also include providing support for supervisors both through training courses and sharing of processes so that the supervisor and the institution are more equally involved in the process (Walker & Thomson, 2010). However these strategies are not widespread and research education curricula are underdeveloped in many institutions (McCallan & Nayar, 2011). One aspect of an integrated approach to researching to learn in the context of Doctoral studies is peer support for writing through institutionally initiated writing groups.

Writing as learning

Writing, and particularly research writing, is part of knowledge development. Once considered a transparent activity confined to the final stages of the research degree it is now recognised as an aspect of the thinking process and a skill that must be practised throughout the candidature (Wellington, 2010). The notion that research is writing and writing is an integral part of research (Kamler & Thomson, 2006; McGinn, this volume) is by no means widely accepted. Assuming that writing is a technical process, something that can be developed outside disciplinary content, allows it to be seen as the responsibility of the individual. This is particularly relevant to Doctoral studies where candidates are often expected to already be proficient in academic skills. Additionally, support for writing at Doctoral level is often provided outside the discipline, separated from the candidate's discipline or research culture (Starke-Meyerring *et al.*, 2014). However Doctoral writing involves a process of individual development where candidates move towards writing for a wider readership (Maher *et al.*, 2008) beyond the institution. This implies the purposeful development of skills and places writing at the centre of the research process.

Central to the development of researchers is identity (Cadman, 2005). As a writer's identity is not fixed but in a continual process of becoming it is intricately tied in with writing for an audience. James (2013:113) conveys this in her assertion that *"the writing subject is construed within and through language and discourse"*. She notes how the Doctoral student writes not only to conform to the academic requirements but to an audience. Positioning oneself in relation to this audience so that the writing communicates clearly may be challenging for candidates as they develop their researcher identity. James (2013:119) suggests supporting candidates to meet this challenge by *"repositioning writing and drafting as a central concern of postgraduate research student becoming and pedagogy"*. Thus research writing involves not only *"text work"* but also *"identity work"* (Kamler & Thomson, 2006:15) as the members develop into researchers and contribute to knowledge development in their fields.

Placing writing at the centre of research pedagogy however, involves more than audience considerations. Writing has a social dimension; it develops in a climate of interaction (Elbow, 1998) and research writers need to talk about their writing in order to develop their ideas. This discussion also needs to take place in a safe environment. Research writers must take risks and operate amid many uncertainties as they progress through their candidature. Some studies have drawn attention to threshold concepts in Doctoral study (Humphrey & Simpson, 2012; Kiley & Wisker, 2009). These are major conceptual challenges for learners that may cause them to feel *"stuck"*, challenged and confused at certain points and unable to continue (Kiley & Wisker, 2009:432). The liminal phase that leads up to the threshold may cause a loss of confidence and contribute to candidates deciding to abandon their studies. Peer-learning approaches as described by Boud and Lee (2005) are one way in which candidates can navigate through such difficulties to the next stage by drawing on the support provided by peers. Writing groups, which help build confidence and self-belief in addition to writing skills, can support writing development. While some writing groups are established within the disciplinary context (Lassig *et al.*, 2009), studies predominate about groups instigated outside the discipline with or without the cooperation of supervisors (Guerin *et al.*, 2012; Aitchison, 2010). Various informal approaches to encourage writing have also emerged such as blogs and the *Shut up and write!* concept (Mewburn *et al.*, 2014), which brings writers together in one place to focus on individual writing. These initiatives contribute to the notion that teaching writing is not always considered a supervisor role and, given its importance as integral to research, institutions could aim for greater integration of writing development into Doctoral studies.

Learning in writing groups

Writing groups contribute to the development of capable researchers by providing a safe environment where writing can be shared in a supportive environment. They have been found to contribute to improved productivity and quality of research writing (Caffarella & Barnett, 2000; Maher *et al.*, 2008). They bring to the fore the importance of writing and the relational side of peer work. They enable both *"writing in"* – experimental writing and discussion around a text, and *"writing out"* – writing for a wider community of scholars and for publication (Aitchison & Lee, 2010; Kamler, 2008).

The notion of peer learning as pedagogy (Boud & Lee, 2005) appreciates the value of learning through group discussion about writing. This pedagogy involves writing that is *"both produced through social interaction and is the outcome of social interaction"* (Aitchison 2010:86). Writing development is partly attributable to the safe zone available in a group. As members become comfortable within the group they are more likely to take risks and experiment with writing and, in the process learn from each other. Forming a group and expecting it to continue on its own however is not always a recipe for success. Writing groups face the problems experienced by any small group in relation to – *"small group dynamics, continuity, regeneration, leadership and purpose"* (Aitchison & Lee 2006:276). Haas (2014) found that to be sustainable – to continue to meet without direction and input – groups require 1) members of similar motivations and 2) some guidance in how to run meetings. Perhaps what contributes most to the success of any collaborative group is the degree of trust developed between members. This is often described as a sense of community (Cotterall, 2011), where members are comfortable with the group, which enables freedom of expression. This sense of trust may only develop over time and depend on group dynamics, motivations and some direction at the start.

Another value identified in writing groups is the diversity within the group (Guerin *et al.*, 2012), (see also Danaher, this volume) as it is considered to help develop writing for a broader readership outside the discipline (Aitchison, 2010). According to Aitchison and Lee (2010) this diversity is welcomed as it allows for horizontal power distribution with students having expertise in their own research fields. Other studies however, see more value in reducing diversity among group members as commonalities assist in developing the discourse of the discipline. In one group set up by a supervisor in an education faculty (Lassig *et al.*, 2009) a key strength was seen in members being within the same discipline. Thus it seems for groups to thrive a certain level of consistency among members' world-views and motivations is required, but otherwise diversity may be considered to be a factor that enhances learning.

Giving and receiving feedback

Feedback in research learning contexts is typically provided by supervisors as they comment on writing produced by candidates. Cadman and Cargill (2007) highlight useful categories of feedback for supervisors to focus on as: argument, voice, language and structure. They suggest that limiting comments to one or two of these categories avoids overwhelming candidates with too much information. These categories are also a useful way to separate out different kinds of feedback for different discussions. Actual feedback provided by supervisors is analysed in only a small number of studies (Kumar & Stracke, 2007; Velautham & Picard, 2010). These explorations enable some insight into feedback processes in Doctoral education contexts. They highlight for example, that comments expressing the supervisor's opinion were most important for the candidate's writing development (Kumar & Stracke, 2007). In offering an opinion the supervisor acknowledged that there could be a different interpretation thus allowing the candidate to reject the suggestion if they wished. They also note that approaches to feedback cannot be applied equally in all cases and more work is needed to analyse feedback depending on the relationships existing between those giving and receiving it.

One aspect of quality feedback in higher education is its dialogic nature. Dialogic feedback involves the receiver of the feedback not only being given feedback but also having the opportunity to engage in discussion about the feedback (Nicol & Macfarlane-Dick, 2006). The informal peer-led writing group is a suitable space for this discussion notwithstanding some reported negative aspects of peer-feedback. One of these is that multiple sources of feedback can confuse the writer and impede the development of their own voice (Aitchison, 2014). Others relate to how feedback may be disregarded if students do not feel confident of the skills of their peer-reviewer. One study found that feedback was most valued when candidates perceived that the feedback provider *"believed in their potential, cared about their improvement of skills, and tried to be helpful"* (Can & Walker, 2011:526). Feedback provided in a peer context will vary according to the skills and relationships within the group but the dialogue around feedback provides an opportunity for both givers and receivers to negotiate as they learn through the process. It has been noted that an important aspect of peer-feedback is that the student learns as much by giving feedback and by watching and listening to feedback given to others, as they do by receiving feedback on their own work (Caffarella & Barnett, 2000).

Writing development is key to learning research skills and writing ability is crucial to the development of active researchers after Doctoral studies (Sinclair *et al.*, 2014). However the processes around peer-feedback are complex and, while work with peers can provide powerful and useful assistance to writing development, it also involves emotion and identity work (Caffarella & Barnett, 2000). Aitchison and Mowbray (2013:868) describe writing development as *"a journey of emotional as well as intellectual labouring"*. This affective side of both researcher development and writing development is a major factor in successful completions for Doctoral candidates but has received scant attention in the literature (Wellington, 2010).

Analyses of feedback given by peers in the context of a research-writing group are rare (Aitchison & Lee, 2010), especially when provided from the student rather than the facilitator point of view. There is a need to understand how feedback works in such groups and how it contributes to researcher and writer development. As research education has developed so the importance given to writing has increased. Writing groups in institutional contexts can contribute through mentorship, the building of a supportive environment and the particular kind of dialogic feedback that is enabled. This chapter explores members' experiences in a writing group that began as a research education support initiative but then became self-sustaining and has supported most members through to completion of their research degrees.

The group

This case study of a writing group examines, from the perspectives of members, this long running, peer-led group at a point where the group is nearing the end its life. I am an original member of the group and, because it was so valuable to my Doctoral experience, have for some time wanted to document our experience. The other group members feel similarly grateful for its existence and have enthusiastically become involved in this study which has allowed us to reflect on our time in the group and its benefit in our studies.

Groups are often considered to evolve in a cyclical fashion as they form, develop and perform their purpose then disband (Galanes *et al.*, 2004). This group, now at a mature stage has evolved through three stages of varying duration and with indistinct and overlapping characteristics:

1) Easing in – During the early months of its first year the group participated with other Doctoral candidates in a series of workshops on the social philosophy of research led by a Research Learning Adviser. This arrangement aligned with Conrad's (2005:38) definition of a structured programme: *"group activities with a curricular character where topics, issues or skills are dealt with in a systematic manner"*. After the workshop series, a core group of eight continued to meet fortnightly facilitated by the same adviser. Each two-hour meeting included an agenda and general discussion as well as providing feedback on the written work of two group members. An online discussion forum was used for communication and as a place to share papers comments. Meeting minutes, taken by group members in rotation, were also posted to this forum. In

this stage we discussed how the group would run producing a written document. It set down some group norms and included sections on:

* Participation – If you can't come, contribute online;
* Contributing work – Submit writing one week prior to meeting; and
* Commenting on the work of others – Comments were to focus on the key critical argument of the work and be posted to the forum ahead of meeting times. Positive comments about the work should precede any suggestions for improvement.

Early in the group's life members posted their research proposals for comment but later the main text type became drafts of thesis chapters or argument summaries. These activities were initiated by the facilitator but she encouraged others to lead different aspects of our activities and gradually prepared the group to function without her. The end of this stage was marked by her withdrawal from meetings and the departure of two members who had completed their studies.

2) Engaging – The remaining six members of the group continued to meet fortnightly. Members presented thesis chapters or shorter writing for comment by the group, some more often than others. Meetings reduced to one-hour duration. Papers were distributed a few days prior to meeting and the conversation focused on only one member's writing at each meeting. With the smaller group, emails replaced the online forum as the main method of communication. In this stage our focus was on the group rather than any one individual as leader (Stupans, 2013) and a collaborative form of leadership emerged with members taking on different tasks and roles, as required; and while some spoke more than others in meetings, all took part and contributed writing to the group.

Over this period there were changes in candidature for group members. Several changed supervisors, one changed academic departments and one moved to a different institution. Initially meetings were held on a campus of the Australian university where most members were enrolled but during the final year the group decided to find a more neutral location. We chose to book a room in the State Library as a convenient space to meet. This stage, in which the group has functioned independently of an institution, is when it has consolidated as an informal learning space and demonstrated its success as a peer-led group. I was one of three members who completed their studies in this stage but we continued to attend meetings, providing feedback and contributing our other writing projects, such as journal articles.

3) Easing out – As the remaining two original members neared completion of their Doctoral studies we attempted to attract new members in order to prolong the life of the group. We approached three or four people, most of whom attended only one or two meetings. One of these *trial memberships* was successful and about a year ago, we recruited another member. We continue to meet regularly but will most likely stop meeting when this newest member completes her studies.

Design of the study

Memory work (Peseta, 2007), a process of reflection and discussion in a group context informs this analysis (chapter) of the phenomenon of the writing group. The approach, which originated in the work of feminist researcher Frigga Haug *et al.*, (1987:34), is *"an intervention into existing practices"* where the group pauses to look for *"indications of how [they] have participated actively in the formation of [their] past experience"*. In its original context, memory work was intended to be emancipatory for groups of women grappling with power structures in society. For our group, emancipation was both a result of the research activity and a feature for individuals over the life of the group as they struggled with the process of completing a research degree and gained confidence as they emerged with a Doctoral qualification. The research process enabled the group to celebrate our success and understand the learning that has taken place for each of us as individuals and as researchers. Researching to learn in the group in this way has also had a wider impact as we apply, in our different professional contexts, the skills, knowledge and dispositions gained through taking part in the group.

The study began with members individually writing a reflection on our experiences in the group, guided by a set of questions we had jointly devised. Ex-group members were approached but only one previous member, the original facilitator, responded. Her comments were gathered through an informal conversation, while I took notes, which were subsequently checked with her for accuracy. Other data sources included the written set of group norms adopted by the group in its early days and some of the written comments on work provided by members. The study participants thus included the current six group members and the original facilitator. To provide a measure of anonymity we all chose a pseudonym and these are shown in Table 1 along with more details of our backgrounds and disciplinary affiliations. I chose the name Gemma and Michelle, the original facilitator is only the participant in the study not currently part of the group.

Pseudonym	Age	Gender	Ethnic affiliation	Previous academic degree	Discipline	Employment
Diana	81	F	Hungarian born, naturalised Australian	Masters	PhD Nursing	Retired from nursing during candidature
Roslyn	69	F	Anglo Australian	Masters	PhD English	Writer
Vanessa	51	F	Anglo Australian	Masters	PhD Public Relations	Academic (Communication)
Gemma	59	F	Anglo Australian	Post-graduate diploma	Professional Doctorate Higher Education	Academic (Language and Learning)
Richard	63	M	Australian Hungarian	Masters	PhD Journalism	Academic (Communication)
Georgie	35	F	Anglo Australian	Masters	PhD Art History	Full-time student and Freelance Researcher/ Arts Writer
Michelle	41	F	Australian	PhD	PhD Women's studies	Academic (Research Education)

Table 1: Participants in the study.

The written reflections formed the basis of a whole group discussion, which, once recorded and transcribed, contributed another level of data to the study. The aim of the group discussion was to create a collective interpretation, enabling a move towards generalising individual experiences (Jansson et al., 2008). This group analysis of reflections involved members in the role of co-researchers (Bosanquet et al., 2014) in the study. This strategy, enabling a blurring of the roles of researcher and researched, suited the group as we have developed a level of trust and mutual understanding over our time together. However, the collaborative approach to the study was limited to analysing the initial reflections in the whole group discussion and commenting on drafts of this chapter. As a member of the group, my role could be described as participant researcher (Brannick & Coghlan, 2007), because I wrote a reflection on my time in the group and took part in all discussions. However the other members were happy for me to take responsibility for the design of the research, much of the analysis and the writing of this account. The study was granted ethics approval by the university at which I am employed.

Building a cohesive group

This group has served as one support mechanism among a range of strategies used by members to complete their candidature and engage in early career researcher activities. The group discussion revealed that members showed commitment to regular meetings by commenting on the work of others. That this was sustained over the long term may be due to a "specific kind of relationship" that developed among members – not exactly close friendships – there was little interaction outside the group, but more of a personal connection than many professional relationships. This is shown when Richard, who had stopped attending except for social events, says: "I feel guilty about leaving, … you probably think I've got everything I can out of it and now I've ditched you..." (Group discussion). The level of commitment felt by Richard is indicative of the connections that had built between members over time. Reasons for attending regularly emerged as more than simply to give and receive feedback on writing and included commitment to the group. However, while motivation for taking part was partly based in this collegial spirit, it was also dependent on the kind of feedback members received on their writing.

The following sections explore some of the conditions for effective feedback on writing evident in the group's reflections. First, I report on how the group was formed and how the members' motivations for continuing to attend contributed to the way feedback processes worked.

Facilitating effective feedback

Initial facilitation by a Research Education Adviser (Michelle) was important to the success of the interactions around feedback in the group. In the early stage, and quite subtly, she helped the group establish and build the sense of community and mutuality that has sustained it over the long term. In the group discussion members recalled Michelle's approach to leading the group:

Gemma.   *She talked about norms and values and things like that.*

Roslyn.   *And there's a sense of flying the nest that she kind of, um ...[attended to]*

Richard.   *Yes, and her actual teaching, you know, the first bit, was really good, you know, we really wanted to do it together.*

(Group discussion)

Aitchison and Lee (2010:266) assert that a skilled facilitator who recruits members, monitors group dynamics, and develops a set of transparent practices around giving and receiving feedback, is crucial to a group's success. While details of the development of processes, such as agreeing on norms, have faded from collective memory they are evident in the routines that continue to underpin group meetings. For instance the member whose writing is under discussion is asked first to nominate a focus for the meeting. This allows them to steer the discussion in ways most useful for their writing development. Feedback usually begins with a series of positive comments and suggestions about structure, and argument generally precede those that deal with sentence level features of the writing. The maintenance of group processes such as these indicates how the group has developed as a community of practice supporting writing development for its members.

Diversity and group cohesiveness

With members' ages ranging from mid 30s to early 80s and most having extensive work experience, there was similarity but also diversity within this *mature-aged* group. While members studied in different disciplines, *"There was enough similarity in [members'] topics that … being from different disciplines didn't interfere too much"* (Michelle, reflection). Members however, saw disciplinary diversity as a definite advantage in the group:

Gemma.   *And our – from what we write, I think, we're saying that that's enhanced by having inter-disciplinarity …*

Vanessa.   *Absolutely. You know, if I'd stayed in my little blinkered view of the world, my thesis wouldn't be anywhere near as …*

Roslyn.   *Vibrant*

Vanessa.   *Engaged as, you know, umm, yeah, it would have been a very formulaic response like all the rest.*

(Group discussion)

There was also an interest in diversity as a topic of study indicating another common thread between group members. Most members were studying groups or individuals with a marginalised status in society: asylum seekers, palliative care nurses, refugees and immigrants, international students and indigenous artists. This interest in the needs of diverse others could well have translated into an awareness of the needs of others within the writing group.

This sensitivity to the needs of others can be seen in the following extract where the group probes the topic of gender. Roslyn reassures Richard that being the only man in a group of women has not been the issue it might have been in a different group:

Roslyn.   *I think you also identify with a minority group …*

Richard.   *Several (laughter) …*

Roslyn.	But you take them on, you don't take on that sort of generic white male macho thing, and so that's why you fit – why you belong.
Vanessa.	It does open up the question for me as to, had there been more men, and different men, whether the group would have been different.
Diana.	Well, we had one man come along once and he never came back again.
Vanessa.	Yes, he didn't like it – [man's name].
Gemma.	Yes, that may be gender, but it may also be the well-developedness of this group.
Richard.	It would have been a very hard group ...
Vanessa.	To break into ...

(Group discussion)

It appears that the similarities within our group and the personalities involved led to the development of positive relationships that transcended the many differences in political positions, cultural affiliation and age and professional background.

The language in these extracts also indicates the closeness that has developed in the group. Vanessa finishes Richard's sentence in this extract and in the previous one Roslyn offers a word (vibrant) for Vanessa to complete her sentence. These indicators of the familiarity that has developed in the group, a feature dependent on regular contact over time are also indicators of the development of a professional community through collegial interactions (Bartholomew, this volume).

Vanessa noted a similarity among members that may not apply to all Doctoral candidates: *"I think we're all more comfortable in our own skins, that there was, you know, that we didn't think people were going to pinch our ideas"* (Group discussion). This commonality indicates that while a range of political positions and opinions in a group is beneficial, for sustained existence writing group members need to have a similar level of commitment to each other and to group processes.

Crucial to this account is Michelle's facilitation of the group through its early stage of formation. The processes that evolved supported the group to continue and sustain it today. The range of similarities among group members and their diversity in terms of background and research topics contributes a mix of features that together build a learning community that has been sustained over time. The informal and mutual learning that has taken place in the group illustrates how a student-led initiative such as this can complement the work of supervisors and research education specialists.

In the next section I demonstrate how feedback was enhanced and facilitated by the level of emotional support and identity work that took place in the group.

A context for effective feedback

Feedback on writing was the main work of the group. Each meeting involved the sharing of, and discussion around, feedback provided on one member's writing. Separating feedback from other group processes becomes somewhat artificial as it is so deeply integrated into the affective context and supported by the relationships that have developed over time. Sharing writing with peers builds a space for experimentation and allows for the exploration of questions of identity and authority (Kamler & Thomson, 2006:152). Over time, through regular feedback and sharing, group members were able to gain a sense of how to write in their discipline and it was by articulating the disciplinary differences that this was possible. Although our group was interdisciplinary, members felt that we were able to develop a sense of writing in our own disciplines through differentiating our work from that of others in the group. Through learning about the different research traditions we were each tapping into, we were able to build a sense of writing in our own disciplines. Comments on writing were often prefaced by phrases such as: *"I'm not sure how it is in your topic or discipline, but for me..."*

Feedback in the group was further enhanced and facilitated by the affective side of learning in the group. In the next section I focus on how the group provided emotional support and managed tensions that arose before touching on some specific approaches to feedback that group members have developed. These details of group processes show how emotional work, associated with developing a researcher identity, could be accessed in this informal learning space.

Emotional support

Kamler and Thomson (2006) describe Doctoral writing as a complex process of forming a writer and researcher identity. The vulnerability and the emotional work involved in this identity-building is a feature of Doctoral studies and, even after publications have been achieved, writers can lack confidence. The group assisted us to gain confidence as writers, offering: *"emotional support, offering encouragement and boosting confidence and morale during what were often stressful times. There is not one of us who has not burst into tears at least once during a group meeting. I believe my completion would have been close to impossible without the support of the group"* (Roslyn reflection). Roslyn highlights how we were helped through the inevitable times of crisis (Kiley & Wisker, 2009) in our candidature and were able to gain support through the care for each other that developed over time.

Gaining confidence as a writer can be a slow process and despite the supportive atmosphere in the group, offering writing for comment is not always easy. Georgie articulates this: *"Sometimes there's a small part of me that feels nervous, as though some really big mistake is going to be exposed and the members will think I'm a fraud!"* (Georgie reflection). Group members dealt with this fear of *"being exposed as a fraud"* through receiving and acting on feedback on their writing and gradually building confidence. We also benefitted through actively providing support and by observing other members giving feedback (Caffarella & Barnett, 2000). Observing feedback given by others enabled mutual learning of positive feedback processes among the group.

Managing conflict

Most groups experience conflict; that it exists is not so important as how it is resolved, which can contribute to successful group interaction (Fujishin, 2007). While the diversity in the group did lead to heated discussions at times, group members did not refer to conflict as such in the group. There were some tensions, however, around the giving and receiving of feedback. Georgie observed some discomfort in this area: *"I also get the impression that certain members aren't comfortable with either providing or accepting 'constructive' feedback and this can sometimes raise feelings of awkwardness"* (Georgie reflection). This observation from the newest group member revealed tensions that may not have been acknowledged by others.

Diana was affected by comments on her writing but reports how she dealt with this herself over time in the group: *"There was only one occasion when I got upset by being drilled. I found they were right and I was way off the mark. As it happened I eventually welcomed critique leading to my own ability to critique myself. Initially I thought I was being judged when it was really helpful commenting"* (Diana reflection). This extract shows how changes in self-belief can take time to develop. It also hints at how tensions within the group may have been suppressed in face-to-face meetings but resolved by individuals in different ways outside the group. This is appropriate in a group of professional adults where members are expected to be able to put aside personal differences as they focus on the work of the group.

Reciprocity – a distinctive style of interaction

Feedback on writing took different forms for different participants but because of the close relationships tended to be reciprocal. Guerin (2014:131) describes peer exchanges in writing groups as *"reciprocal gift giving"* as peers learn by giving and receiving feedback and incorporating it into their writing. Watching others give and receive feedback is also an important learning process. For Georgie the most useful feedback was: *"Always sentence structure, how to simplify and clarify my writing and how to make argument flow better"* (Georgie reflection). However the feedback process often involved more than text editing. This reflection from Roslyn suggests interaction with the writer is as important as the text: *"The most common, and most useful, comments took the form of a query: What do you mean by this? What are you trying to say here? How does this fit into the bigger picture? Discussion might then shift to suggestions on how to better express the point being made"* (Roslyn reflection). Vanessa also reflected on her questioning approach: *"I think I have been able to run a critical eye over the arguments being made, and pose questions to make the writer think more deeply about the issues, often playing devil's advocate to assist them in strengthening the justification for the position they have taken"* (Vanessa reflection).

In these extracts both Roslyn and Vanessa focus on Cadman and Cargill's (2007:186) categories of *"argument"* and *"voice"* emphasising argument development and dialogue with the writer whose work is being reviewed. While Roslyn and Vanessa use questions to push the writer to think in different ways rather than to locate faults in the surface features of the writing, other group members *do* tend to focus on features such as word choice and grammar. The fact that comments are provided on different aspects of the writing just enriches the feedback provided on the text. In the light of these comments Kumar and Strake's (2007:) preference for *"suggestions for improvement"* over *"judgments on the work"* goes only part way to understanding the importance of the context in which the feedback is given. For this group the spirit in which the feedback was given and received was paramount. It relied on the level of trust that had developed between group members over time and on the teaching skills and knowledge about learning held within the group. The trust among peers in the group has enabled *"learning from multiple voices"* (Aitchison 2014:51) as members build their writing skills.

Vanessa summarises what she has learned about providing feedback in the group: *"I think the main thing I have learned from the process of giving and receiving feedback, is to understand the person behind the work you are reviewing. Knowing what they want from the session is important, and understanding how they are likely to respond to comments, so you can phrase them appropriately is essential. But this can only come from knowing the person well"* (Vanessa reflection). Vanessa shows how, knowing the person to whom she is giving the feedback is important because it helps her to moderate what she says to suit the receiver. Such knowledge is rarely possible in more formal or public situations where feedback on writing is provided. This approach to feedback takes into account Kamler and Thomson's (2006) connection between identity and texts produced by scholarly writers. Because developing a research writer's voice is so closely tied up with identity and emotions, matching feedback to the person in this way can only happen in a supportive environment such as that which can be developed in a writing group.

Conclusion

This chapter has examined an informal peer-led writing group high-lighting feedback as a central activity largely inextricable from other group processes. Through developing supportive relationships over time, sharing leadership roles and building on their diversity, our group managed tensions and remained open to new members joining. The sense of mutual trust and the development of personal connections helped to build our researcher and professional identities as we took part in the reciprocal process of giving and receiving feedback on writing. While it is not possible to generalise from one case, this study suggests that informal learning in peer-led groups can complement the support provided by supervisors. Facilitated groups, led either by research learning advisors or supervisors are rarely sustainable over the long term and peer-led groups, with careful facilitation at the outset, and, given the right mix of diversity and uniformity among members, can make a valuable contribution to the process of researching to learn. A further benefit is the contribution they can make to healthy institutional writing cultures (Kamler & Thomson, 2006) as they provide a supportive learning community for Doctoral candidates and early career researchers to develop as research writers. The skills in providing feedback developed in the supportive group environment also have wider application and can continue to be of value to individuals in a range of professional contexts.

About the author

Helen Benzie is Language and Learning Coordinator, Learning and Teaching Unit at the University of South Australia. She can be contacted at this email: helen.benzie@unisa.edu.au

Bibliography

Aitchison, C. & A. Lee (2006). Research Writing: Problems and Pedagogies. *Teaching in Higher Education*, Vol. 11, No. 3, pp. 265-278.

Aitchison, C. (2010). Learning Together to Publish: Writing Group Pedagogies for Doctoral Publishing. In C. Aitchison; B. Kamler & A. Lee

(Eds.), *Publishing Pedagogies for the Doctorate and Beyond*. London & New York: Routledge, pp. 83-100.

Aitchison, C. (2014). Learning From Multiple Voices: Feedback and Authority in Doctoral Writing Groups. In C. Aitchison & C. Guerin (Eds.), *Writing Groups for Doctoral Education and Beyond*. London: Routledge, pp. 51-64.

Aitchison, C. & C. Guerin (2014). Writing Groups, Pedagogy, Theory and Practice: An Introduction. In C. Aitchison & C. Guerin (Eds.), *Writing groups for doctoral education and beyond*. London: Routledge, pp. 3-17.

Aitchison, C. & A. Lee (2010). Writing in Writing Out: Doctoral Writing as Peer Work. In M. Walker & P. Thomson (Eds.), *The Routledge Doctoral Supervisor's Companion*, London: Routledge, pp. 260-269.

Aitchison, C. & S. Mowbray (2013). Doctoral Women: Managing Emotions, Managing Doctoral Studies. *Teaching in Higher Education*, Vol. 18, No. 8, pp. 859-870.

Bosanquet, A.; J. Cahir; C. Jacenyik-Trawoger & M. McNeill, (2014). From Speed Dating to Intimacy: Methodological Change in the Evaluation of a Writing Group. *Higher Education Research and Development*, Vol. 33, No. 4, pp. 1-14.

Boud, D. & A. Lee (2005). 'Peer Learning' as Pedagogic Discourse for Research Education. *Studies in Higher Education*, Vol. 30, No. 5, pp. 501-516.

Brannick, T. & D. Coghlan (2007). In Defense of Being "Native": The Case for Insider Academic Research. *Organizational Research Methods*, Vol. 10, No. 1, pp. 59-74.

Cadman, K. & M. Cargill (2007). Providing Quality Advice on Candidates Writing. In C. Denholm & T. Evans (Eds.). *Supervising Doctorates Downunder*, Sydney: Australian Council for Educational Research pp. 182-191.

Caffarella, R. S. & B. G. Barnett (2000). Teaching Doctoral Students to Become Scholarly Writers: The Importance of Giving and Receiving Critiques. *Studies in Higher Education*, Vol. 25, No. 1, pp. 39-52.

Can, G. & A. Walker (2011). A Model for Doctoral Students' Perceptions and Attitudes Toward Written Feedback for Academic Writing. *Research in Higher Education*, Vol. 52, No. 5, pp. 508-536.

Conrad, D. (2005). Developing the Intellectual and Emotional Climate for Candidates. In C. Denholm & T. Evans (Eds.), *Supervising Doctorates Downunder: Keys to Effective Supervision in Australia and New Zealand*, Camberwell, Victoria: ACER Press, pp. 36–44.

Cotterall, S. (2011). Doctoral Students Writing: Where's the Pedagogy? *Teaching in Higher Education*, Vol. 16, No. 4, pp. 413-425.

Elbow, P. (1998). *Writing Without Teachers*. Oxford: Oxford University Press.

Fujishin, R (2007). *Creating Effective Groups: The Art of Small Group Communication*. Lanham, Boulder, New York: Rowman & Littlefield.

Galanes, G. J.; K. Adams & J. K. Brilhart (2004). *Effective Group Discussion*. New York: McGraw Hill.

Guerin, C.; V. Xafis; D. V. Doda; M. H. Gillam; A. J. Larg; H. Luckner; J. Nasreen; A. Widayati & C. Xu (2012) Diversity in Collaborative Research Communities: a Multicultural, Multidisciplinary Thesis Writing Group in Public Health. *Studies in Continuing Education*, Vol. 35, No. 1, pp. 65-81.

Haas, S. (2014). Pick-n-mix: A Typology of Writers' Groups in use. In C. Aitchison & C. Guerin (Eds.), *Writing Groups for Doctoral Education and Beyond*. London: Routledge, pp. 30-47.

Haug, F.; S. Andresen; A. Bünz-Elfferding; K. Hauser; U. Lang; M. Laudan; M. Lüdemann; U. Meir; B. Nemitz; E. Niehoff; R. Prinz; N. Räthzel; M. Scheu & C.Thomas (1987). *Female Sexualization : a Collective Work of Memory*. London: Verso Press.

Humphrey, R. & B. Simpson (2012). Writes of Passage: Writing up Qualitative Data as a Threshold Concept in Doctoral Research. *Teaching in Higher Education*, Vol. 17, No. 6, pp. 735-746.

James, B. (2013). Researching Student Becoming in Higher Education. *Higher Education Research & Development*, Vol. 32, No. 1, pp. 109-121.

Jansson, M.; M. Wendt & C. Åse (2008) Memory Work Reconsidered. *NORA – Nordic Journal of Feminist and Gender Research*, Vol. 16, No. 4, pp. 228-240.

Kamler, B. (2008). Rethinking Doctoral Publication Practices: Writing From and Beyond the Thesis. *Studies in Higher Education*, Vol. 33, No. 3, pp. 283-294.

Kamler, B. & P. Thomson (2006). *Helping Doctoral Students Write: Pedagogies for Supervision*. London: Prentice Hall.

Kiley, M. & G. Wisker (2009). Threshold Concepts in Research Education and Evidence of Threshold Crossing. *Higher Education Research and Development*, Vol. 28, No. 4, pp. 431-441.

Kumar, V. & E. Stracke (2007). An Analysis of Written Feedback on a PhD Thesis. *Teaching in Higher Education*, Vol. 12, No. 4, pp. 461-470.

Lassig, C.; M. E. Lincoln; L. H. Dillon; C. M. Diezmann; J. L. Fox & Z. Neofa (2009). *Writing Together, Learning Together: the Value and Effectiveness of a Research Writing Group for Doctoral Students*. Paper presented at the Australian Association for Research in Education 2009

International Education Research Conference, National Convention Centre, Canberra.

McCallan, A. & S. Nayar (2011). Postgraduate Research Supervision: a Critical Review of Current Practice, *Teaching in Higher Education*, Vol. 17, No. 1, pp. 63-74.

Maher, D.; L. Seaton; C. McMullen; T. Fitzgerald; E. Otsuji & A. Lee (2008). Becoming and Being Writers: the Experiences of Doctoral Students in Writing Groups. *Studies in Continuing Education*, Vol. 30, No. 3, pp. 263-275.

Manathunga, C. (2005). The Development of Research Supervision: Turning the Light on a Private Space. *International Journal for Academic Development*, Vol. 10, No. 1, pp. 17-30.

Mewburn, I.; L. Osborne & G. Caldwell (2014). Shut up & Write!: Some Surprising Uses of Cafes and Crowds in Doctoral Writing. In C. Aitchison & C. Guerin (Eds.), *Writing Groups for Doctoral Education and Beyond*. London: Routledge, pp. 218-232.

Nicol, D. J. & D. Macfarlane-Dick (2006). Formative Assessment and Self-regulated Learning: a Model and Seven Principles of Good Feedback Practice. *Studies in Higher Education*, Vol. 31, No. 2, pp. 199-218.

Peseta, T. (2007). Troubling Our Desires for Research and Writing Within the Academic Development Project. *International Journal for Academic Development*, Vol. 12, No.1, pp. 15-23.

Sinclair, J.; R. Barnacle & D. Cuthbert (2014). How the Doctorate Contributes to the Formation of Active Researchers: What the Research Tells Us. *Studies in Higher Education*, Vol. 39, No. 10, pp. 1972-1986.

Starke-Meyerring, D.; A. Pare; Y. S. King & N. El-Bezre (2014). Probing Normalized Institutional Discourses About Writing: The Case of the Doctoral Thesis. *Journal of Academic Language & Learning*, Vol. 8, No. 2, pp. A13-A27.

Stupans, I. (2013). Developing Student Contemporary Leadership Capacity Through Teamwork. In C. Nygaard; J. Branch & C. Holtham (Eds.), *Learning in Higher Education: Contemporary Standpoints*, Faringdon, Oxfordshire: Libri Publishing, pp. 45-58.

Velautham, L. & M. Picard (2010). *Reshaping HDR Supervisor Writing Advice Through Unpacking Discourses*. Paper presented at the 33rd HERDSA conference, Melbourne.

Walker, M. (2010). Doctoral Education as Capability Formation. In M. Walker & P. Thomson (Eds.), *The Routledge Doctoral Supervisor's Companion*, London: Routledge, pp. 29-37.

Walker, M. & P. Thomson (Eds.) (2010). *The Routledge Doctoral Supervisor's Companion : Supporting Effective Research in Education and the Social Sciences.* London Routledge.

Wellington, J. (2010). More Than a Matter of Cognition: an Exploration of Affective Writing Problems of Post-graduate Students and Their Possible Solutions. *Teaching in Higher Education,* Vol. 15, No. 2, pp. 135-150.

Chapter Eleven

Forms of Capital and Transition Pedagogies: Researching to Learn Among Postgraduate Students and Early Career Academics at an Australian University

P. A. Danaher

Introduction

This chapter contributes to this anthology about learning to research and researching to learn in higher education by exploring one approach to researching to learn enacted by a group of postgraduate students and early career researchers at one Australian university. This group constitutes an informal learning community whose members support one another in developing research success and in the ongoing processes of being and becoming effective researchers. Indeed, the community is now in its 11th year as a group with the same continuing name, although during that period it has experienced considerably varied membership. Yet the author also highlights potentially dynamic tensions between individual empowerment and institutional socialisation in relation to the group members.

At this point it is timely to indicate that, despite the community's name (the Postgraduate and Early Career Researcher group), membership relates more strongly to a sense of affiliation and mutual support than to a strict adherence to particular roles, which in any case are fluid. From the perspective of the physical sciences in Australia, the usual career trajectory is for a period of full-time Doctoral candidature to be followed by one or more postdoctoral fellowships and then by an academic position combining teaching and research duties. For these individuals, being early career researchers denotes the period of five years after the award of the Doctoral qualification. In education (the core discipline represented by the group), by contrast, most academics move into higher education after successful school teaching careers, and they generally begin their new careers by completing their doctorates part-time while conducting university teaching full-time.

This recognition of the fluidity of membership categories notwithstanding, "postgraduate students" and "early career academics" constitute two distinct groups of university researchers. In this chapter "postgraduate students" are candidates enrolled in research higher degrees, particularly Doctoral programmes, while "early career academics" denote researchers in the first few years after completing their Doctorates. Together "postgraduates and early career academics" are taken to be usually highly accomplished individuals in previous phases of their lives who are currently undergoing a process of transition into the expectations and responsibilities of contemporary academic staff members and researchers in universities (see also Piihl *et al.*, this volume).

Their previous accomplishments notwithstanding, postgraduate students and early career researchers often face multiple challenges in adjusting to their unfamiliar roles and understanding the contextually specific "rules of the game" that they now need to "play" (Austin, 2010; Bedeian *et al.*, 2010; Levine *et al.*, 2011). Despite having considerable knowledge and skills acquired from their prior formal education and careers, they must demonstrate their capacities to teach, research and provide service contributions against the wider perspective of academic work intensification (Harding *et al.*, 2010) and heightened competition among universities (Abramo *et al.*, 2012).

Becoming successful in research is a crucial element of these postgraduate students' and early career academics' work (MacDonald *et al.*, 2014). As was noted above, some university staff members undertake their Doctorates while working full-time as academics; others have completed their Doctorates and need to develop their postdoctoral research journeys while acquiring experience in exploring the synergies between university-level teaching and research. For both of these groups, developing knowledge about research almost always generates a parallel process of researching to learn, whereby they acquire new understandings of the character of contemporary academic work environments and of their desired and actual positions within those environments. From this perspective, researching to learn is seen as applying the experiences and outcomes of one's research endeavours in other elements of academic life, such as supervising one's own postgraduate students and explicating the "rules of the game" of being and become authentic and successful academics and researchers.

These propositions are illustrated in this chapter by means of selected data from the author's autoethnographic study (see also Bartholomew, this volume). This continuing study explores the intentions, activities and outcomes of an informal learning community of postgraduate students and early career academics in an Australian university (see also Danaher, 2008; Harreveld & Danaher, 2009). The author is both the researcher and a member of the community. The project's focus is on investigating the community's experiences as a manifestation of broader influences on contemporary academics' work and identities (see also McGinn, this volume) and of their strategies in engaging with those influences.

The chapter's particular contribution to extending this research project is to elucidate some of the dimensions and implications of "researching to learn". This elucidation is progressed by outlining how the postgraduate students and early career academics use the informal learning community to inform their ongoing learning about academic life and their continuing processes of be(com)ing university researchers. This analysis is framed in turn by the interrelated ideas of forms of capital (Bourdieu, 1986) and transition pedagogy (Kift et al., 2010). This analysis also identifies dynamic tensions evident in the data – specifically between individual empowerment and institutional socialisation for and of these postgraduate students and early career academics. The chapter consists of the following five sections:

1. a literature review and conceptual framework;

2. the study's research design;

3. a description of the informal learning community;

4. selected findings from the study;

5. identified implications of the findings for understanding current and potential future manifestations of researching to learn.

Furthermore, reading the chapter you will:

1. learn about the selected concepts (forms of capital and transition pedagogy);

2. become acquainted with an informal learning community of postgraduate students and early career researchers in an Australian university;

3. consider some suggested implications of this autoethnographic study for broader approaches to researching to learn in contemporary higher education.

Literature Review and Conceptual Framework

A growing body of scholarship is devoted to investigating the aspirations, experiences and outcomes of postgraduate students and early career academics. With some notable exceptions, which highlight the positive aspects of these researchers' work (Jones *et al.*, 2012), much of that scholarship focuses on the often daunting challenges confronting individuals moving from their previous occupations to new careers (a trajectory that is common with education academics in Australia, as was noted above), with unfamiliar jargon and generally implicit "rules of the game". There is a corresponding recognition of the requirement for these individuals to develop distinctive identities and to enact increasingly effective agency in their roles (Sutherland & Taylor, 2011). They need to do this in order to contest and move beyond their state of *"academic fringe-dwelling"* (Sutherland-Smith *et al.*, 2011:330) and of inhabiting *"the foothills"* (Savage, 2013:190) of academic work. Moreover, despite important disciplinary and national differences, these challenges and this need have a thought-provoking international consistency and similarity (McAlpine & Åkerlind, 2010).

One particular indicator of the challenging character of postgraduate students' and early career academics' work is the large number of accounts of communities of practice and learning communities being developed to assist these researchers to navigate these transitions as effectively and smoothly as possible. These accounts (Cox, 2013; Foote, 2010; see also Benzie, this volume; McGinn, this volume) confirm the complexity of what the community members are striving to accomplish and the need for multiple mechanisms of support for that striving.

As was noted above, researching to learn is a crucial dimension of postgraduate students' and early career academics' personal and professional journeys at this stage of their development. From this perspective, acquiring research confidence is vital but not necessarily assured for these researchers (Hemmings, 2012). Similarly, enacting approaches to research leadership that help to enable and empower beginning researchers in this fundamental aspect of their work is considered invaluable but often in short supply (Lee & Rolley, 2014). One strategy claimed as being successful entails assisting postgraduate students and early career academics to publish systematic literature reviews from their research (Pickering & Byrne, 2014).

Conceptually, two key notions and the interplay between them are elaborated in this chapter. The first concept is forms of capital, and in particular Bourdieu's (1986) enduringly useful distinction between cultural and social capital (see also Piihl *et al.*, this volume). Helpfully, Webb *et al.* (2002:x) synthesised Bourdieu's understanding of cultural capital as referring to "*A form of value associated with culturally authorised tastes, consumption patterns, attributes, skills and awards. Within the field of education, for example, an academic degree constitutes cultural capital*". Bourdieu (1986:248) defined social capital as "*the aggregate of the actual or the potential resources which are linked to possession of a durable network or more or less institutionalized relationship of mutual acquaintanceship or recognition*". In combination, cultural and social capital specifically, and forms of capital more broadly, can be seen as constituting contextually specific currencies. These currencies in turn are indispensable elements of postgraduate students and early career academics being able to use their research to learn how to survive and thrive in their new occupational environments. Indicators of community members acquiring and deploying such capital and currencies included their references to networks of fellow researchers that they had joined and were learning how to mobilise, and also their explicit understandings of the "rules of the game" framing academics' work and identities.

The second concept is transition pedagogy (see also Coombes, this volume). This notion was elaborated to analyse the educational experiences and outcomes of first year undergraduates (Kift *et al.*, 2010). Nevertheless transition pedagogy is helpful also in explaining both the challenges facing postgraduate students and early career academics and their strategies for moving beyond those challenges. Explicitly with regard to the link between transition pedagogy and forms of capital, Kift *et al.* (2010:12) noted that *"A transition pedagogy intentionally and proactively takes account of and seeks to mediate the reality of commencing cohorts diverse in preparedness and cultural capital"*. More generally, Kift *et al.* (2010:11) identified five constituent principles of transition pedagogy – *"Transition, Diversity, Design, Engagement, and Evaluation & Monitoring"*. When they are deployed effectively and sustainably, these principles can *"facilitate student engagement, mediate learning support and address the development of discipline knowledge and learning skills which are contextualised and embedded through the curriculum"* (see also Picard & Guerin, this volume). In doing so, these principles highlight the navigation of occupational and professional transitions as entailing the acquisition of contextually relevant forms of capital. Although, as was noted above, this concept was elaborated with regard to first year undergraduate students' experiences, the findings below demonstrate its applicability to postgraduate students and early career academics. Potential evidence of transition pedagogy being enacted in practice included community members applying a retrospective and/or a prospective lens to reflect on their progress to date and/ or on their career-related aspirations, as well as their engaging in assessment with varying degrees of formalisation of what they had learned and of their effectiveness in carrying out that learning.

Research Design

Given the author's dual role as researcher and as a member of the informal learning community of postgraduate students and early career academics with whom this chapter is concerned (Dwyer & Buckle, 2009), the research project's research design demonstrated some of the features of autoethnography (Boylorn & Orbe, 2014).) The data corpus underpinning the broader study of which this chapter forms a part constituted a bricolage (see also Coyle, 2010; Wibberley, 2012) of several sources:

publicly available documents; informal electronic mail communications; individual observations; and theoretically informed reflections by the researcher. In keeping with the study's autoethnographic character, all these sources were filtered through the author's framework of interpretation. Data analysis combined thematic analysis and discourse analysis (Oswick, 2012). The analysis was directed at addressing two key research questions. The first question was: "Which approaches to becoming successful researchers were exhibited by the postgraduate students and early career academics?". The second question was: "How did those approaches to becoming successful researchers inform the researchers' learning about their work and identities underpinning their occupationally transitional roles?"

Formal ethics approval was not sought for this research project. This decision reflected some of the broader complexities of conducting and publishing research about a community of which one is a member (see also Benzie, this volume). In this study, given the absence of a formal and clearly defined membership, it would have been impossible to have gained approval from all community members for the research to proceed. Accordingly, and as was noted above, the study is an autoethnographic study, reporting the author–researcher's experiences and observations as a community member and eschewing any claims that those experiences and observations were necessarily the same as those of other members. In adopting this position, the author is conscious of the potential risk of appearing to appropriate the group's activities and outcomes into his individual representations of the community. At the same time, he is aware that the community has achieved some significant successes in enabling members to draw on their research knowledge to learn about be(com)ing effective academics. It would be ironic, even paradoxical, if the community's self-consciously emergent and open design were to prevent community members from writing about it and from sharing with potentially interested members of other groups information about its existence and operations.

A Description of the Informal Learning Community

The informal learning community of postgraduate students and early career academics in an Australian university under review in this chapter has a number of distinctive features (see also Danaher, 2008; Danaher & Harreveld, 2009). The community began in 2004 as a group of early career academics and some of their research higher degree students in the then Faculty of Education who sought to devise ways of boosting their confidence and building their capacity in the sometimes unfamiliar and even hostile terrain of academic research. The author was invited to join the group in 2005 as a more experienced researcher and research leader (and subsequently the doctoral programmes coordinator in the then Faculty of Education) and has been an active member continuously since then.

As was noted above, the group's membership continues to develop and evolve over time. One membership pattern has been for individuals to participate actively in the community while completing their doctorates and sometimes in the early stages of their postdoctoral careers. Another pattern has been for individuals to arrive at the university having completed their doctorates and to participate in the group as early career or sometimes as more experienced researchers. Some people attend one or two meetings and do not return; others remain actively committed to the community over several years.

Current practice is to hold fortnightly meetings designed to share information about, and to engender enthusiasm for, research and publishing. Each meeting has a different chairperson, elected at the end of the previous meeting, whose tasks include framing the agenda of the next meeting, providing copies of relevant readings and facilitating discussion during the meeting to ensure that all participants have opportunities to articulate their viewpoints. Over the past decade, agenda items have clustered around a wide range of topics. These topics have included "Provocation" (discussing a relevant "hot topic" in designing and conducting research) and "Sharing the joy" (celebrating one another's research successes). Topics have also traversed "Spotlight" (considering one member's current research project or else a particular research debate or issue of interest to several members) and "Theoretical angle iron" (evaluating a specific concept or aspect of research). Meetings have included as well opportunities to present practice versions of forthcoming confirmation of doctoral candidature proposal presentations and conference paper presentations.

Meeting participants from multiple sites are linked using technologies such as videoconferencing, teleconferencing, Skype and SeeVogh, with varying degrees of effectiveness (see also Picard & Guerin, this volume). Meeting attendance also differs considerably, with as few as four or five and as many as 25 to 30. Such attendance is entirely voluntary, although there is a strong sense of communal commitment to the group and hence regret at missing meetings. The group has existed long enough for distinct membership patterns to have emerged. One such pattern entails some individuals attending every meeting that they are able to attend. Another pattern includes those who attend regularly for certain periods (such as at particular times during their candidatures as doctoral students) and less often while they are working to finalise their doctoral dissertations or during peak periods of teaching and assessing their students. Importantly, while the group began in the then Faculty of Education, its focus has steadily broadened to embrace other disciplines, and a recurring feature has been ongoing interactions with and participation by the active engineering education research group at the same university.

In addition to the fortnightly meetings, since November 2006 the group has conducted a series of research symposia, initially annually and more recently biannually; to date, 14 such symposia have been held. The recurring element of these symposia has been the opportunity for group members to present their research. Different formats for such presentations have been attempted, with current practice being to cluster the programme around hourly sessions of three presentations of 15 minutes each followed by 15 minutes of joint reflection on the three presentations in that cluster. From the outset, symposium themes were selected by group members as a way of maximising programme coherence and of enabling members from diverse disciplinary, methodological and paradigmatic backgrounds to contribute to the overall discussion. To this point, the symposia have averaged 21 presentations co-authored by 28 individuals. Other elements that have been employed in some symposia but not in others have included a book launch, group conversations, keynote speakers, panel discussions, rapporteurs' or respondents' statements, a workshop and a presentation by a publishing editor. The focus has been on presenting a rich array of group members' research projects in a safe and supportive and yet also rigorous and systematic scholarly environment (an approach that parallels the ethos of collegial support manifested strongly in the Learning in Higher Education research symposia).

Another vital element of the group's activities and outcomes is a series of edited research publications originating from, and sometimes extending beyond, individual research symposia. To date, three special theme issues of a peer-reviewed academic journal and seven edited research books published by national and international publishers have been published, with an average of 14 peer-reviewed articles or chapters written by an average of 22 authors per special theme issue or edited book. Moreover, 12 further reported edited publications are currently in varying stages of preparation, with another four edited books in the early stages of planning.

As is elaborated in the next section of the chapter, these three significant components of the group's operations are intended to facilitate success for both individual group members and the community as a whole. At the same time, these components are designed to enable that research success to maximise the group members' contextually specific learning in their new occupational environments. That simultaneous process is analysed in relation to the intersecting concepts of forms of capital (Bourdieu, 1986), particularly cultural and social capital, and transition pedagogy (Kift *et al.*, 2010), as articulated earlier in the chapter.

Findings

The findings selected for inclusion in this section of the chapter have been clustered around the two research questions posed earlier in the chapter, informed by the study's conceptual framework (the implications of which are canvassed in the next section of the chapter). These findings are also attentive to the interrelated themes of practice, theory and evaluation in relation to this informal learning community.

With regard to the first research question, "Which approaches to becoming successful researchers were exhibited by the postgraduate students and early career academics?", several strategies to enhance such research success were manifested. For instance, requested topics to discuss during the group's fortnightly meetings generally centre on specific aspects of research, including different research paradigms and methods and varied techniques of data collection and analysis. Many of those topics were also represented in presentations in the group's research symposia and associated peer-reviewed publications. Particular examples of these topics have ranged from statistical significance and critical discourse analysis to anecdotes as tools for critical reflection and researcher–research participant relationships to photo elicitation interviewing and transcriptions of interviews. In other words, an important set of strategies to enhance group members' research success has centred on the content, concepts and methods associated with their respective research higher degree studies and/or their current and prospective research projects. Members have been free – and encouraged – to deploy their developing scholarly agency to identify areas for individual development and also to share the results of that development with fellow group members, consistent with the principles and practices of an informal learning community.

Another strategy used by group members to extend their research knowledge has been to interact with, and to acquire understanding from the expertise of, university colleagues holding particular roles. These colleagues and their accompanying roles include a departmental librarian, a research librarian, directors of the office of research and the office of graduate studies, a former research ethics and integrity manager, departmental associate deans (research) and directors of research centres and initiatives. Some of these colleagues are regular attendees at the fortnightly meetings; others have participated in panel discussions and/or have presented at one or more of the group's research symposia. Once again, group members have asked these colleagues questions specifically targeted at their research interests as well as more general inquiries designed to expand their broader awareness of research parameters, principles and processes.

Yet another strategy is centred on the growing corpus of edited, peer-reviewed publications produced by group members. After each research symposium, opportunities are communicated to serve as co-editors of future such publications. In total, 15 different individuals have been co-editors of the three special theme issues of a peer-reviewed journal and the seven edited research books published to date, with several more individuals involved in co-editing the publications currently in production and in preparation. Informal, on-task mentoring (see also McGinn, this volume) is provided to these co-editors by more experienced members of the community to help in guiding them through the complex, at times challenging but ultimately rewarding tasks associated with editing a research publication. For many of these individuals, this opportunity has been their first experience of academic editing, which in turn has contributed to their knowledge about research.

An equivalent strategy has applied to the group members who have contributed as authors to these edited research publications. A supportive yet rigorous approach has been adopted to ensure that participants have felt encouraged and enabled while also adhering to appropriate scholarly standards of excellence and quality. For instance, authors are invited to participate in two writing workshops for each publication, one earlier in the process when approximately 1,000 words have been written, and the other when a complete draft text of the publication has been prepared. Again in a parallel with the Learning in Higher Education research symposia ethos and techniques, these workshops are carefully structured to provide constructive and meticulous feedback designed to enhance the appropriateness of the text when it undergoes anonymous peer review. Likewise, the publication editors work closely with authors to ensure that they engage wholeheartedly and appropriately with the recommendations of the reviewers, while retaining their authorial agency. In undergoing this process, members of the informal learning community enact the authentic roles and responsibilities of scholars in their own right.

Moreover, as was noted above, group membership is entirely voluntary, and the group is self-supporting and self-sustaining. At the same time, as the group has developed it has attained greater recognition within the university, and successive departmental leaders have encouraged its activities (such as by funding external keynote presenters at some of the research symposia). This recognition and encouragement constitute endorsement of the group's effectiveness in assisting large numbers of its members to develop and display research success.

In terms of the second research question, "How did those approaches to becoming successful researchers inform the researchers' learning about their work and identities underpinning their occupationally transitional roles?", one response relates to the tenor and type of discussions at many of the group's fortnightly meetings. These discussions have traversed the challenges and opportunities attending postgraduate students and early career academics and the kinds of strategies gleaned from more experienced colleagues as well as from scholarly literature likely to assist their socialisation and transition into their new occupational trajectories. Reflections include the need to learn new vocabulary, new institutional structures, new expectations and imperatives, and new working arrangements. These discussions are accompanied and enriched by reference to relevant and sometimes provocative readings (Debowski, 2012; Hirschkorn & Geelan, 2008; Shaw, 2013; Teelken, 2012).

Another response pertains to the broader context of the group members' academic work; group membership forms just one part of a wider set of their activities and outcomes. Many members have drawn on their knowledge about research in general, and their membership of the group in particular, in staff meetings, research higher degree supervision training workshops, teaching and learning forums and similar congregations. They have used these opportunities to highlight specific aspects of the work and identities of contemporary academics, including postgraduate students and early career academics. In doing so, they have sometimes referred to certain elements of the group's operations as supporting their learning about the dispositions, knowledge, skills and values attendant on being an academic today.

Yet another response refers to two observed and interrelated commonalities among most (if not all) group members that from the author's perspective are crucial to successful and sustainable transitions from previous occupations to this new professional environment. The first commonality is a palpable sense of agency, understood simultaneously as primary responsibility for thriving in this environment residing with the individual academic and as personal capability to discharge that responsibility. The second commonality is an equally palpable sense of community that is understood in terms of mutual and shared interests in individuals and the institution surviving and thriving together. This sense of community is manifested among other ways in an ongoing commitment to group membership and to supporting fellow group members during the fortnightly meetings and the biannual research symposia, and also in helping to celebrate and value the associated edited research publications. As one simultaneous illustration of these two commonalities, one group member (a full-time Doctor of Philosophy candidate) has presented a series of papers at the group's research symposia that explicitly draws on various identified transition points in her journey from novice to more experienced researcher, and that implicitly demonstrates the interplay between individual responsibility and communal support identified above.

Finally, the group has been in long enough continued existence for an assessment to be made of its longer-term effectiveness in assisting its members to learn about the work and identities of contemporary academic and research life. While those members exhibit considerable diversity in terms of career aspirations and trajectories, a number of them have made the successful transition from full-time doctoral students to tenured academics, and many of them have experienced success of varied kinds, including occupational promotion, supervising their own doctoral students to completion, holding particular leadership positions and being recognised externally as well-regarded researchers. In different ways, community membership has enhanced their understandings of being and becoming researchers, and has also added considerable value to their developing dispositions, knowledge and skills.

Implications for Researching to Learn

How does this parallel process of developing research knowledge and researching to learn on the part of members of this informal learning community relate to the conceptual framework underpinning that presentation of findings? Firstly, with regard to forms of capital (Bourdieu, 1986), cultural capital has been manifested through such markers as the publication of peer-reviewed articles in special theme issues of journals and of chapters in edited research books, which have particular and increasing currency in the working environments of contemporary academics. Similarly, social capital has been acquired and mobilised through the development of scholarly networks and partnerships derived from membership of the group itself. Social capital has been generated as well by such mechanisms as interacting with external keynote presenters at some of the group's research symposia and with the co-editors of and the fellow contributors to the edited research books. These forms of capital are indispensable to group members being enabled to demonstrate success in research and simultaneously to use the outcomes of that research experience and knowledge to learn increasingly capably and confidently about being an academic.

Secondly, the chapter has important implications for researching to learn in terms of transition pedagogy (Kift *et al.*, 2010:11), and more particularly in relation to its five constituent elements *"Transition, Diversity, Design, Engagement, and Evaluation & Monitoring"*. These five elements have been manifested in varied ways, although for the most part informally rather than formally. For instance, there is considerable diversity pertaining to research interests, methods, paradigms and theories within the group that makes for engaged and lively discussions about a variety of research approaches; that engagement, while taking diverse forms, is a vital ingredient of the group's success. At the same time, the design and evaluation and monitoring dimensions are far more emergent and implicit than they are systematic and explicit. This is not to deny the value of a more formalised approach to some or all of these elements in the future, but rather to reflect the group's developing character and ethos to date. Certainly the transitions undergone by group members, like the transitions of first year undergraduate students, are: times of doubt and uncertainty, fluidity of roles and responsibilities, and responsiveness to individual and institutional support.

More broadly, it is appropriate to highlight that these intertwined processes of developing research success and researching to learn, and that the underlying enactment of forms of capital (Bourdieu, 1986) and of transition pedagogy (Kift *et al.*, 2010), are neither automatic nor easy outcomes. On the contrary, group members demonstrate continued industry and resilience to maintain group commitment at the same time that they discharge their other, multiple responsibilities as postgraduate students and early career academics. Many of them have referred to the ongoing competing demands that they need to juggle, while recognising that these demands apply to the work of all academics regardless of degree of experience and longevity.

More specifically, there was evidence in the findings of a degree of discursive dissonance (Harreveld, 2002) in group members' experiences and reflections on those experiences. Some members identified this dissonance as representing a kind of potentially dynamic tension, both within the group itself and more widely across the terrain of contemporary academic work and identities. A particular example of this dissonance and this potentially dynamic tension was the interplay between the themes of individual empowerment and institutional socialisation for and of these postgraduate students and early career academics. Many of the group's strategies outlined above and group members' responses to those strategies reflected efforts to facilitate individual empowerment. Furthermore, highlighting personal responsibility for that empowerment accords with many group members' assumptions about appropriate approaches to developing research success and researching to learn. This is the proposition that the strongest obligation for charting professional growth rests with the individual professional who will benefit from such growth. However, at least some group members were less comfortable with selected perceived elements of institutional socialisation, including a view that some types of research activities and outcomes were more highly valued than others. While there was a recognition that this inequality was largely derived from national and international pressures and trends, there was nevertheless some disquiet that group members' efforts at individual empowerment might be counteracted by these identified aspects of institutional socialisation. This disquiet accorded with unsolicited remarks made separately to the author by two colleagues at another Australian university who had both moved from the school system to the university sector anticipating increased collegiality and a lively discourse about ideas, and yet both communicated a sense of disappointment at finding instead heightened individual competition for career progression and promotion.

Conclusion

Some of the author's critical self-reflections on selected experiences and outcomes of an informal learning community at an Australian university concerned with helping its members to achieve research success have been presented in this chapter. Simultaneously the group members have sought to use the results of their research success to inform their learning about the ongoing work of being and becoming postgraduate students and early career academics. In doing so, the chapter has been designed to contribute to new understandings of practice, theory and evaluation in relation to the goals and operations of contemporary universities.

In terms of practice, the group's strategies encapsulate its contextually specific approach to building its members' capacities and confidence as postgraduate students and early career academics. None of these strategies is new or revolutionary, but they are based on clear principles (such as collegiality, reciprocity and professional agency) and they have generated some demonstrable successes (represented by the community's research symposia and the associated peer-reviewed research publications) for group members and the institution as a whole. The discussion in this chapter has emphasised the group's status as an informal learning community, with both the strengths and the limitations of such a focus.

With regard to theory, the author has deployed the two concepts of forms of capital (Bourdieu, 1986), particularly cultural and social capital, and transition pedagogy (Kift et al., 2010), as theoretical resources to frame the chapter's findings and to inform the identified implications of those findings. These resources also help to highlight the study's broader relevance and wider significance, not least because they resonate with other groups of postgraduate students and early career academics seeking to enhance their outputs. Both concepts have been demonstrated to assist in explaining the processes of acquiring research knowledge in the context of the group, and they have also reinforced their utility in aiding the corresponding interpretation of researching to learn on the part of group members.

Finally, in relation to evaluation, while no formal evaluation of the group's effectiveness has been undertaken, some indicators have been adduced to signify the group's success in facilitating members' research knowledge and their corresponding researching to learn. Quantitatively these indicators include the number of attendees at the fortnightly meetings, the number of presenters and audience members at the biannual research symposia and the number of contributors to the edited research publications. Qualitatively these indicators include the group's longevity and the calibre of the external keynote speakers who accept invitations to present at the symposia. Thus the impact and the quality of the group's activities and outcomes can be assumed to constitute part of its members' ongoing efforts to develop research success and thereby to research to learn against the backdrop of current academic work and identities in contemporary universities.

Acknowledgements

The author acknowledges gratefully the generous and insightful feedback on an earlier version of this chapter provided by Professor Michelle McGinn and Dr Jens Smed Rasmussen. Professor Paul Bartholomew, Dr Cally Guerin and Professor Claus Nygaard have been encouraging and facilitative editors of this volume and also provided detailed feedback on the draft chapter. All feedback received is highly valued; some has been held over for future publications owing to word count limitations here. The fellowship and goodwill of all participants in the 12th Learning in Higher Education research symposium in Adelaide, Australia from 23 to 27 November 2014 represent an enduringly successful model for supporting scholarly writing and professional learning that has enhanced the quality of the chapter.

About the Author

P. A. Danaher is Professor in Educational Research in the School of Linguistics, Adult and Specialist Education, and Associate Dean (Research and Research Training) in the Faculty of Business, Education, Law and Arts, at the Toowoomba campus of the University of Southern Queensland, Australia. He is also currently Adjunct Professor in the School of Education and the Arts, Higher Education Division, CQUniversity, Australia. He can be contacted at this email: patrick.danaher@usq.edu.au

Bibliography

Abramo, G.; T. Cicero & C. A. D'Angelo (2012). The Dispersion of Research Performance within and between Universities as a Potential Indicator of the Competitive Intensity in Higher Education Systems. *Journal of Informatics*, Vol. 6, No. 2, pp. 155-168.

Austin, A. E. (2010). Expectations and Experiences of Aspiring and Early Career Academics. In L. McAlpine & G. S. Åkerlind (Eds.). *Becoming an Academic: International Perspectives*, Basingstoke: Palgrave Macmillan, pp. 18-44.

Bedeian, A. G.; D. E. Cavazos; J. G. Hunt & L. R. Jauch (2010). Doctoral
    Degree Prestige and the Academic Marketplace: A Study of Career
    Mobility within the Management Discipline. *Academy of Management
    Learning & Education*, Vol. 9, No. 1, pp. 11-25.

Bourdieu, P. (1986). The Forms of Capital. In J. Richardson (Ed.), *Handbook
    of Theory and Research for the Sociology of Education*, New York:
    Greenwood Press, pp. 241-260.

Boylorn, R. M. & M. P. Orbe (Eds.) (2014). *Critical Autoethnography:
    Intersecting Cultural Identities in Everyday Life*. Walnut Creek: Left Coast
    Press.

Cox, M. D. (2013). The Impact of Communities of Practice in Support of
    Early-Career Academics. *International Journal of Academic Development*,
    Vol. 18, No. 1, pp. 18-30.

Coyle, A. (2010). Qualitative Research and Anomalous Experience: A Call for
    Interpretative Pluralism. *Qualitative Research in Psychology*, Vol. 7, No. 1,
    pp. 79-83.

Danaher, P. A. (2008). Teleological Pressures and Ateleological Possibilities
    on and for a Fragile Learning Community: Implications for Framing
    Lifelong Learning Futures for Australian University Academics. In D.
    Orr, P. A. Danaher, G. R. Danaher, & R. E. Harreveld (Eds.). *Lifelong
    Learning: Reflecting on Successes and Framing Futures*: Keynote and
    Refereed Papers from the 5th International Lifelong Learning Conference,
    Yeppoon, Central Queensland, Australia, 16-19 June 2008: Hosted by
    Central Queensland University, Yeppoon: Lifelong Learning Conference
    Committee, Central Queensland University Press, pp. 130-135.

Debowski, S. (2012). *The New Academic: A Strategic Handbook*. Maidenhead:
    Open University Press.

Dwyer, S. C. & J. L. Buckle (2009). The Space Between: On Being an
    Insider–Outsider in Qualitative Research. *International Journal of
    Qualitative Methods*, Vol. 8, No. 1.

Foote, K. E. (2010). Creating a Community of Support for Graduate
    Students and Early Career Academics. *Journal of Geography in Higher
    Education*, Vol. 34, No. 1, pp. 7-19.

Harding, N.; J. Ford & B. Gough (2010). Accounting for Ourselves: Are
    Academics Exploited Workers? *Critical Perspectives on Accounting*, Vol. 21,
    No. 2, pp. 159-168.

Harreveld, R. E. (2002). *Brokering Changes to the Knowledge Base of
    Twenty-Three Members of a Cohort of Adult Literacy Teachers in Central
    Queensland*. Unpublished Doctor of Philosophy dissertation, Faculty

of Education and Creative Arts, Central Queensland University, Rockhampton.

Harreveld, R. E. & P. A. Danaher (2009). *Fostering and Restraining a Community of Academic Learning: Possibilities and Pressures in a Postgraduate and Early Career Researcher Group at an Australian University.* Paper presented at the 13th biennial conference of the European Association for Research on Learning and Instruction, Vrije Universiteit, Amsterdam.

Hemmings, B. (2012). Sources of Research Confidence for Early Career Academics: A Qualitative Study. *Higher Education Research & Development*, Vol. 31, No. 2, pp. 171-184.

Hirschkorn, M. & D. Geelan (2008). Bridging the Research–Practice Gap: Research Translation and/or Research Transformation. *Alberta Journal of Educational Research*, Vol. 54, No. 1, pp. 1-13.

Jones, G.; J. Weinrib; A. Scott Metcalfe; D. Fisher; K. Rubenson & I. Snee (2012). Academic Work in Canada: The Perceptions of Early-Career Academics. *Higher Education Quarterly*, Vol. 66, No. 2, pp. 189-206.

Kift, S. M.; K. J. Nelson & J. A. Clarke (2010). Transition Pedagogy: A Third Generation Approach to FYE: A Case Study of Policy and Practice for the Higher Education Sector. *International Journal of the First Year in Higher Education*, Vol. 1, No. 1, pp. 1-20.

Lee, G. A. & J. X. Rolley (2014). Early-Career Researchers: What's in It for Us? *Journal of Advanced Nursing*, Vol. 70, No. 5, pp. 955-956.

Levine, R. B.; F. Lin; D. E. Kern; S. M. Wright & J. Carresse (2011). Stories from Early-Career Women Physicians Who Have Left Academic Medicine: A Qualitative Study at a Single Institutions. *Academic Medicine*, Vol. 86, No. 6, pp. 752-758.

MacDonald, A.; V. Cruickshank; R. McCarthy & F. Reilly (2014). Defining Professional Self: Teacher Educator Perspectives of the Pre-ECR Journey. *Australian Journal of Teacher Education*, Vol. 39, No. 3, article 1.

McAlpine, L. & G. S. Åkerlind (Eds.) (2010). *Becoming an Academic: International Perspectives.* Basingstoke: Palgrave Macmillan.

Oswick, C. (2012). Discourse Analysis and Discursive Research. In G. Symon & C. Cassell (Eds.). *Qualitative Organizational Research: Core Methods and Current Challenges*, London: Sage Publications, pp. 473-491.

Pickering, C. & J. Byrne (2014). The Benefits of Publishing Systematic Quantitative Literature Reviews for PhD Candidates and Other Early-Career Researchers. *Higher Education Research & Development*, Vol. 33, No. 3, pp. 534-548.

Savage, L. (2013). A View from the Foothills: Public Engagement among Early Career Researchers. *Political Studies Review*, Vol. 11, No. 2, pp. 190-199.

Shaw, V. N. (2013). *Navigating the Academic Career: Common Issues and Uncommon Strategies.* Charlotte, NC: Information Age Publishing.

Sutherland, K. & L. Taylor (2011). The Development of Identity, Agency and Community in the Early Stages of the Academic Career. *International Journal for Academic Development*, Vol. 16, No. 3, pp. 183-186.

Sutherland-Smith, W.; S. Saltmarsh & H. Randell-Moon (2011). Research Mentoring on the Edge: Early Career Researchers and Academic Fringe-Dwelling. In *HERDSA 2011: Research and Development in Higher Education: Reshaping Higher Education Vol. 34: Refereed Papers from the 34th HERDSA Annual International Conference*, Milperra: Higher Education Research and Development Society of Australasia, pp. 330-339.

Teelken, C. (2012). Compliance or Pragmatism: How Do Academics Deal with Managerialism in Higher Education? A Comparative Study in Three Countries. *Studies in Higher Education*, Vol. 37, No. 3, pp. 271-290.

Webb, J.; T. Schirato & G. R. Danaher (2002). *Understanding Bourdieu.* Crows Nest: Allen & Unwin.

Wibberley, C. (2012). Getting to Grips with Bricolage: A Personal Account. *The Qualitative Report*, Vol. 17, article 50.

Chapter Twelve

Learning Through Auto-Ethnographic Case Study Research

Paul Bartholomew

Introduction

This chapter contributes to the anthology by showing how taking a reflexive approach to the lived experience of research leads to new learning for the researcher. This new learning cascades from engagement with the researcher's professional community through formalised and non-formal communication processes. From this engagement, lived experiences can be analysed and new meaning discerned. Specifically, case studies of practice, used as data, can be reflexively interrogated to build new under-standing. Thus, case study research – a process of building new knowledge from experience, can provide a valuable opportunity for learning. In this chapter, I apply this logic to auto-ethnographic case study research to demonstrate how reflexive analysis of cases from our own practice context can lead to new knowledge. In my case, this context is academic practice in higher education. My chapter is therefore an example of researching to learn. Reading this chapter you will:

1. learn how we can consider case studies of our practice (narrative accounts) as data to be reflexively analysed and how that reflexive analytical process can be regarded as a legitimate research activity that yields new learning;

2. be presented with a new typology of case study research that seeks to integrate a range of typologies found in literature;

3. be presented with a new variant model of experiential learning that shows how academic practice can be enhanced through auto-ethnographic case study research that includes engagement with a professional community.

This chapter shows how academic practitioners can become better teachers in higher education and thus become more effective in enhancing students' learning experiences and outcomes through taking a more explicit case study research-informed approach to reflecting on their practice. By so doing, I contend that academic staff can model reflective practice to the students they teach while enhancing their practice through self-actuating professional development activity.

Maréchal (2010:43) describes autoethnography as *"a form or method of research that involves self-observation and reflexive investigation in the context of ethnographic field work and writing"*. Through this chapter I show how the researcher, in parallel with focusing on their area of research, can reflect on their experience of the research process itself and learn as a consequence.

Stake (1995:xi) defines case study as *"the study of the particularity and complexity of a single case, coming to understand its activity within important circumstances"*. With reference to this definition, I write this chapter from the context of having been engaged in a piece of auto-ethnographic case study research whereby I considered how my academic professional development (a single longitudinal case) had been advanced through opportunities made available to me over a period of ten years as a result of the impact of the 2003 United Kingdom White Paper: *The future of higher education* (DfES, 2003) (the important circumstances of Stake's definition). This White Paper was a UK Government publication that laid out National educational policy in relation to supporting the scholarly activity of learning and teaching in higher education.

However, this chapter is not about my case of professional development; rather, the chapter shares how my use of case study research as a method to explore the impact of the White Paper on my academic development led to new learning and development through the process of write-up. To clarify then, this chapter offers a proposition that case study research not only allows for the development of new understandings relating to a particular context but also how the *process* of conducting case study research leads to new learning which is additional to, and separate from, the context being researched – i.e. the act of *conducting* case study research is a learning experience in its own right. Case study may be regarded by some academics as an illegitimate research method because it does not yield generalisable results; if true for case study research generally, this must be regarded as being particularly true where the research in question relates to a single case – as has been the case with my own auto-ethnographic approach. Accordingly, in the first part of this chapter, I mount a defence of case study research using and extending Flyvbjerg's (2006) paper: *'Five Misunderstandings about Case Study Research'*.

The definition of 'case study' attributed to Stake (1995) above is just one of many worthy of inclusion in discussion and, in order to articulate my work with wider conceptions of case study research, I synthesise prominent definitions into a common schema within which I have located my own auto-ethnographic case study work. This schema, presented later in the chapter, represents theorisation as a consequence of undertaking the formal write-up of my case study research. As I share my views on the potential for the *writing* of a case study as route to additional learning, I argue that it is necessary for a distinction to be made between 'case study' and 'case study research'. Indeed, it is the write-up, the *codification* of collected data that is fundamental to the process of learning – rather than the simple reporting of a case.

Defending case study research

In his defence of case study research *'Five Misunderstandings About Case Study Research'*, Flyvbjerg (2006) points to Campbell and Stanley (1966:6) as an indicator of early scepticism of case study research; they concluded that *"such studies have a total absence of control as to be of almost no scientific value"*. Of course, the inclusion of the word 'scientific' in their tirade is significant, with its allusion towards incompatibility with a positivist standpoint. They go on to write *"Any appearance of absolute knowledge, or intrinsic knowledge about singular isolated objects, is found to be illusory upon analysis"* (Campbell & Stanley, 1966:6). Through my broad agreement with Flyvbjerg (2006) below, I challenge this view – contending that the case study's *"contextual proximity"*, or what Flyvbjerg (2006) refers to as *"proximity to reality"*, offers the opposite of being *"illusory"*;

I contend that case study research, through its sharing of rich contextual detail, communicates a particular form of authenticity – one that is no less a legitimate source of new knowledge than could be argued for less granular (less finely detailed), more broadly framed, research approaches. There is an additional reason to feel relaxed about offering a challenge to Campbell and Stanley's position of 1966: as Flyvbjerg (2006) notes, Campbell later made an about-face to become a staunch advocate of case study research.

Unsurprisingly (given its title), central to Flyvbjerg's 2006 paper is the critique of five contentions in relation to case study research referred to as "five misunderstandings"; I cite each below, offer my own critique and then reflect on the thoughts offered by Flyvbjerg (2006). By doing so, I use Flyvbjerg's paper as an overarching framework to mount my own defence of case study methodology and thus underpin my advocacy of case study research as a valuable tool for learning through research.

Misunderstanding 1

"General, theoretical (context-independent) knowledge is more valuable than concrete, practical (context-dependent) knowledge." (Flyvbjerg, 2006:221). As will be made clear within this chapter, I contend that for auto-ethnographic case study research, the primary "user" of the research is likely to be the researchers themselves, as a vehicle for professional development through structured reflection. In my case, my overarching reflection upon my academic development is simply a narrative account (a *product*) and I contend that the *process* of studying the case transforms the narrative of a case study account to case study *research*. A process that has allowed me, as a user of the case study to make sense of my learning and to construct new understanding from my reflexive engagement with the associated study process. In this way, writing-up of the case becomes an integral part of the case study research activity and not just an abstracted commentary upon it. With that in mind, and by way of commenting on the "misunderstanding" written above, it is the specificity of *"concrete, practical (context-dependent) knowledge"* (Flyvbjerg, 2006:221) that makes case study research much more valuable than more general forms of knowledge.

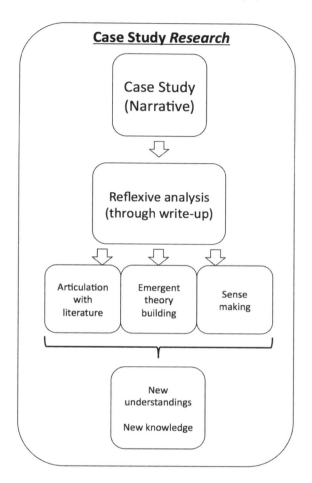

Figure 1: Diagrammatic representation of the proposed relationship between a (simple) case study and case study research. Production of a case study narrative is just the initial stage of case study research.

Flyvbjerg (Flyvbjerg, 2006:221) speaks partly to this when he reflects on the writing of Peattie (2001): "*The case story is itself the result. It is a 'virtual reality,' so to speak*". I'm not sure I agree with the latter part of this statement, that the notion that the case story is some form of "virtual reality", as that would infer the narrative, the case story, is a full encapsulation of the context. Rather, my view is slightly different – I'm contending that the case, when written with reflexive analysis, transcends an encapsulation and "augments" reality because the act of writing-up the narrative offers an opportunity for new reflexive analyses; this creates new understandings, new knowledge if you will, from that process. This proposal is diagrammatically represented as Figure 1 and the idea is explored further throughout the remainder of this chapter.

Theorisation around case study research included as part of this chapter, particularly the modelling of a typological schema for case study research, can itself be considered as an output of such reflexive analysis when brought to bear on the overarching case study of academic professional development. The theorisation of the relationships between professionalism, communities, scholarship and learning as offered later in the chapter represents another example of how researching one's practices is inclusive of the write-up process itself – as it emerged from my process of sense-making when reflecting on the specifics of my case. In other words, the act of writing-up the narrative accounts of how my academic practice had developed through the opportunities I had as a consequence of the White Paper of 2003 led to new learning and the generation of new models and theories.

This notion of theories emerging, as a case is examined, is labelled by Simons (2009:22) as a 'theory-generated case study'. She aligns such work with grounded theory and constructivist grounded theory approaches or *"some other interpretive lens that leads to an eventual theory of a case"*. I don't fully align my conception of my reflective practice with this notion, but I do contend that nascent theories have emerged from a consideration of my context.

For his part, Flyvbjerg (2006:224) responds to the statement he introduces as "Misunderstanding 1" modifying it to the following: *"Predictive theories and universals cannot be found in the study of human affairs. Concrete, context-dependent knowledge is, therefore, more valuable than the vain search for predictive theories and universals."* I agree with the broad thrust of this statement but find the *"universals cannot be found in the study of human affairs"* part to be a little too certain. I believe that broader methodologies of social research that seek to investigate and disseminate aggregate findings are not without worth and *can* be "found", they just offer a differently framed picture, for a different audience and thus have a different use.

Misunderstanding 2:

"*One cannot generalize on the basis of an individual case; therefore, the case study cannot contribute to scientific development*" (Flyvbjerg, 2006:221). This "statement of misunderstanding" pre-supposes that whenever a finding cannot be generalised, it is not a valid contribution to knowledge. As discussed above, a case study is rich in context, which contributes to its authenticity. Such authenticity, by virtue of its "proximity to reality" is a good approximation of an experienced truth, or at least some part of it. Sometimes a case can be highly indicative of a more generalisable phenomenon, whereby the specificity of context is the very thing that makes it generalisable. Flyvbjerg (2006) refers to this specificity of context when discussing sampling strategies; he refers to "critical cases" whereby the purpose of selection is "*To achieve information that permits logical deductions of the type. 'If this is (not) valid for this case, then it applies to all (no) cases'*" (Flyvbjerg, 2006:230). He goes on to describe a case drawn from occupational medicine in which a study is conducted to find out whether working with organic solvents correlates with incidents of brain damage. Rather than use a large sample of companies utilising organic solvents, a single case was studied where adherence to all regulations, safeguards and best practice guidance was complied with – the logic being that if a correlation was found in this case, then logically it would be found in all cases.

This was the logic that I applied to justify a single-case approach to investigating the impact of the White Paper of 2003. I contended that my professional development, the narrative account, was a critical case. I was one of only eight people in the United Kingdom who benefited from each of the initiatives that cascaded from that Government White Paper. Thus, if evidence of impact of the White Paper could not be found in my academic practice, then one might contend that it is unlikely that the White Paper had any wide impact.

Returning to Flyvbjerg's rebuttal of the statement (Misunderstanding 2), he modifies it to: "*One can often generalize on the basis of a single case, and the case study may be central to scientific development via generalization as supplement or alternative to other methods. But formal generalization is overvalued as a source of scientific development, whereas 'the force of example' is underestimated*" (Flyvbjerg, 2006:228). I agree with the first sentence, but the second runs the risk of being a rather sweeping generalisation itself. It would perhaps be more appropriate to insert a qualifier to the second sentence: *"But, without consideration of caveats, formal generalization is overvalued as a source of scientific development, whereas 'the force of example' is underestimated."*

My understanding of the logic behind Flyvbjerg's contention is that formal generalisation is overvalued because of its "fragility"; that is to say a generalisation will always be tentative and will always have the potential to be "broken" by a single case that contradicts the generalised finding. Of course, this underpins the scientific method and leads one to understand why researchers try to disprove a null hypothesis when conducting scientific work. However, I think Flyvbjerg goes further than this and argues that outside of case study approaches, hypotheses (and thus null hypotheses) are constructed from data sets that are absent of the necessary detail that would make generalisation viable. I don't disagree with that, but I believe that the users of such generalised findings are mostly aware of the limitations and apply the necessary caveats. Of course, this might not always be the case, but in those situations the fault does not lie with the researcher or their attempts at generalisation; rather, the fault lies with the user/interpreter of the research and their inability or lack of willingness to apply the necessary caveats to make the research useful. So, when Flyvbjerg contends that generalisation is overvalued, I want to ask "by whom?"

Misunderstanding 3:

"The case study is most useful for generating hypotheses; that is, in the first stage of a total research process, whereas other methods are more suitable for hypotheses testing and theory building" (Flyvbjerg, 2006:221). In terms of my rebuttal of this "misunderstanding", there is considerable overlap with the arguments made above. Can hypotheses be tested with case studies? Yes they can; the value of critical cases (organic solvent exposure; White Paper of 2003) to test a hypothesis has already been argued above. Can a case study build theory? Yes it can, as demonstrated by Simons' (2009) nomenclature of case study research, which includes "theory-generated" cases. Additionally, Dooley (2002:335) states: *"The researcher who embarks on case study research is usually interested in a specific phenomenon*

and wishes to understand it completely, not by controlling variables but rather by observing all of the variables and their interacting relationships. From this single observation, the start of a theory may be formed". Dooley (2002:335) also draws on Herling *et al.* (2000:338) to contend that case study research is an *"essential methodology for applied disciplines"* and goes on to describe it as a way of undertaking *"theory building or theory testing"* (Dooley, 2002:338). Dooley also cites Torraco (1997:123) who defines theory-building as *"the process of modelling real-world phenomenon"* – a definition conceptually close to the process of reflexive analysis leading to new understanding that is shown as part of the case study research process illustrated in Figure 1. Flyvbjerg's alternative is: *"The case study is useful for both generating and testing of hypotheses but is not limited to these research activities alone."* (Flyvbjerg 2006:229) This time, I am in full agreement with the alternative statement.

Misunderstanding 4:

"The case study contains a bias toward verification, that is, a tendency to confirm the researcher's preconceived notions" (Flyvbjerg 2006:237). Although I would concede that preconceived notions are embedded within case studies, I would also contend that all qualitative research is always subjectively framed at some level or another. Furthermore, I hold the view that transparent subjectivity is a strength of qualitative methods and particularly so for case study approaches. For case studies, particularly auto-ethnographic case studies, those preconceptions form part of the data to be researched; they are a result, perhaps even a representation, of the lived experience being recounted. I don't agree that case studies necessarily allow a bias towards verification; rather the process of case study research includes a development of thinking that starts with a simple narrative account of a lived experience and moves towards higher levels of understanding as sense is made of the experience. This "sense making" emerges from a process of reflexive analysis that is a form of theory building, whereby new ideas and new models, constructed to attempt to explain experiences, emerge from the writing process allowing the researcher/writer to iterate the narrative account, layering ever-increasing meaning upon the narrative artefact.

Above, I took issue with Flyvbjerg's (2006) idea of the construction of a "virtual reality"; I contend that the writing process, the act of reflexive analysis leads to an "augmented reality" characterised by new ideas, new theories and new models that would not have come into being without the researcher having had the opportunity to undertake such reflexive analysis. So, as the case (narrative account) is researched, new perspectives are articulated with the case and the narrative account itself is iterated. Each iteration takes the final work further away from an unarticulated position; thus, rather than reinforcing *preconceptions*, the process facilitates *conception*, making the final work a *post-conceived* artefact.

In the model I am proposing in this chapter, the very point of writing-up the case is to research it, to develop new understandings in relation to the experiences being recounted. This search for *new* understanding means that case study research has little structural propensity towards verification and much structural propensity towards modification. I therefore find I am in agreement with Flyvbjerg (2006:237) when he offers the following statement as an alternative to "Misunderstanding 4": *"The case study contains no greater bias toward verification of the researcher's preconceived notions than other methods of inquiry. On the contrary, experience indicates that the case study contains a greater bias toward falsification of preconceived notions than toward verification"*. Although my argument falls short of contending that a case study has a greater bias towards falsification, my construct of "iteration" can accommodate "falsification" as the iterated position.

Misunderstanding 5:

"It is often difficult to summarize and develop general propositions and theories on the basis of specific case studies" (Flyvbjerg, 2006:235). For my purposes, this is the point at which my use of Flyvbjerg's framework becomes subject to the law of diminishing returns. I find Misunderstanding 5 to have considerable conceptual overlap with points I have already raised, but nonetheless it is useful to offer a rebuttal of this Misunderstanding by way of constructing a summary for this section. Firstly though, for the sake of completeness, I offer Flyvbjerg's (2006:241) suggested alternative statement: *"It is correct that summarizing case studies is often difficult, especially as concerns case process. It is less correct as regards case outcomes. The problems in summarizing case studies, however, are due more often to the*

properties of the reality studied than to the case study as a research method. Often it is not desirable to summarize and generalize case studies. Good studies should be read as narratives in their entirety." I'm in broad agreement with this statement having already offered arguments that support it but I summarise as follows:

* summarising case studies can be problematic as their strength lies in their contextual proximity. As such, the process of summarising will inevitably lead to loss of the very detail that I have argued sets case study methods apart from other forms of social research;

* developing propositions from case studies: The development of general propositions from case studies (including a single case study approach) is possible, especially where the research focuses on a "critical case" whereby the case has contextual properties that allow for generalisation by virtue of it being highly indicative of the phenomenon being researched;

* it is possible to develop theory from case studies: I have argued that "case studies" are rich narratives that describe lived experiences (perceived realities) and that "case study *research*" augments this reality by applying a process of reflexive analysis to the case. This analysis seeks to create new understanding by articulating the representation of the lived experience (the narrative) with new thinking informed by literature and engagement with communities. This process creates new knowledge *from* the case as theory is built and models are developed to try to make sense of the world around us. Case studies are particularly strong in this regard because their contextual proximity (Flyvbjerg's "proximity to reality") affords them with detail that make them a better approximation of the world than data sets that emerge from less granular forms of social inquiry.

In this chapter I set out a particular conception of case study research, placing semantic distance between the term "case study" and "case study *research*". Given there are a number of conceptions of case study research to be found in literature, how does my conception articulate with the view of others? The following section seeks to make that articulation.

Case study research methods – variations on a theme

Many authors have offered their own conceptions of what case study/case study research is and what variants of the method there may be. Often they share their conceptions with a label (a qualifying word) and a broad definition of the sub-type. Although I'm not opposed to such construction of these concept labels, I think there is a tension inherent within their construction. Firstly the labels can be seen as a semantic device, simply the appropriation of a word that is used to convey the sense of a method that is at variance with more commonly held understandings; and secondly they are exactly the sorts of constructs we should expect people to make as they try to make sense of their experiences. When people write about case study research, so theories and models emerge as a consequence of their thinking and writing – this is exactly analogous to the process of theory generation discussed in the earlier sections in this chapter. By way of example (and inevitably given what I have contended), I undertake just such activity below, by outlining a variety of case study typologies as I have found them in literature, integrating them into a common schema that incorporates my own ideas.

Exploring case study typologies

When exploring literature in relation to case study research, one quickly uncovers a variety of forms of the method – each with its own "label" (as indicated in italics below). Stake (1995) makes reference to *intrinsic* case studies – undertaken for the intrinsic interest in the case. He contrasts this with *instrumental* case studies undertaken to explore a particular research question or interest. Stake also makes references to *collective* cases and implicitly (through the use of a scenario of a teacher researching the case of a single student) *single* cases.

Bassey (1999:62) makes reference to *theory-seeking* and *theory-testing* case studies. He makes reference to them within the context of what has been described above as "critical cases", i.e. the particularity of the case (Bassey refers to "singularity") makes it reasonable to assume that the case is likely to be *"typical of something more general"*. Bassey attempts to tie his nomenclature with that of other authors; he relates his *theory-seeking* term with Yin's (1993) concept of *exploratory* case study and his *theory-testing* term with Yin's (1993) concept of *explanatory* case study. Furthermore, he relates both *theory-seeking* and *theory-testing* to Stake's (1995) concept of the *instrumental* case study. Bassey (1999:62) also refers to *story-telling* and *picture-drawing* case studies. He sees these terms as broadly interchangeable and sees the story-telling process as being analytical *"aimed at illuminating theory"*; he links this with Yin's (1993) concept of the *descriptive* case study and what Stake (1995) refers to as *intrinsic* case study. I take a different view. For me, the story-telling part of the case is the descriptive non-analytical part of case study research – it forms the data *to be* analysed. The activity that creates new meaning and generates theory is that which goes beyond the story-telling, beyond describing. So, although I agree that Bassey's *story-telling* and Yin's descriptive *typologies* are related, my constructs of story-telling and description puts these at some semantic distance from Stake's *intrinsic* case study concept. For me, an intrinsic case study, one studied for the inherent interest, would be one that is closely examined, studied, analysed; one that leads to, in my terms, the greatest augmentation of reality.

Additionally, Merriam (1988) with Bassey (1999) and Simons (2009) make mention of *evaluative* case studies. Of course, evaluation can be the purpose of case study research but I'm not convinced the purpose of the research on its own should define it as a type. Merriam (1988), like Yin (1993) offers up the *descriptive* type of case study and throws *interpretative* into the mix too. Mindful though that through this writing I have the opportunity to generate theory, to build my own models, I feel compelled to reflect on what I have learnt about case studies and try to build a model of case study research to advance my understanding.

Modelling a schema of case study research typologies

As I explored the typological words and tried to articulate them with my own understanding of what case study research had come to mean to me, I found that I could group the words (concept labels) into sets and that I was able to add my own concept labels to these sets. This allowed me to begin to build a graphical model made up of two parts. Firstly, I felt that some of the typologies put forwards by other authors pertained to case study as a "method". Secondly I felt some of the typologies spoke to case study research in terms of its "focus". As my model developed I found that both "method" and "focus" had three components (see Figures 2 and 3).

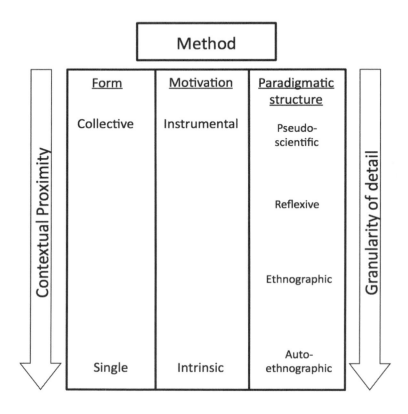

Figure 2: "Method" facet of a typological schema for case study research.

For "method" it was useful to aggregate typologies into "form", "motivation" and "paradigmatic structure". It was then possible to arrange the typologies according to their "contextual proximity" (what Flyvbjerg called "proximity to reality") and the granularity of detail collected. A collective case study drawn from many cases would not, I contend, seek to collect the specifics of a single case; rather, such a study would report with reference to aggregate data. Hence, the contextual proximity to any lived experience (a reality) would be less than would be the case for a single-case study. I also contend that instrumental case study research processes

– those constructed to answer a particular pressing question are more likely to adopt pseudo-scientific methods and thus be more likely to make use of multiple cases as a source of data. Auto-ethnographic work is likely to be related to a single case (the researcher's lived experience) and would likely be intrinsic in its motivation.

Dooley (2002:338-339) takes a somewhat positivist view on what case study research should "look like" and states that *"Case study research, like all other forms of research, must be concerned with issues such as methodological rigor, validity, and reliability. This is accomplished through the six elements below.*

- *Determine and define the research questions*
- *Select the cases and determine data-gathering and analysis techniques*
- *Prepare to collect data*
- *Collect data in the field*
- *Evaluate and analyze the data*
- *Prepare the report".*

Although I would not argue that case study research *could* "look like" this, it does not always need to. There will be a range of paradigms that underpin case study research and I postulate that each would lead to a chosen (paradigmatic) structure as shown in the third column of Figure 2.

I shall now discuss the "focus" facet of the modelled schema:

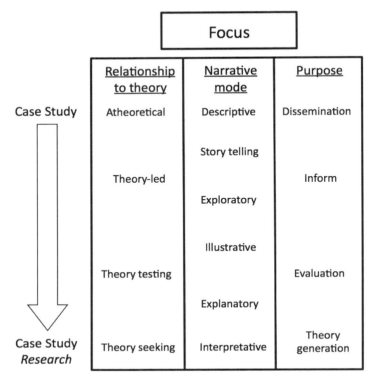

Figure 3: "Focus" facet of a typological schema for case study research.

The second facet of my schema relates to the "focus" of case study research. I found it useful to aggregate the various typologies put forward by the authors I have referenced above according to their statements about "relationship to theory", "narrative mode", and "purpose". Bassey (1999), Dooley (2002) and Simons (2009), among others, write of the relationship to theory when discussing case study research, hence this is incorporated within the "focus" facet of my schema. Earlier in this chapter, I have contended that a case study is just a narrative account – the raw data that through reflexive analysis becomes part of case study *research*. This argument is reflected in my schema. A purely descriptive case, perhaps conducted purely for the purpose of disseminating the experience, could (and perhaps would) be atheoretical. It is reflexive analysis that differentiates case study research from a report, in that the former leads the researcher to make sense of the world and generate theories and models informed by that new thinking. I therefore place "theory-seeking" case study work at the "case study research" end of the spectrum.

Authors such as Merriam (1988) and Yin (1994) have introduced case study typologies that speak to the narrative mode, the way in which the researcher interrogates and presents the data (the case) – for me, there was a sense of alignment between narrative modes that were more descriptive and those that may seek to move beyond "description" and into "interpretation"; this is reflected in my schema. Some authors seek to classify case study research according to its purposes. Merriam (1988), Yin (1994), Bassey (1999) and Simons (2009) all make reference to the potential for case study research to be evaluative in its purpose. I have added the "purpose of dissemination" into my schema because I believe that, although simple descriptive narrative accounts that are atheoretical can communicate a series of events, they are unlikely to serve a wider purpose on their own.

Simons (2009) refers to formative case studies, included here as "inform". These case studies are close to simple narrative accounts but are written to be shared within a specific context, to inform a particular audience about the specifics of a particular phenomenon. I have placed "evaluation" even further towards the research end of the spectrum because of its potential to test theory – i.e., when it is postulated that a particular educational intervention might have some impact. Evaluative case studies are useful for measuring impact and the evaluation questions will emerge from a starting hypothesis. I see theory generation as being at the most extreme end of case study research; indeed I contend that this is the defining feature of case study *research*.

Exploring professionalism

Central to this discussion is the contention that the auto-ethnographic variant of case study research that I undertook, leads to learning and professional development – i.e. researching to learn. Before considering the nature of professional development (in the context of academic practice in higher education), it is useful to first consider what is meant by "professionalism". This is by no means an uncontested concept. Freidson (1994:169) offers the view that *"much of the debate about professionalism is clouded by unstated assumptions and inconsistent and incomplete usages"*.

Evans (2008) explores this by borrowing (and developing) the term "professionality" from Hoyle (1975), usefully creating some semantic distance between the terms "professionalism" and "professionality". She ties the former to notions of socio-political structures that define expectations for professional behaviour and capability, going on to build an argument that links "professionalism" to a *"quality of service"* (Hoyle, 2001:146) or *"quality of practice"* (Sockett, 1996:23); hence "professionality" is tied to the attitudes and values a professional has in respect of their respective practice.

"Professionalism" has broadly been described above as subscribing to, and working within, the "service" and "practice" parameters that have been negotiated between "professionals", an associated professional body and (often) wider society through the proxy of authoritative agencies. "Professionality", Evans (2002:6-7) contends, is different from this socio-political construct of "professionalism" and relates to the ideological and attitudinal disposition of the "professional". Evans defines it as *"An ideologically-, attitudinally-, intellectually-, and epistemologically-based stance on the part of an individual, in relation to the practice of the profession to which s/he belongs, and which influences her/his professional practice"*. The distinction between these two facets of broader conceptions of professionalism is useful in that it allows for clear differentiation between these two otherwise conflated facets.

However, Evans (2008) is careful to remind us that these two facets of professional practice – professionalism and professionality – are not divorced; they are intimately related and mutually reinforcing. The parameters that define professionalism are socio-politically constructed, but the members of the profession themselves contribute to this construction. Thus the values held by members of a profession – aspects of their collective professionality, become manifest within the socio-political constructs of the profession they help to build (such as codes of conduct or professional frameworks). Evans (2008:9) explains this link between professionalism and professionality in the following terms: *"I perceive professionalism to be what may perhaps best be described as, in one sense, the 'plural' of individuals' professionality orientation: the amalgam of multiple 'professionalities' – professionality writ large."*

Scholarship of teaching and learning

Engagement by academics in "scholarship of teaching and learning" is related to the concept of professionality. Evans (2008) discusses a link between professionality and professionalism through the plurality of *professionalities* – that is to say professionalism is an inevitable output of the existence of a community of professionals. If we accept a notion of professionalism as a plurality of professionalities, how do individual professionalities relate to one another? How are professional value sets, ideas, models and theories of a community of professionals shared? In my profession, higher education academia, Shulman (2000) makes reference to two communities – "discipline-based" and "professional educator-based" with the latter being a community of academic practice. Although this latter community is theoretically open to all those who teach in higher education, it is not the case that every academic chooses to be active within this community. Historical emphasis on disciplinary research as the primary academic activity still exists today and a largely mono-focal approach to carrying out disciplinary research is tolerated or even rewarded.

However many academics *do* choose to engage in what Boyer (1990:16) described as being a *"broader, more capacious"* conception of academic scholarship – one that comprises a scholarship of discovery, of integration, of application, and of teaching. Although this conception of scholarship of academic practice is now broadly accepted (Trigwell & Shale, 2004; Haigh, 2010), some earlier discussion (for example Kreber, 2002) called for clearer distinction between *scholarly teaching* (what might today be referred to as research-informed teaching) and the *scholarship of teaching* (research practices that seek to shed light upon what effective teaching is and how it is constructed). Kreber (2002:159) offers some examples of responses (as an output of a Delphi process) that speak to this difference:

> *"Excellent teachers need not be scholars of teaching"*; and *"Scholarly teaching is intended to impact on the activity of teaching. The scholarship of teaching is intended to result in a formal peer reviewed communication in appropriate media or venues".*

I find this distinction a little sharp and somewhat false. Yes, excellent teachers need not be scholars of teaching, but they don't teach in a vacuum and will draw, even if only through conversation with colleagues, from the professional community of academic practice (the plurality of their own and colleagues' professionalities) to some extent. This certainly does not necessitate engagement in what we might call the pedagogic research "end" of the scholarship spectrum, but it does not mean they do not indirectly benefit from such research or what Kreber (2002) is referring to as scholarship of teaching. Conversely, those who engage in the scholarship of teaching are not excluded from engaging in "scholarly teaching" or from participating in the community of academic practice in a more indirect manner (in addition to more formal participation modes).

Modelling scholarship

I propose that scholarly teaching and the scholarship of teaching are not mutually exclusive positions but are the poles of a spectrum of engagement with the professional community of academic practice. The "scholarly teaching" pole is characterised by engagement in innovative teaching practice (with the intention of enhancing the student learning experience) and informal engagement in the professional community of academic practice through community networking and informal dissemination of their practices. The "scholarship of teaching" pole is characterised by formal engagement in the professional community of academic practice through pedagogic research and formal dissemination of findings through publication.

Reflecting on the concept of case study research I offered in the first part of this chapter, I find that it is easily accommodated within a (spectrum) model of scholarly teaching/scholarship, sitting squarely at the scholarship of teaching "end" of the spectrum (Figure 5).

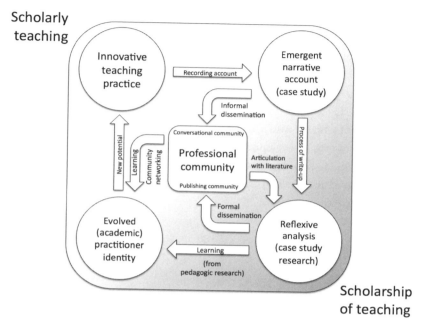

Figure 5: A model to demonstrate a spectrum of mode of (practitioner) engagement with a professional community of academic practice.

A key implication of the model (Figure 5) is that the professional community (of academic practice) is itself made up of sub-communities: the "conversational community" and the "publishing community". Of course, participation in one sub-community is not mutually exclusive of participation in the other, nor does it necessitate participation in the other. Thus, community members might never publish (pedagogic research) nor draw ideas (directly) from such publications; other community members may never teach or network with (teaching) practitioners but they are still members of an overarching community of academic practice.

Functionality of the wider community, in terms of supporting the development of individual professionality and thus (the academic practice facet of collective) professionalism, is dependent on at least some of the members engaging in the full spectrum of community engagement – these "Full Engagement Scholars" act rather like academic community "bees" cross-pollinating both ends and allowing the whole community to bloom. Building on the argument above, three types of community member emerge: "Excellent Teachers" (Kreber's (2000) scholarly teachers), "Peda-gogic Researchers" (those who research learning) and "Full Engagement Scholars" (those who do both).

Excellent Teachers

These members teach and inform their practice through reflecting on their own teaching experience and through informal engagement with the conversational sub-community of academic practice. Their zone of engagement within the full spectrum of community activity is shown below as Figure 6a.

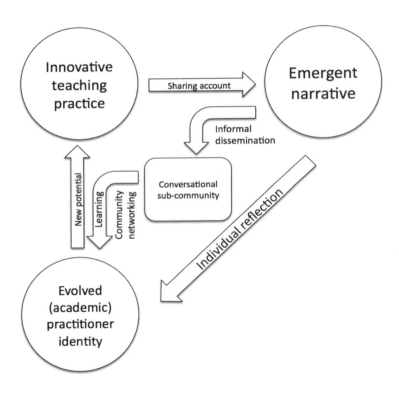

Figure 6a: Community engagement of Excellent Teachers.

Pedagogic Researchers

These members research and inform their practice through reflecting on their research experience, analysing their findings and articulating their thinking with the published and conversational outputs of the (full) community of academic practice. Their zone of engagement within the full spectrum of community activity is shown below as Figure 6b.

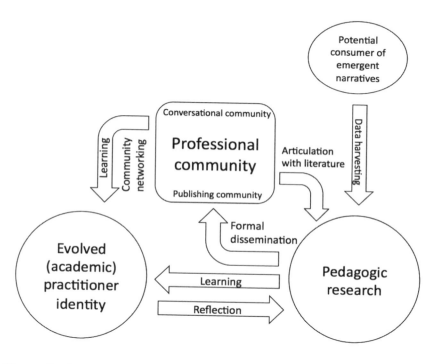

Figure 6b: Community engagement of Pedagogic Researchers.

Full Engagement Scholars

Although the activities of the Excellent Teacher and Pedagogic Researcher members still lead to outputs of learning and evolution of identity through reflection on teaching experiences *or* research experiences, it is only the "Full Engagement Scholars" who populate the full spectrum of activity described in Figure 5. This has important ramifications for the efficacy of practices that have the potential to lead to academic professional development (learning).

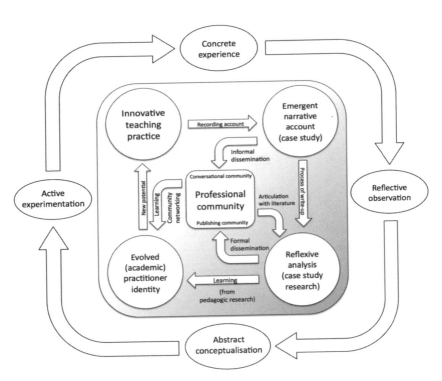

Figure 7: Mapping of my model of professional community engagement with the Kolb (1984) cycle of experiential learning (using case study research as an example).

The context in which I am discussing learning is self-evidently "experiential" in nature whereby personal and professional development emerges from a process of reflecting and learning from experience. A striking feature of my full model (Figure 5) is the degree to which it aligns with Kolb's (1984) experiential learning cycle (Figure 7). Not only does my model offer a useful extension to Kolb's cycle of experiential learning by modelling how individual learning is dependent on participation in a professional community, but it also demonstrates that the "partial" engagement undertaken by both the "Excellent Teacher" members and the "Pedagogic Researcher" members restricts their capacity to learn from experience. This is because "Excellent Teachers" limit their opportunities for abstract conceptualisation, while the "Pedagogic Researchers" limit their opportunities for active experimentation that leads to them acquiring concrete experience.

Only the "Full Engagement Scholars" have the potential to draw full learning potential from engagement with community activities because they research their own practice, articulate their experience with the formal and informal outputs of the full professional community and as teachers they have the opportunity to practise what they have discovered and to learn from that experience.

Conclusion

Reflecting on one's academic practice is a cornerstone of professional development as a higher education practitioner. The writing-up of narrative accounts of facets of our academic practice provides valuable data sets that we can exploit by embracing case study research. I contend that taking the time to undertake a process of reflexive analysis on our experiences as laid out in Figure 7 gives us valuable opportunities to learn from research. Like Hayes (in this volume), I contend that learning from research is most powerful when one "lives research". Auto-ethnographic case study research emerges from the study of lived experiences as case study narratives are made sense of through a process of reflexive analysis that includes articulation with a professional community.

Furthermore, I contend that my interpretation of case-study research, when used as a vehicle for professional development, can be used to embrace the tenets of scholarly teaching *and* the scholarship of teaching, enabling practitioners to benefit to learn maximally from their experiences and thus become "Full Engagement Scholars". Thus, it is members of this group of academics who maximise their potential to learn from research and thus enhance the academic practice they are able to offer the students they teach.

About the author

Professor Dr. Paul Bartholomew is Director of Learning Innovation and Professional Practice at Aston University, Birmingham, England. He can be contacted at this email: p.bartholomew@aston.ac.uk

Bibliography

Bassey, M. (1999). *Case Study Research in Educational Settings*. Buckingham: Open University Press.

Boyer, E. (1990). *Scholarship Reconsidered: Priorities for the Professoriate*. New Jersey: Carnegie Foundation for the Advancement of Teaching.

Campbell, D. T. & J. C. Stanley (1966). *Experimental and Quasi-experimental Designs for Research*. Chicago: Rand McNally.

Department for Education and Skills (DfES) (2003). *The Future of Higher Education*. London: TSO, January 2003, Cm 5735.

Dooley, L. M. (2002). Case Study Research and Theory Building. *Advances in Developing Human Resources*. Vol. 4, No 3, pp.335-354.

Evans, L. (2002). *Reflective Practice in Educational Research: Developing Advanced Skills*. London: Continuum.

Evans, L. (2008). Professionalism, Professionality and the Development of Education Professionals. *British Journal of Educational Studies*, Vol. 56, No 1, pp. 20-38.

Flyvbjerg, B. (2006). Five Misunderstandings about Case-Study Research. *Qualitative Inquiry*, Vol. 12, No. 2, pp.219-245.

Freidson, E. (1994). *Professionalism Reborn: Theory, Prophecy and Policy*. Cambridge, Polity Press, in association with Blackwell Publishers.

Haigh, N. (2010). *The Scholarship of Teaching and Learning: a Practical Introduction and Critique*. Wellington, New Zealand: AUT University and Ako Aotearoa.

Herling, R. W.; L. Weinberger & L. Harris (2000). *Case Study Research: Defined for Application in the Field of HRD*. St. Paul: University of Minnesota, Human Resource Development Research Center.

Hoyle, E. (1975). Professionality, Professionalism and Control in Teaching. In V. Houghton *et al.* (Eds.) *Management in Education: the Management of Organisations and Individuals.* London: Ward Lock Educational in association with Open University Press.

Hoyle, E. (2001). Teaching: Prestige, Status and Esteem, *Educational Management & Administration*, Vol. 29, No. 2, pp. 139–152.

Kolb, D. A. (1984). *Experiential Learning: Experience as the Source of Learning and Development.* Englewood Cliffs, NJ: Prentice Hall.

Kreber, C. (2000). How University Teaching Award Winners Conceptualise Academic Work: Some further Thoughts on the Meaning of Scholarship. *Teaching in Higher Education*, Vol. 5, No. 1, pp.61-78.

Maréchal, G. (2010). Autoethnography. In A. J. Mills; G. Durepos & E. Wiebe (Eds.) *Encyclopedia of Case Study Research, Vol. 2.* Thousand Oaks, CA: Sage Publications, pp. 43–45.

Merriam, S. B. (1998). *Qualitative Research and Case Study Applications in Education.* San Francisco: The Jossey-Bass Education Series and The Jossey-Bass Higher Education Series.

Peattie, L. (2001). Theorizing Planning: Some Comments on Flyvbjerg's Rationality and Power. *International Planning Studies*, Vol. 6, No. 3, pp. 257-262.

Shulman, L. (2000). Inventing the Future. In Hutchings, P. (Ed.) *Opening lines: approaches to the scholarship of teaching and learning.* California: The Carnegie Foundation for the Advancement of Teaching.

Simons, H. (2009). *Case Study Research in Practice.* Sage Publications.

Sockett, H. T. (1996). Teachers for the 21st Century: redefining professionalism, *NASSP Bulletin*, May, 1996, pp. 22-29.

Stake, R. E. (1995). *The Art of Case Study Research.* California: Sage

Torraco, R. J. (1997). Theory Building Research Methods. In R. A. Swanson & E. F. Holton (Eds.) *Human resource development research handbook: Linking research and practice.* pp. 114-138. San Francisco: Berrett-Kohler.

Trigwell, K. & S. Shale (2004). Student Learning and the Scholarship of University Teaching. *Studies in Higher Education*, Vol. 29, No. 4, pp.523-536.

Yin, R. K. (1993). *Applications of Case Study Research.* London: Sage.